BOURDIEU AND SOCIAL SPACE

Edited by Noel B. Salazar, University of Leuven,
in collaboration with ANTHROMOB, the EASA
Anthropology and Mobility Network

WORLDS IN MOTION

This transdisciplinary series features empirically grounded studies that
disentangle how people, objects, and ideas move across the planet. With
a special focus on advancing theory as well as methodology, the series
considers movement as both an object and a method of study.

Bourdieu and Social Space

Mobilities, Trajectories, Emplacements

Deborah Reed-Danahay

berghahn
NEW YORK · OXFORD
www.berghahnbooks.com

First published in 2020 by
Berghahn Books
www.berghahnbooks.com

Library of Congress Cataloging-in-Publication Data

A C.I.P. cataloging record is available
from the Library of Congress
Library of Congress Cataloging in
Publication Control Number: 2019030599

British Library Cataloguing in Publication Data

A catalogue record for this book is available from the British Library

ISBN 978-1-78920-353-0 hardback
ISBN 978-1-80073-641-2 paperback
ISBN 978-1-78920-354-7 ebook

https://doi.org/10.3167/9781789203530

Contents

Preface

My desire to write this book arose from my conviction that although social space is central to Bourdieu's theory of practice and has important implications for studies of spatiality and mobility, it has received insufficient attention in comparison with other aspects of his work. I made reference to social space in my first book on Bourdieu, *Locating Bourdieu* (Reed-Danahay 2005b)—in which I explored topics such as location, point of view, and positionality—but I have since come to better appreciate the key role of social space in his work. My engagement with Bourdieu's concept of social space deepened in tandem with two ethnographic research projects dealing with migration and mobility that I began after completing *Locating Bourdieu*: one on former Vietnamese refugees in Texas (Reed-Danahay 2008; 2010; 2012; 2015b; see also Brettell and Reed-Danahay 2012); and an ongoing ethnographic project I began in 2014 on French citizens living in London, which is just beginning to yield publications. *Bourdieu and Social Space* includes revised and expanded versions of material that originally appeared in two previous publications (Reed-Danahay 2015c and 2017b).

I began to develop the idea for this book in 2012 during a sabbatical at Cambridge University, while holding a Yip Fellowship at Magdalene College. Conversations about Bourdieu's work with Tim Jenkins and Derek Robbins while I was in Cambridge strengthened my resolve to pursue this project. I am very grateful for the support of the Humanities Institute at the University at Buffalo for a Fellowship during the 2013–14 academic year that granted teaching release in spring of 2014, enabling me to devote a semester to further exploration of the ideas that shape this book. An NEH Senior Summer Stipend in 2014 was a welcome source not only of financial support but also encouragement for this project, and I began to compose some of the chapters during that summer. This book has benefited from research funding from the European Commission and its Erasmus+ program for my Jean Monnet Chair (2015–18) on the topic of "Citizenship, Mobility, and Belonging in the European Union." Although writing this book was not the central activity of the Jean Monnet Chair, which was primarily that of teaching and research on the European Union, various opportunities to observe the EU at closer range afforded by this position helped me shape the chapter in this book on the European Union as Social Space.

My thinking about Bourdieu and social space has also benefited greatly from two collaborative working groups in which I was fortunate to participate and further develop my ideas about social space. In the context of a collaboration that started with a Wenner-Gren workshop in 2007 bringing together French and American scholars working in each other's countries, organized by Susan Carol Rogers and Anne Raulin (see Raulin and Rogers 2012), I began to articulate how Bourdieu's concept of social space can help us understand the processes through which social groups referred to as "communities" come to be viewed as social realities (Reed-Danahay [2012] 2015a). My participation in another long-term working group, convened by Vered Amit and focused on concepts of sociality (see Amit 2015), which I joined in 2009, was instrumental in helping me deepen my understanding of the relationships between social space and sociality, with particular reference to Bourdieu's work (Reed-Danahay 2015c).

My work on this book has benefited from numerous exchanges with scholars when I have had the opportunity to present my ideas either at conferences or in invited lectures. In addition to all of the colleagues involved in the two working groups mentioned above, I am particularly grateful to Stefan Helgesson and the Research Program in World Literatures at Stockholm University for inviting me to deliver a keynote at their meeting in February 2018 as I was completing this book. This very much informed my approach to Bourdieu's thought as a form of "world-making," which I develop in Chapter One. That visit also led to useful discussions about Bourdieu with Bo Ekelund and Raoul Galli at a key moment in this project. I want to thank Osman Kocaaga, an advanced PhD student at Kirklareli University who was in residence at the University at Buffalo during the 2016–17 academic year to study Bourdieu's ideas under my supervision through the auspices of a grant from the Turkish Scientific and Technological Research Council (TUBITAK). We had many stimulating exchanges about Bourdieu's oeuvre during that year. I am grateful to Noel Salazar for having faith in this project and to Marion Berghahn for her support in publishing this book. Tom Bonnington and Lizzie Martinez at Berghahn have been helpful guides in preparing the final product. Two anonymous reviewers of the manuscript helped make it better, although I take full responsibility for any remaining imperfections.

Thanks to all of my friends, those in Buffalo and those in other parts of North America, in Europe, and in India. They know who they are, and I hope they realize how much I appreciate their moral support and encouragement over the years. My family means everything to me and I am grateful for their love and support. I became a grandmother while writing this book and bask in the joy of having little Gideon in our lives.

Note on citations of Bourdieu's work: Because this book traces the idea of social space both over time in Bourdieu's work and across various topics about which he wrote, it has been necessary to pay close attention to the original French sources rather than rely solely on translated versions of Bourdieu's work. Translations have often appeared many years after the original French versions, and frequently involved reworkings of the material or slight alterations in what was included or excluded in them. Although my reading and analysis comes primarily from the original French sources, I will draw upon the English versions of Bourdieu's writings for quotes and references for the convenience of Anglophone readers of this book. Occasionally, however, I reference the original French versions when there is a need to point out subtleties of argument and translation. In order to be clear about the chronology of the original versions, I will employ both publication dates when citing sources, with the original version appearing first and the English translation second (original/translation).

Bourdieu, Social Space, and Mobility

> As a body and biological individual, I am, in the way that
> things are, situated in a place: I occupy a position in physical
> space and social space.
> —*Pascalian Meditations* (1997/2000c, 131)

How is social mobility related to geographic mobility? How is mobility related to power and symbolic domination? What are the emotional implications of mobility and immobility? These are questions that Pierre Bourdieu addressed in his work. Bourdieu's concept of social space, which I view as the basis of his work, is highly relevant for critical issues in the humanities and social sciences regarding mobility and related processes of social inclusion and exclusion. Even more so than field, social space expresses articulations between physical spaces, embodied habitus, and sociality. Bourdieu's most significant contribution for spatial and mobility studies is that he developed a conceptual framework for connecting social practices and modes of sociality with physical space. As architectural historian Hélène Lipstadt (2008, 38) has pointed out, Bourdieu has much to contribute to "the spatial study of lives." In this book, I show that spatiality is integral to the development of Bourdieu's theory of practice and impossible to separate from the idea of habitus.

Although I agree with Charles Lemert (2006, 231) that social space is Bourdieu's "second most inventive concept" after that of habitus, its meaning remains elusive. Ideas of spatiality permeate Bourdieu's writings in ways that produce an almost *doxic*, invisible, and elusive quality for the reader. Grasping what Bourdieu means by social space, a concept that he was less explicit in defining than that of habitus or field, requires a broad view of the ways he approached spatiality and its relationship to sociality. It is important to put Bourdieu's disparate writings, which often reach different audiences and thereby shape somewhat different interpretations and understandings of his work in various disciplines, into dialogue with each other to show their connections. A thorough comprehension of Bourdieu's theory of social space must take into account the wide corpus of his writings on different topics and in multiple realms—from Algeria and rural France, to art and literature, to language, to French education and academia, to the housing market, and to the state. In order to understand the relationship between physical space and social space in Bourdieu's thought, it is particularly important to draw out the connections between the ways in which he developed ideas of social space in his more ethnographic writings and in his other work.

My aim in writing this book is to provide a comprehensive overview of Bourdieu's theory of social space across the span of his career, with a particular focus on the implications of his thought for understandings of mobility.[1] In Chapter One, I provide a critical analysis of Bourdieu's concepts of "habitus," "capital," "field," and "symbolic power" in relationship to social space. This chapter considers Bourdieu's own "world-making" in the construction of his theoretical approach. In Chapters Two through Four, I trace the chronological development of Bourdieu's thought on social space from the earliest ethnographic writings on peasants in France and Algeria to his later writings on the state. I then extend Bourdieu's ideas in order to apply them to a consideration of the European Union as a social space in Chapter Five. In each of these realms, the implications of viewing mobility and immobility in terms of social space(s) are explored. In this book's Conclusion, I connect Bourdieu's theory of social space to the emerging focus on emplacement in mobility studies and argue for an ethnographic approach to mobility that is informed by the concept of social space.

The study of geographic mobility is not usually considered to have been a major focus of Bourdieu's work. However, although it is true that Bourdieu did not address international migration extensively in his research and writing, he was interested in movements across space that are associated with mobility—conceived of as a much broader concept than migration. His work speaks to the relationships between social and geographical mobility and location. If, as Noel Salazar has proposed (2018), mobility is about boundary crossing, then we can see Bourdieu's contributions to mobility studies in his concern with symbolic classifications of social, linguistic, and geographic boundaries. Bourdieu's theory of social space includes the analysis of trajectories across spatial and social boundaries and the workings of symbolic power that produce immobility.

The term "migration" refers primarily to geographic movement across physical space, whereas "mobility" and "immobility" can signal movement or the lack thereof in either social positioning or physical space. Mobility can equally refer to human movement across space, in as simple a gesture as walking, and to social movement or social mobility whereby a person or group rises or falls in their position or status. Migration is often understood as a form of mobility that involves a more "permanent" relocation—the end of a trajectory in which someone was not mobile, became mobile, and then stopped being mobile again after "settling." However, this vastly oversimplifies the experiences of mobile people. Many questions are left unaddressed when something is labeled as migration. These include that of why the person moved, why some people move and others don't, questions of the temporal aspects of migration (when, for how long), as well as questions about social agency (was the mobility one of privilege and choice, or was it forced). All of these questions also need to be viewed as lying upon a continuum rather than either/or. For example, economic migrants who are frequently juxtaposed with refugees may also be "forced" to seek a better economic situation even when a clear-cut situation of persecution cannot be demonstrated. Due to national origins, socioeconomic status, or other factors, the ability or desire to move may be understood as associated with more or less privilege regarding travel (cf. Amit 2007).

Bourdieu addressed immigration most explicitly both in his early research in Algeria (especially in his coauthored publications with Abdelmalek Sayad)[2] and in his later collaborative work on social suffering (Bourdieu et al. 1993c). It is significant, however, that Bourdieu did not include immigrants in his analysis of French national social space in his major work *Distinction* (1979b/1984a). Despite many gaps in his attention to migrants and other mobile people, Bourdieu did provide insights on issues of belonging, and of both mobility and immobility, which I extend in my analysis of his work to explore their potential applications. Bourdieu's perspective is useful in understanding the positionings in and thresholds of social space that are associated with belonging and affinity—with feeling (and being perceived by others as) "at home," but also feeling close affinities with others in the same social position (and similar habitus). For Bourdieu, this was important for political mobilization in order to lessen social inequality. Bourdieu assumed that people want to feel at home and that mobility is connected to desires for the emotion of happiness that this entails. He described situations in which people can feel out of place and not at home due either to their own mobility or to the world changing around them.

A perennial problem in scholarship on Bourdieu is the sheer volume of his writings and the range of his interests, which has led to partial readings and sometimes to what he referred to as "fast readings" (1989a/1996c, 434, fn12) of his work. Bourdieu's concept of social space is most often associated with his book *Distinction*, which draws little attention to the relationship between social and physical space. Bourdieu's relevance for the "spatial turn," an influential trend in the social sciences and humanities since the late 1980s that interrogates the relationship between power and spatial organization, is rarely acknowledged.[3] Those who have identified a more recent "mobility turn" linked to an explicit concern with inequality also rarely cite Bourdieu's work.[4] Sheller (2017) suggests that the mobilities turn extended the spatial turn by incorporating the relational aspect of space, yet overlooks Bourdieu's contributions to this very idea.

Most scholarship that does recognize Bourdieu's writing on social space fails to fully appreciate the ways in which his approach links the study of physical space and that of a more relational social space. Among anthropologists, Bourdieu's relevance for spatiality is most often taken from his analysis of the Kabyle house, in work deriving from very early in his career that was published in various places, including *Outline of a Theory of Practice* (1972a/1977c). Henrietta Moore (1986) was one of the first social anthropologists to use Bourdieu's spatial approach, which she applied to a study of gender among the Marakwet of Kenya. Moore relies primarily on Bourdieu's analysis of the Kabyle house, and does not utilize his broader concept of social space that appears elsewhere in his work. Nageeb (2004) drew upon Bourdieu's concept to understand Muslim women's construction of social space in Sudan, and stretches it to locate social agency among these women while also incorporating both the spatial and social structural aspects of Bourdieu's approach. Such work has drawn attention to Bourdieu's relevance for feminist theory, and this has been noted by several authors who take up his emphasis on point of view and position-taking in social space to better understand gendered forms of agency and symbolic violence (see Butler 1997; Adkins and Skeggs 2005; see also Bourdieu 1998b/2001). In much of this literature, however, the emphasis is not on physical space, but on positionings in a more abstract social space.

One strand of attention to Bourdieu's concept of social space comes out of geography, urban planning, and architecture (e.g., Hillier and Rooksby 2002; Lipstadt 2008; Webster 2011), where the emphasis is placed on geographic or physical space.[5] Speller's book *Bourdieu and Literature* (2011) addresses the topic of social space in Bourdieu's writings on literature, but does not place them in the broader context of his other sociological and ethnographic work. In sociology and related disciplines, Bourdieu's concept of social space has most often been associated with the method of correspondence analysis he used in *Distinction*.[6] A retrospective volume dedicated to *Distinction* (Coulangeon and Duval 2013) focuses primarily on Bourdieu's contributions to social class theory and includes discussions of social space, but pays little explicit attention to the physical or geographical aspects of that concept in Bourdieu's thought. Because *Distinction* does not address physical space in relationship to social space as much as does other work by Bourdieu that I discuss in subsequent chapters, the wider implications of social space in his overall theory are occluded when this book is taken as the primary source for understanding Bourdieu's concept of social space.

My position in this book is that social space is the key to understanding Bourdieu's work. Bourdieu's most cited concepts are habitus and cultural capital, with the consequence that less attention is paid to his broader view of the social world in which these two concepts have meaning. Bourdieu deployed social space in order to conceptualize the ways in which groups form and take shape in society, and to explore metaphors of social distance and proximity. Among scholars who focus on the relational aspect of social positionings in Bourdieu's concept of social space, there is a tendency to downplay his attention to geographic space. This has resulted in an overemphasis on Bourdieu's deployment of "field" at the expense of attention to social space.[7] There is evidence of Bourdieu's interest in the concept of social space across all of his work (from peasant societies to the housing market in contemporary France); whereas "field" is a more focused concept that Bourdieu used primarily in contexts of what he referred to as "differentiated," or class-stratified, societies.[8] The idea of field, which became more explicit in Bourdieu's work over time, is a framework intended to explain the ways in which power and knowledge coalesce in particular realms of society (education, literature, politics, journalism) that are understood as relatively autonomous "fields." Bourdieu viewed field as a region in social space. Although I view social space as a more useful concept for mobility and spatial studies than field, the two complement each other, and I will address the relationship between field and social space in greater detail in Chapter One.

Although not always in reference to Bourdieu's approach specifically, the term "social space" appears in scholarship in phrases like "social space of postmodernism" (Rouse 1991), "social space of ethnic identity" (Smith 1992), "transnational social fields" (Levitt and Glick Schiller 2004; Wimmer and Glick Schiller 2002; Amelina et al. 2012), and "transnational social spaces" (Pries 2001; Faist 2012; Faist and Özveren 2004). There are some important differences, however, in Bourdieu theory of social space and these uses of the term.

The dominant approach in migration studies since the 1990s has been a "transnational" one (Gupta 1992; Basch, Glick Schiller, and Blanc 1994; Hannerz 1996). It is viewed by most of its proponents as leading to a way out of the so-called "container" problem of methodological nationalism. Transnationalism emphasizes the ongoing ties that migrants maintain with the country from which they moved. In an early iteration of this concept,

Basch, Glick Schiller, and Blanc proposed that one of its major premises was that "transnationalism is a process by which migrants, through their daily activities and social, economic, and political relations, create social fields that cross national boundaries" (1994, 22).

Those who focus on transnationalism have sought to identify transnational spaces and transnational behaviors. There has, however, been a lack of appreciation of Bourdieu's contributions to understandings of spatiality in publications dealing with transnational social space. Pries claims that Bourdieu's concept of social space was primarily a spatial metaphor and not "an explicit concept of the relations between social and geographic space" (2001, 19). As the explication of Bourdieu's theory of social space conveyed in this book will show, such an interpretation can only be understood as based on a very narrow reading of Bourdieu's work. Thomas Faist defines transnational social spaces as "relatively stable, lasting, and dense sets of ties reaching beyond and across borders of sovereign states" (2004, 3). He adopts an actor-oriented transactional approach that views social space in terms of networks among individuals. This use of social space does link geographical space and social relationships but bears little resemblance to Bourdieu's approach. As in the case of Faist's approach, ethnographic studies that have been inspired by the concept of transnational social space emphasize social ties among mobile people living abroad with other coethnics (e.g., Wiles 2008; Richter 2012), which is different from attention to the position of habitus in social space.

The uses of Bourdieu's work by migration specialists who posit transnational social fields also miss some important aspects of his work. Although influenced by Bourdieu's idea of fields as sites of struggle, the concept of transnational field is primarily an ego-centered idea that uses network as a metaphor. Nina Glick Schiller has written that transnational social fields are "networks of networks that stretch across the borders of nation-states" (2005, 5). Bourdieu did not envision social fields in this way; he saw them, as I have noted earlier in this book, as regions within a wider social space. Unless the concept of transnational social field also takes into account the dispositions of habitus and the forms of capital that come into play in these fields, it retains an actor-oriented focus that, while avoiding methodological nationalism, risks adopting a methodological individualism.

Another term that has gained momentum in recent years is that of translocality (Conradson and McKay 2007; Greiner and Sakdapolrak 2013; Low 2016). Low defines a translocal space as one in which "a person who lives in two or more locations often separated by national boundaries and distance has emotional, linguistic, and material access to both simultaneously" (2016, 174). This is a primarily ego-centered perspective in which the body is a "mobile social field" (ibid., 5). Low addresses Bourdieu's approach to space in developing what she calls a framework of "spatializing culture," but limits her analysis of his work to that published in the 1970s (especially the work on the Kabyle house). She views translocal space as compatible with ideas of transnationalism, but suggests that it has the potential to elucidate emerging affiliations that "bind people and places together" (ibid., 181).

Overview of Bourdieu's Concept of Social Space

I believe that Bourdieu's concept of social space is good to "think with" because it encourages us to view geographic mobilities and emplacements in relationship to movements and positions in social space. Social space is an idea that Bourdieu developed in tandem with that of habitus—an embodied orientation to the world, which includes dispositions, tastes, points of view, and so on. He viewed habitus as a position in social space. The concept of social space expresses articulations between physical space and sociality. The following brief overview of what Bourdieu meant by social space will help set the stage for what is to be discussed in greater detail in subsequent chapters.

For Bourdieu, physical and social space are closely related. He wrote in *Pascalian Meditations*, "social space tends to be translated, with more or less distortion, into physical space, in the form of a certain arrangement of agents and properties," and argued that physical space is "reified social space" (1997/2000c, 134). Places or spatial localizations that people inhabit are related to the position of their habitus in social space. It is important to realize that Bourdieu did not view social space as the physical place where social interactions occur. In this, he differs from those who consider physical space associated with human activity and materiality as social space. For Bourdieu, social space is an underlying structure of symbolic classifications that is expressed and constructed by positionings of and relationships between habituses in physical space. The concepts of habitus and social space are central to Bourdieu's theory of practice, through which he attempted to trouble the conceptual division between social structure and social practices. Social space is not, however, a given that people enter into; it is also composed by them. Social space is produced through the combination of various social actors engaged in social practices—their points of view, their positions, and their strategies.

Spatial practices imply spatial choices, which are connected to the dispositions of habitus and associated forms of capital (1993c/1999b). The main thread in all of Bourdieu's work is the idea that social space is constituted by the habituses of social agents in it and, in turn, their position in social space shapes their understandings of what is possible (their aspirations). This affects their trajectories and strategies. Bourdieu imagined the social world as a social space that is a "system of relations" (1989c, 16), and a social hierarchy in which there are more or less dominating and dominated social positions. Habitus is not an attribute of an autonomous individual, but of a person who is positioned in social space and whose value, power, and trajectory within that social space can only be understood in a relational sense, in relationship to other habituses within the social space. Bourdieu's concepts are designed from the perspective of the social analyst, not the individual social actor. However, the social actor has a position and point of view in social space in relationship to others who are engaged with or enclosed by that social space or a field within it.

In his analysis of France as a national social space, Bourdieu considered social space to be coterminous with the limits of the nation-state. In other writings, however, he occasionally used the term "social space" to apply to more localized social units, such as a city or a region.[9] Even though he frequently took social space to be national social space (e.g., *Distinction* [1979b/1984a]), Bourdieu regarded emplacement or displacement in social space not primarily in terms of the territorial boundaries of the nation-state but, rather, in terms of commonsense ideas about the social world, its composition, and its hierarchies that are fostered by the state and its institutions (especially education).

Bourdieu was particularly interested in perceptions of distance and proximity in social space among social actors within it. These are related to the dispositions and affinities of habitus. These are also related to geographic distances. It is important to take into account, however, that social interactions among people in close physical proximity may hide social distances and underlying social hierarchies. Bourdieu wrote of geographic and social space:

> It is true that one can observe almost everywhere a tendency toward spatial segregation, people who are close together in social space tending to find themselves, by choice or by necessity, close to one another in geographic space; nevertheless, people who are very distant from each other in social space can encounter one another and interact, if only briefly and intermittently, in physical space. (1989c, 16)

The taken for granted divisions of geographic space (such as center and periphery) must be viewed, according to Bourdieu, as "the effect of distance in social space, i.e. the unequal distribution of the different kinds of capital in geographical space" (1985b, 726, fn5).

Bourdieu addressed the materiality of social space not only in his attention to physical space and place but also through visual images that he incorporated into his published works. He depicted physical or geographic space (which was also social space) in his diagrams of the Kabyle house (1958; 1970a) and the Béarnaise house (1962); maps of villages and resettlement camps in Algeria (1958; Bourdieu and Sayad 1964a); and a map of Paris depicting the trajectory in social space of characters in a nineteenth century French novel (1975). Bourdieu also published photographs he took during fieldwork in rural France (1962) and in Algeria (2003a).

Because perceptions of distance and proximity in social space inform and are constructed by relations of inequality and social domination, Bourdieu's approach to social space has important implications for understandings of the circulation of people and ideas in the contemporary world. The lens of social space helps illuminate the relationship between spatial practices and position in social hierarchies—that is, the ways in which some people have more privileges associated with mobility than others. Social space also helps us explore social processes related to immobility, emplacement, and mooring. An important contribution of Bourdieu's theory of habitus and social space is his attention to emotions. Bourdieu viewed the habitus as shaping both thinking and feeling. He paid attention in his work to feelings of being in or out of place, either socially or physically or both, and the consequences of this for those who are in dominated positions in society. Bourdieu also, however, described his own privileged position in academia that resulted from social and geographical mobility, as connected to his feeling out of place.

Mobility and Reflexivity: Bourdieu's Trajectory

Distance and proximity in social space underlie not only Bourdieu's research questions, but also his reflexive methodology, in which the researcher should be aware of his or her position or point of view in social space. In comments about his former collaborator Abdelmalek Sayad, Bourdieu (2008b/2013, 299) wrote: "Research in social science, where analytical procedures are less strictly codified than elsewhere, always depends largely, for better or worse, on the habitus, more or less corrected and controlled, of the person conducting it." Bourdieu felt that a truly scientific sociology and anthropology depended on reflexivity on the part of the researcher, and by this, he meant being able to analyze one's own position in social space—including one's proximities and distances from those studied. Advocating a stance of "participant objectivation" (Bourdieu 2003), Bourdieu argued that being aware of one's own position in social space would aid the researcher in being careful not to mistake their own point of view for that of their interlocutors.

We can learn a great deal about Bourdieu's concept of social space by looking at how he applied the concepts of social space, field, and habitus to his own career trajectory in his *Sketch for a Self-Analysis* (2004a/2007). Completed toward the end of Bourdieu's life and published posthumously, this book was intended primarily for a younger academic audience who were themselves struggling with and questioning their role as researchers. Bourdieu wrote of his "path through social space," which linked two incompatible "social worlds" (2007, 1), by which he meant the world of academia and the world of rural Béarnaise society in which he spent his childhood. This had led to his split habitus (*habitus clivé*), whose two parts were often contradictory, leading him to have impulses at cross-purposes with each other. As a child, he tells us, Bourdieu desired recognition at school, but also disdained educational institutions.

Bourdieu viewed the dispositions he acquired as a child in rural France as the product both of his family upbringing and of regional characteristics (such as language, values, postures, and so on). He describes his family history and the mobilities experienced by his parents and grandparents in terms of loss, insecurity, and some emotional suffering. Bourdieu's father was a humble man who had left the life of sharecropping (to which he was born) to be first a mail carrier and then a clerk in the post office. In spite of his social mobility, Bourdieu's father felt guilty about his social distance from farmers in the township where they lived. Bourdieu's mother came from a family with higher social status, but suffered, like others in the petite bourgeoisie, from class insecurity. Although her father had come from a prosperous and well-established peasant family, he remained one of the lesser members of it and struggled financially while taking on several different ventures related to the rural economy.

Like the figure of "the stranger" analyzed by Georg Simmel (Wolff 1950) who is physically close but socially remote, Bourdieu felt a social distance from his colleagues in academia despite his spatial proximity to other scholars with whom he interacted. He felt that he had acquired, and retained throughout his life, certain habits of thought and language that marked him with a regional form of masculinity that was somewhat alien in the Parisian academic milieu in which he later found himself. He had migrated from a rural milieu to an urban and academic one; and much like any migrant, he experienced social distance. This emotional response of social distance is associated with not feeling "at home." Bourdieu wrote that he became aware of his own habitus through the gaze of others—especially those in Paris, but also beginning with his *lycée* days in the city of Pau—when fellow students and colleagues from higher social milieu would react to him. Because he was not a peasant child, Bourdieu was teased in primary school, yet also felt scorned in Paris many years later because of his provincial and lower-class background by the majority of academics who came from higher social strata.

At *lycée* in Pau, where he boarded during the week, Bourdieu felt conflicted because although he desired to learn and read and was a good student, he also tended to make trouble and organize pranks, for which he was frequently disciplined.[10] As he came to feel an affinity with more urban children, he realized he was becoming more distant from his rural peers. Playing rugby permitted him to express a form of masculinity that could counter the interest in learning. Bourdieu was encouraged by both parents to pursue an education. On his father's side, this had to do with a left-leaning support for the Republican values of French education; while on his mother's, it had to do with a desire for social advancement and position.

In this "self-socioanalysis," Bourdieu discussed his movements in social space through an analysis of his own habitus and the axes of rural versus urban, higher versus lower social class status, Paris versus provinces, and also in terms of gender and sexuality (as when he distinguished himself from Foucault partly on the basis of Foucault's homosexuality in contrast to his heterosexuality). At the same time, he described his positions in the fields of philosophy, anthropology, and sociology. He explained the possible position-takings available to him through discussion of key figures and stances in each field, showing both his distances from and proximities to them and including stories about his interpersonal relations with several intellectuals. Bourdieu concluded that his "choice" of leaving the field of philosophy and turning toward anthropology and sociology was one based in his habitus. The themes that Bourdieu addressed in his self-analysis are all present in his approach to social space that will be approached in more detail in the chapters to follow.

Trajectory, Bourdieu wrote, is

> A series of successively occupied positions by the same agent (or the same group) in a space which itself is constantly evolving and which is subject to incessant transformations. . . . Biographical events are defined as just so many *investments* and *moves* in social space." (1986b/2000a, 302)

Bourdieu was an internal migrant in France, who was both geographically and socially mobile as he moved from being a child of modest origins in the region of Béarn to a highly respected figure in the world of Parisian academia and beyond. He was both a "scholarship boy" living "at the friction point between two cultures" (Hoggart [1957] 1992, 224) and a "class traveller" (Löfgren 1987, 88) who faced alienation and feelings of being out of place.[11] Although both Richard Hoggart and Orvar Löfgren use a vocabulary of "class cultures" to discuss the boundary crossing of such figures, Bourdieu's approach is to posit the acquisition of a secondary habitus and new positionings in the wider social space. This leads to a situation of having a "split habitus" and never truly feeling at home in the world. Bourdieu's reflections on his life trajectory illustrate quite succinctly how closely habitus and social space are linked in his theory of practice. As Bourdieu argued in his essay "The Biographical Illusion" (1986b/2000a), a person's habitus should not be viewed in terms of unique individual traits and freely made choices. Habitus is a position in social space and has a social trajectory related to the choices and aspirations available.

Placing Bourdieu and Social Space

Bourdieu's concept of social space draws upon several different strands in social theory and philosophy, and constitutes a synthesis of anthropological approaches that emphasize physical space as a reflection of social organization and belief systems, and sociological approaches that focus on social positioning within a stratified and heterogeneous society. In this final section of the Introduction, I place Bourdieu in relationship to earlier thought about social space that influenced him and consider how his contemporaries used this concept in ways that were similar and different from his own.

The phrase "social space," which can be traced back to Durkheim,[12] appears frequently in recent scholarship, although, as I have previously shown (Reed-Danahay 2015c), its meanings and uses are quite varied—especially regarding the degree to which emphasis is placed either on the material and built environment or on issues of social distance or proximity. The paradigmatic view prevalent in social theory during most of the nineteenth and into the early twentieth century was that a social group was associated with a geographical territory and that this relationship was a central part of social structure and sociality. This was expressed in the approaches of Émile Durkheim and Marcel Mauss, who were fundamental figures in the development of ideas about social space and its relationship to physical space that continue to influence social thought today. Durkheim's emphasis on cognitive and empirical aspects of social life, as well as collective representations and systems of classification (Durkheim [1912] 1995; Durkheim and Mauss 1963), led him to see the built environment and its organization as reflecting social organization.[13]

Although Bourdieu distanced himself from structuralism in a now-famous comment he made about having been a "blissful structuralist" (1980b/ 1990, 9) when composing his classic essay on the Kabyle house, it is important not to ignore the influence of Claude Lévi-Strauss (who was in turn influenced by Durkheim) on Bourdieu's approach to social space. In his own extensive writings on the subject (see especially [1958] 1963), Lévi-Strauss outlined an approach to social space in traditional societies that linked social space and social time to perceptions of time and space. According to Lévi-Strauss, there is a relationship between social structure (as "surface structure") and "spatial structure," but these are not identical. In clarifying this point, he wrote:

> A large number of native societies have consciously chosen to project into space a schema of their institutions. . . . Study of these spatial phenomena permits us to grasp the natives' own conception of their social structure; and, through our examinations of the gaps and contradictions, the real structure, which is often very different from the natives' conception, becomes accessible. ([1958] 1963, 332)

When using the concept of social space (*l'espace social*), Lévi-Strauss referred to the physical or geographical aspects of space, but also to underlying mental systems for the classification of space. These perceptions were products of the social phenomena (underlying structures) that, as he phrased it, "furnished" them. Because he viewed social groups as "cultural units" that were also communication structures, Lévi-Strauss posited that the borders of these units were the thresholds to their social space—the limit where rates and forms of communication weaken.

Lévi-Strauss introduced the element of time to that of social space by pointing out that a spatial configuration could be temporary (as in ritual or dance) or more durable (as in village layout). He employed the idea of "isolates," a concept he borrowed from French demographers who looked at intermarrying groups and their prevalence of cross-cousin marriage, to suggest that cultural isolates can be found in urban as well as smaller-scale societies. Even though Bourdieu described social space as an underlying social structure, his explanation of how physical and social space were connected was, however, quite distinct from that of Lévi-Strauss. Bourdieu was more interested in seeing the interrelationships between social and spatial practices than was Lévi-Strauss, who did not focus on how social practices shape social structure, which was at the heart of Bourdieu's theory of practice (see Bourdieu 1972a/1977c). Bourdieu also went beyond the approach of Lévi-Strauss by exploring social space in wider scales of societal organization such as the nation-state. Lévi-Strauss maintained that anthropological research should confine itself to social space in face-to-face societies. When Marc Augé asked him during a published interview, "Is an ethnology of the modern world possible?" Lévi-Strauss replied that it was important to identify

> Limited areas [*aires*] where ethnological research feels able to operate because it finds there conditions which correspond to its needs: relative continuity in time, continuity within a space, and direct communication between people. The site may be a country village, a district within a town, or even the point of intersection of two or three streets in a metropolis of thousands or millions of inhabitants; these are all places where spatial proximity gives rise to habits or encourages their continuance. (Augé 1990, 90)

This statement illustrates the ways in which Lévi-Strauss viewed social space as a space of interaction, which differs from Bourdieu's understanding of social space as a space of positions and position-takings. Although it can be discerned from the observation of social interaction, social space for Bourdieu is the underlying social structure. Another key difference is that for Bourdieu, the social structure is not entirely a cognitive structure, as it was for Lévi-Strauss, but also one that is embodied and constructed through social practice. One commonality between the two theorists was their interest in the question of the threshold of social space and its relationship to communication. This was primarily a threshold in physical space for Lévi-Strauss, whereas for Bourdieu, social space was not entirely coterminous with the physical space of a collectivity. As I point out repeatedly in subsequent chapters, Bourdieu often referred to whatever social space he was describing as "enclosed," which echoes Lévi-Strauss's emphasis on "isolates."

When Bourdieu was creating his own view of social space that would become more explicitly articulated in his work during the 1980s, other scholars in France influenced by Durkheim and Lévi-Strauss were also developing ideas of social space. One of these figures was anthropologist Georges Condominas, who overlapped with Bourdieu in the late 1950s and early 1960s in Paris, although I am not sure if they had any contact with each other. Condominas was a Southeast Asian specialist who produced an influential book called *L'Espace Social—A propos de l'Asie du Sud-est* (1980) that offered a critical perspective on the concept of culture and proposed that social space be used instead. Condominas offered a comprehensive history of concepts of social space that cited many of his contemporaries in anthropology, but made no mention of Pierre Bourdieu. Condominas proposed that social space was composed of the social relations of a group. Similarly to Lévi-Strauss, he viewed social space in terms of limits to social action and communication and argued that social space, which he called "lived space," was both inhabited physical space and "used space" in an economic sense (1980, 13—my translations). He focused primarily on peasant societies, similar to Bourdieu's ethnographic work in the 1950s and 1960s, where one could identify what Lévi-Strauss referred to as "social isolates" as social spaces.

The idea of spatial settings as comprised of physical boundaries and communication networks, which may or may not coincide with the values and traditions associated with social space central to Lévi-Strauss's idea of cultural isolates, was also present in Paul-Henri Chombart de Lauwe's work, another influence on Bourdieu. Chombart de Lauwe utilized the concept of social space in his study of Paris. He viewed social space as the physical manifestation of collective representations and divisions in social life. Although Bourdieu does not cite him, he was acquainted with him[14] and probably read his work. Chombart de Lauwe viewed urban ethnography and sociology as an emancipatory enterprise that would help "the inhabitant of a large city situate themselves in a specific space" (1965, 28—my translation). He described social space as determined in part by symbolic representations of social difference and noted that there was a relationship between the types and locations of residence of people in Paris and particular habits and behaviors (which recalls Bourdieu's concept of habitus). As Ann Buttimer explains, Chombart de Lauwe introduced a hierarchy of urban social spaces that captured an ever-widening dimension of the "orbits of group social activity" (Buttimer 1969, 421), suggesting also that there are "thresholds in space beyond which certain groups cannot travel without experiencing frustrations, tensions, and feelings of anomie" (ibid., 421). This corresponds to Lévi-Strauss's emphasis on the weakening of communication at the boundaries of cultural "isolates" (social spaces).

Bourdieu's understanding of social space also draws from the ideas of Maurice Halbwachs ([1950] 1980) on the importance of "spatial frameworks" and the relationship between space and collective memory, as well as from Gaston Bachelard's ([1958] 1964) attention to the "poetics" of space and the emotional component of affinity as linked to physical surroundings. Another strand of influence on Bourdieu is the focus on distance and proximity in social space that developed in sociology. Although he did not explicitly address the links between this work and his own approach, there is also much in common between Bourdieu's concept of social space as a space of distances and proximities and that of Georg Simmel (Wolff 1950), as well as Pitirim Sorokin (1927) and urban sociologist Robert E. Park (1924 and 1952).

Whereas those writers focus primarily on the analysis of social interaction, another figure who influenced Bourdieu's thought, Kurt Lewin ([1939] 1967), was more interested in articulating social space as something to be understood by looking at what he referred to as the "topography" of individuals. Lewin described this as "relative positions which the different regions of activity of persons, or groups of persons bear to each other" (ibid., 8). Bourdieu's concept of trajectory in social space draws upon Lewin's concept of "life-space," although Lewin, a social psychologist, was more in-

terested in the individual as a generator of the social space than was Bourdieu—who viewed social space as the underlying social hierarchy and viewed
social practices in social space as the product of habitus. The major influence of Lewin on Bourdieu's concept of social space, as others have pointed
out,[15] is this relational aspect in which social groups are viewed in terms of
social actors taking different positions within them relative to each other.

Another major influence on Bourdieu's concept of social space, and especially the ideas of being in one's place or knowing one's place, was the
work of Erving Goffman, who is frequently cited by Bourdieu. Goffman developed the concept of "territories of the self" (Goffman 1971) and "regions" (Goffman 1959) as a way to explore an individual's social space and
its contours and limits. Goffman was primarily interested in face-to-face
interaction, and his contributions to spatial theory rely upon observations
of encounters in physical space. Although Bourdieu drew heavily from Goffman's work, he was more interested in the underlying social space that informs visible social interactions in physical space.

Two French scholars who were contemporaries of Bourdieu have received much more attention in scholarship on social space, and it is, therefore, instructive to end this brief review of influences on Bourdieu's work
with a consideration of the similarities and differences between Bourdieu's
approach and theirs. The first is Michel de Certeau, who has been highly influential in studies of spatiality and sociality. Certeau distinguished between
space (*l'espace*) and place (*lieu*) in his discussion of spatial practices and
spatial stories but used the phrase "social space" only rarely in his work. A
space, for Certeau, is a "practiced place" (1984, 117), which he likens to a
word when it is spoken, or a street that has been walked upon. Like Bourdieu, he was critical of the idea of the autonomous individual and wrote
that "each individual is a locus in which an incoherent (and often contradictory) plurality of such relational determinations interact" (ibid., xi). Also
like Bourdieu, Certeau used the terms "practice," "structure," and "trajectory." In contrast to Bourdieu, however, Certeau was more interested in
"tactics" utilized by the marginalized and dominated in order challenge
forces of domination. In his criticisms of Bourdieu, Certeau zoomed in on
the notion of habitus (charging that it masked tactical behavior in most
instances) and failed to acknowledge the spatial aspects of Bourdieu's work
or its relationship to his own (ibid., 45–60).

Among scholars interested in the relationship between space and society, the phrase "social space" is most often associated with Bourdieu's
contemporary Henri Lefebvre.[16] Although there are many affinities between
their approaches, there are also significant differences. Both scholars investigated the ways in which distance and proximity to power could occur in
both social and physical space. Lefebvre viewed physical, mental, and social

space as domains that cannot be seen to neatly overlap ([1974] 1991, 11), and argued (ibid., 38–39) that space in capitalist societies includes social practice (linked to particular societies and economic structures); representations of space (that associated with planners and architects who create the dominant physical spaces in society); and representational spaces (space as lived and understood through symbols and images by users who are primarily those of the dominated classes in society). Lefebvre was also interested in structural relationships (by which he meant, in the Marxist sense, relations of production) that generate social space. Lefebvre placed more emphasis on the physical and material aspects of social space than did Bourdieu. Bourdieu, like Lefebvre, saw social space in terms of a system of relations, but not so much as relations of production (as did Lefebvre), than as relations of power based on different forms of capital (economic, cultural, social, and symbolic). I return to a discussion of the relationship between Lefebvre and Bourdieu in my discussion of Bourdieu's theory of the state and state space in Chapter Four.

As Marchetti (2011, 17) has observed, current thinking about social space interrogates the relationship between physical and social space. This is central to Bourdieu's approach and, as I have shown, has a long history going back to Durkheim. An important question regarding social space that was taken up by Bourdieu is the degree to which the physical environment, or geographic space, should (or can) be analytically separated from the more abstract idea of one's position in an imagined social space that has to do with moral values, status, prestige, affinity, identity, and so on. In Chapter One, I consider the ways in which Bourdieu's concept of social space works to address the articulation of physical space and a social space related to social organization and social hierarchy.

NOTES

1. Bourdieu's relevance for mobility or spatial studies is a topic that has received scant attention among Bourdieusian scholars, as evidenced in volumes dedicated to his legacy. See, for example, Encrevé and Lagrave (2003); Swartz and Zolberg (2004); Susen and Turner (2011); Coulangeon and Duval (2013); Leclercq, Lizé, and Stevens (2015); and Medvetz and Sallaz (2018). An exception is the recent volume edited by Thatcher et al. (2015).

2. Sayad, for his part, wrote extensively about immigration (see Sayad [1991] 2004), and Bourdieu wrote the preface to Sayad's book on immigration.

3. Key texts in the literature on the "spatial turn" that bear mentioning include Soja (1989); Massey (2005); Warf and Arias (2009); Tally (2013). In anthropology, see Ardener (1993); Pellow (1996); Gupta and Ferguson (1997); Low and Lawrence (2003); Coleman and Collins (2006); Baudin and Bonnin (2009); Roberts (2012);

and Low (2016). Several recent books that signal the growing interdisciplinary interest in spatial studies and are otherwise good reference points for approaches to space in social theory nevertheless fail to recognize Bourdieu's contributions. See Claval (1984); Simonsen (1996); Zieleniec (2007); Marchetti (2011); and Susen (2014). Of these, only Susen mentions Bourdieu, but very briefly.

4. See, for example, Urry (2000); Cresswell (2006); Sheller and Urry (2006); Franquesa (2011); and Faist (2013). Recent work aimed at conceptualizing an anthropology of mobility and immobility includes Svašek (2012); Salazar and Jayarim (2016); Bon and Repič (2016); and Salazar (2018). Bourdieu's relevance for mobility studies in anthropology is generally viewed primarily in terms of his concept of capital, adapted as "mobility capital," rather than his wider concept of social space.

5. Fogle (2011) similarly places emphasis on the built environment and physical space. Painter (2000), who engages in one of the most comprehensive ways with Bourdieu's attention to geography and spatiality in an overview of his reception by and relationship to approaches by geographers, tends, unfortunately, to view Bourdieu's concept of social space as primarily a spatial metaphor in ways that diminish its potential.

6. This can be seen in discussions of Bourdieu's theory of social space in such examples as Crossley (2005) and Hardy (2014). Atkinson (2017) adapts this to a different national context, the United Kingdom, but similarly pays little attention to physical space or place.

7. See Susen and Turner (2011); Grenfell et al. (2011); Gorski (2013); Swartz (2013); and Hilgers and Mangez (2015). An exception to this is Mike Savage's (2011) call for more attention to Bourdieu's contributions to urban sociology, although his focus is on what he refers to as Bourdieu's "field analysis" without a full appreciation of the implications of the wider concept of social space. Although I agree with Hilgers and Mangez (2015b, 1) that habitus has dominated scholarship on Bourdieu, they argue that his theory of fields "lies at the heart of his work," whereas I see field as secondary to the broader concept of social space.

8. Bourdieu's distinction between differentiated and undifferentiated societies is one that recalls Durkheim's division between organic and mechanical solidarity. I have previously offered a critique of this distinction, which is also one between traditional and modern societies in his work (see Reed-Danahay 1995; 2004; and 2005b). A more recent critique of his concept of more or less differentiated societies in relationship to Bourdieu's theory of fields, with implications for its application to postcolonial settings, can be found in Hilgers and Mangez (2015a).

9. For example, Bourdieu referenced the social space of academia in his essay on "Participant-Objectivation" (Bourdieu 2003b) in which the anthropological field, among other disciplinary fields, could be located. He also indicated in that essay that training in a particular discipline could produce shared *doxa* through the same process whereby commonsense notions are instilled in students by national institutions of education.

10. That Bourdieu attended boarding school should not be taken as a sign of high social status, as it might be in other national contexts. In rural France at the time when he was a child, anyone who advanced to high school (and this would be the minority for rural children who typically ended their education after primary school) lived at school at least during the week. This was primarily because of the geographic distances between cities, where such institutions were located, and rural towns and villages.

11. As I noted in *Locating Bourdieu* (Reed-Danahay 2005b, 30 and 168, fn3), the British sociologist Richard Hoggart, of working-class background himself, was influential in Bourdieu's thought. Moreover, Bourdieu was responsible for having Hoggart's translated work published in France. I am grateful to the anonymous reviewer of *Bourdieu and Social Space* who pointed out the relevance of Löfgren's work to this discussion.

12. See in particular Durkheim's *The Elementary Forms of Religious Life* (1995, 339). Claval (1984) mentions this, and also cites Condominas (1980) for having pointed it out. Also see Buttimer (1969) and Claval (1984) for overviews of the history of ideas about social space.

13. Durkheim's contributions to social space have also been noted by Sorokin (1927), and more recently by Anne Buttimer (1969, 418–19), who points to his focus on social differentiation and social morphology. (See also the more recent discussion in Corsín Jiménez 2003.)

14. Based on personal communication with Bourdieu in the early 1980s.

15. Lewin's influence on Bourdieu is usually discussed in terms of his field theory (Lewin 1964), since both Lewin and Bourdieu used the term "field." However, Lewin also wrote about social space. See Friedman (2011) and the chapters in Hilgers and Mangez (2015b).

16. The relationship between the ideas of Lefebvre and Bourdieu is a topic for further exploration, although it is outside of the scope of this book to do so here. The two figures were born a generation apart, with Lefebvre born in 1901 and Bourdieu in 1930, but Lefebvre's most influential writings appeared after the 1970s. Significantly, Lefebvre is not of one of the academics mentioned in Bourdieu's *Homo Academicus* (1984b; 1988b) even though he was quite active in the events of May 1968. Pierce and Martin (2015, 6) claim that Lefebvre was influenced by Bourdieu in the development of his concept of social space, even though he never cited his work.

Bourdieu's World-Making

> To change the world, one has to change the ways of world-making, that is, the vision of the world and the practical operations by which groups are produced and reproduced.
> —"Social Space and Symbolic Power" (1989c, 23)

Bourdieu viewed the power of world-making as symbolic power—that is, the imposition of a point of view and taken-for-granted understanding of the classifications, divisions, and groups in a society. Bourdieu's concept of social space is inseparable from the related concepts of habitus, field, capital, and symbolic power.[1] These are the concepts that Bourdieu used to imagine the social world he analyzed in his writing. Bourdieu found an affinity between his idea of social space and the concept of world-making introduced by Nelson Goodman in his 1978 book *Ways of Worldmaking*. He began to cite Goodman after having publishing *Distinction* (1979b/1984a). In a lecture delivered in 1986 at the University of California, subsequently published in 1989 as "Social Space and Symbolic Power," Bourdieu remarked:

> In fact, there are always, in any society, conflicts between symbolic powers that aim at imposing the vision of legitimate divisions, that is, at constructing groups. Symbolic power, in this sense, is a power of "world-making." "World-making" consists, according to Nelson Goodman (1978), "in separating and reuniting, often in the same operation," in carrying out a decomposition, an analysis, and a composition, a synthesis, often by the use of labels. Social classifications, as is the case in archaic societies where they often work through dualist oppositions (masculine/feminine, high/low, strong/weak, etc.), organize the

perception of the social world and, under certain conditions, can really organize the world itself. (1989c, 22)

As Zeynep Gürsel pointed out in her book on digital news, for Goodman, "representations are central to worldmaking and contribute the understanding but also the building of the realities in which we live" (Gürsel 2016, 13). For Bourdieu, world-making is the product of struggles over creations of reality.

At the same time that he sought to unveil the workings of world-making through the imposition of *doxa* as commonsense understandings of social reality, Bourdieu was himself engaged in an alternative construction of the social world—his own sociological vision of how power operates in social life. In his writing, Bourdieu constructed a social world or universe and analyzed the workings of that world—which he viewed as the social space. Novelists, anthropologists, and sociologists are engaged in this type of world-making, as are the "everyday" people we encounter and whose lives we study and write about.[2]

Bourdieu hoped to change understandings of the social world that masked the ways in which social inequality and social dominance are reproduced. In examining his key concepts, we also, therefore, examine Bourdieu's vision of the world. Bourdieu sought to challenge existing ways of world-making in order to establish a more equitable society. In this chapter, I consider how his writing acted as a form of world-making (by exposing and analyzing how symbolic power operates). Bourdieu stated, "To change the world, one has to change the ways of world-making." Whether or not he was successful, it is clear that Bourdieu hoped his form of social analysis might have the power to change the world for the better by stripping us of some of our illusions.

Bourdieu's theoretical approach was a form of world-making in that, first of all, he viewed all social interaction as informed by an underlying structure. The structure of this world is the social space—which is hierarchical, divided, and a space of struggles for both material and symbolic dominance. Bourdieu's social world was also one in which we are all habituses (positions in social space), even if we see ourselves otherwise as autonomous individuals who freely make choices. Our lives are guided by the dispositions of our habitus, which shapes our aspirations as well as the things from which we distance ourselves or reject. Some people have more power to shape understandings of the social world, which is connected to their symbolic power—the power of representation and the imposition of meaning about the world. Bourdieu viewed the social world as one of competition and struggle in which social actors are either motivated to maximize their own positions in social space or resolve themselves to immobility.

Although some have criticized Bourdieu for seeing all life in terms of power dynamics,[3] I think it is also fair to see him as understanding that people engage in activities not only to get ahead but also to get by.

In order to fully take advantage of Bourdieu's framework and apply it to new social configurations and relationships connected to mobility practices, it is essential to understand how the various elements within it complement each other and are part of an overall view of the social world. In the rest of this chapter, I will discuss Bourdieu's concepts of habitus, field, capital, and symbolic power as they worked together with social space in his thought.

Habitus, Affinity, and Social Distance

For Bourdieu, physical and geographical space are linked through the embodied habitus, which occupies a place in physical space and a position in social space. Habitus and social space cannot be understood without reference to each other.[4] Bourdieu's theory of practice aimed to bridge what he viewed as a false dichotomy between the structure of social space and social practices by proposing a continual process of mutual shaping. Paying close attention to the ways Bourdieu describes the habitus as a position in social space helps avoid interpretations of his work that either exalt the strategies of habitus or view it as overdetermined.[5] Social space is connected to physical space through the habitus as a body, which is in a "place" both physically and socially. Bourdieu wrote in his book *Pascalian Meditations* that "the structures of the social space . . . shape bodies by inculcating in them, through the conditionings associated with a position in that space, the cognitive structures that these conditionings apply to them" (1997/2000c, 183). Although Setha Low (2003, 12) charged Bourdieu with treating the body as "an empty container without consciousness or intention," I challenge such a view here. The embodied aspects of habitus are central to Bourdieu's theory, which posits that habitus engages in social practices that are shaped, if not determined, by the structures of social space.

Many aspects of the habitus that each of us embodies are shared by others who grew up in a similar social milieu. The primary habitus is acquired through informal mechanisms of socialization in a social space from early childhood and onward. People with similar social origins (not only in terms of social class position but also national and regional affiliations) have affinities of habitus. A person can also acquire a secondary habitus through geographic or social mobility, which may result in what Bourdieu called a "split habitus" (*habitus clivé*). When a person acquires a new habitus with new dispositions and orientations to the world, this frequently causes emotional distress because the person no longer feels "at home" in the world. For Bourdieu, as Jean-Louis Fabiani (2016, 94) has observed, the consequences of having a split habitus are generally negative—leading to feelings of displacement rather than to a positive expansion of one's sense of selfhood. Acquiring a secondary habitus is what causes the "split," because the original habitus is durable. Although I agree with Fabiani's point, I also think that an understanding of the consequences of acquiring new orientations and dispositions that result from mobility should be further explored ethnographically. When mobility is understood as an opening up to new experiences (associated with a certain cosmopolitan outlook) and a broadening of the self in positive terms, as in so-called "lifestyle migration" (Benson and O'Reilly 2009), then it is a matter of investigating to what degree the habitus has shifted and what the consequences are for feelings of belonging.

Our embodied habitus informs our everyday, commonsense understandings of our social world and how to behave within it, as well as our aspirations—that is, our understandings of what is possible (and not possible) for us. Bourdieu referred to commonsense understandings of the world as *doxa*. These taken-for-granted assumptions about social reality vary, however, according to the orientations and dispositions of any particular acquired habitus. According to Bourdieu, habitus is not a conscious aspect of identity or action under most circumstances. It is more like, as he put it, a "feel for the game." Habitus is an "invisible reality that can neither be shown nor handled, and which organizes agents' practices and representations" (1991a, 635).

Bourdieu sought to analyze the relationships between time, physical space, and social space in ways that emphasized how social practices generated from habitus (in terms of behaviors, world views, position-takings, and physical locations) are influenced both by the other habituses in a particular social space, and the possibilities (in terms of both "objective" opportunities and "subjective" aspirations) available to each habitus. A person's movement across time and space, and up or down in the social hierarchy, is a product of habitus (entailing both inherited and acquired cultural and symbolic capital). Habitus is not only situated in geographic and social space, therefore, but has a trajectory related to forms of mobility and immobility. A person's relationships to others may change, as they come to feel closer or more socially distant from certain people and as they acquire new forms of capital or enhance the ones they already possess. Bourdieu therefore understood social space not as a static structure but rather as a space in which the positions and positionings of social agents (his term for "individuals") are in motion as their positions may alter in relationship to each other.

Bourdieu evoked the term "point of view" to describe understandings of social reality, which will vary according to habitus because different positions or locations in social space provide different perspectives on the social world. Physical and social space are linked through perceptions of social distance and closeness (or proximity) related to the affinities of habitus—those dispositions (tastes and distastes) and ways of understanding the world and one's position within it that are related to family origins. People who share similar dispositions and worldview are closer in social space. They may also be drawn to each other in physical space when they perceive each other as socially close. Bourdieu argued that the physical places or localizations that people inhabit are related to their position in social space. A person will have understandings of their position in social space and the range of other positions and position-takings in this space. These understandings are related to the disposition of their habitus. The position of any particular person (or agent) in social space is expressed through such physical locations as their place of residence or their business address.

Bourdieu noted that there is quite often geographic segregation so that those distant in social space are also distant in physical space. However, he also observed:

> People who are close together in social space tend to find themselves, by choice or by necessity, close to one another in geographic space; nevertheless, people who are very distant from each other in social space can encounter one another and interact, if only briefly and intermittently, in physical space. (1989c, 16)

Although proximity in social space depends on affinities of shared habitus (or similar habitus), it may be that people brought into close physical proximity with each other might be far apart in social space. Being physically close to those from whom one is distant in social space can be experienced as "intolerable" (1993c/1999b, 128), and this helps to reinforce social divisions by producing feelings that encourage people to keep their physical distance from those who are also perceived as socially distant. Those sharing a particular type of habitus and position in social space will tend to inhabit differently valued geographical settings.

Bourdieu introduced the concept of *lieu* in the collaborative book *The Weight of the World* in order to describe physical location as well as location in social space. It refers to emplacement and means "a place" or "a site." Noting that humans have bodies and, like other material things, occupy space, Bourdieu defined *lieu* as: "The point in physical space where an agent or a thing is situated, 'takes place,' exists; that is to say, either as a localization or, from a relational viewpoint, as a position, a rank in an order" (1993c/1999b, 123). The term "location" or *lieu* thus refers to both social and physical location, and Bourdieu saw each as organized through hierarchy, with any particular location being either of higher or lower position relative to other locations. Physical location comes to express social location because those who possess highly valued symbolic capital are able to dominate and to define what are understood to be the most prestigious physical locations. Bourdieu wrote that "the power over space . . . comes from possessing various kinds of capital . . ." (ibid., 124), so that where you live and where you shop become reified expressions of your cultural capital.

Because social space is inscribed in mental as well as spatial structures, physical space becomes a site for the assertion of power and of symbolic violence. Capital allows those who have it to keep their distance from undesirable people and things, and to get close to desirable people, places, and things. In describing what could be viewed as immobility, Bourdieu wrote that "the lack of capital intensifies the experience of finitude; it chains one to a place" (ibid., 127). People make spatial choices, Bourdieu noted, in order to avoid feeling "out of place"—as in a person in a museum who is not used to visiting museums. Bourdieu (1993c/1999b, 123) characterized American ghettos as examples of *lieux* that can only be explained by social processes that exist elsewhere, in that they are defined in terms of absences of various basic social services like health care.

Because localizations in physical places are connected to positions in social space, those who are homeless therefore have no recognized or legitimate "social existence" (Bourdieu 1993c/1999b, 124). Relative position in social space is also expressed during more "temporary localizations," such as seating arrangements during official ceremonies. These forms of appropriations or consumptions of space can be displays of power. Bourdieu wrote, "The locus and the place occupied by an agent in appropriated social space are excellent indicators of his or her position in social space" (1996a, 11). Those sharing a particular type of habitus tend to dwell in differently valued geographical settings, so that the rich will live in more pleasant and favored neighborhoods within cities.

In some cases, those who are in more elevated positions in social space will interact with others in such a way that their social distance from those with lower positions is downplayed. Bourdieu referred to this as "strategies of condescension" (ibid., 16). The ways in which such behavior is perceived by those lower in the social hierarchy indicate they understand that the social distance is not truly eliminated even when they may approve of the attempt to close the distance. For example, a remark such as "he is not so highbrow, for a university professor" reveals that the speaker understands the distance and qualifies it through the reference to the status of professor. Those who have been, in Bourdieu's terms, "consecrated" with higher status are most able to transgress social boundaries. As he wrote, "He who is sure of his cultural identity can play with the rules of the cultural game" (1982b/1992c, 87).

On the other hand, there is also the possibility of avoiding interactions with those who are perceived to be socially distant. Bourdieu remarked that "social distances are inscribed in bodies or, more precisely, into the relation to the body, to language, and to time" (1989c, 17), and this includes having a sense of one's place (in Goffman's terms). This can lead to a strategy of not wanting to get too familiar and can be perceived by others as either timidity or arrogance, depending on the social context. It is this "sense of one's place" that leads to the feelings of either social closeness or distance (associated with emotions of sympathy or antipathy) that influence forms of affiliation, cooperation, and sociality. This also connects to feelings of belonging, as mentioned above. Bourdieu cited E. P. Thompson's study, *The Making the English Working Class* (ibid., 18), to underscore his point that groups do not exist in any "social reality" but must be constructed. For Bourdieu, each habitus, as a position in social space, views the world as "natural" and accepts various divisions in social space that are part of the social structure. These structurings can be economic, ethnic, national, religious, and so on.

As I have argued elsewhere (Reed-Danahay 2005b), Bourdieu's first uses of the notion of *habitus* in the early 1960s drew both from the more psychological theory of habitus used by Norbert Elias and that of the theory of bodily habits and habitus in the work of Marcel Mauss. For Elias, habitus is a form of "embodied social learning" associated with drives and impulses that determine tastes and habits (Dunning and Mennell 1996, ix). Social habitus is a form of "we-feeling" and is related to group identity (Elias 1987, 225). Mauss used the concept of habitus to refer to customary habits of moving the body and wrote: "In them we should see the techniques and work of collective and individual practical reason . . ." ([1950] 1979, 101).

Max Weber and Erwin Panofsky also influenced Bourdieu in his development of the concept of habitus.[6] Bourdieu was drawn to Panofsky's work on gothic architecture and scholastic mental habits, and he later wrote that it inspired his development of ideas of habitus to include the generation of practices (see Bourdieu 1967 and 1985a) that would be harmonized in a particular social milieu, such as that of scholasticism. Bourdieu interpreted Weber's approach to religion and charisma through a lens of the religious habitus and its points of view (1971). It was also in his analysis of Weber and religion that Bourdieu offered one of his earliest examples of the concept of field (religious field) in relationship to habitus.

In a discussion of the origins of his concepts of field and habitus, Bourdieu explained that both were intended to draw upon the same "generative" idea that Chomsky was developing about grammar. For Bourdieu, the active and "inventive capacities" of habitus are not those of a "universal mind," as he believed was Chomsky's perspective on language; rather, the dispositions of habitus are those of the "acting agent" driven by practical reason (1985a, 13). Bourdieu's theory of field was not that of an autonomous field but a "social space of objective relationships" (ibid., 16) in which cultural production can occur. This meant that positions of social actors in a field must be understood as occurring within social space. Fields are only partially autonomous in that the interactions within them are based on the underlying "objective relationships" between different fields in wider social space resulting from the positioning of habituses in that space. In this Bourdieusian view of the world, there is room for some invention and creativity, which can permit some social actors to develop new fields and sometimes "produce actions or works which go beyond their intentions and their interests" (ibid., 24).

Field

Readers often overlook the distinctions between Bourdieu's understandings of field and social space, and this is largely due to Bourdieu's own use of social space (*espace social*) and social field (*champ*) in both more general and more specific ways.[7] Bourdieu's concept of field has little necessary relationship to any particular place or physical location, and does not articulate physical and social space. Although Bourdieu occasionally seemed to use the concepts of field and social space interchangeably, the field is a region in wider social space (Bourdieu 1985b). Social space is a broader concept than field, and it is only by understanding how the habitus is generated through its position in social space that one can grasp how habitus operates in and constitutes (as well as possibly originating) a field—as in the establishment of the "literary field" in the late nineteenth century in France (Bourdieu 1993b).

Bourdieu's concepts of field and social space complement each other but do not refer to the same thing. Although Bourdieu used social space in his early ethnographic work in what he referred to as "undifferentiated" societies, fields are present in his work primarily when he was referring to "differentiated," class-stratified societies. As I have mentioned above, social space is generated by the operation of the habitus—its points of view, position-takings, and positions (social and physical). However, we can say that habitus is "realized" in fields—taking Bourdieu's point that "any habitus, as a system of dispositions, is only effectively realized in relation to the determinate structure of socially marked positions . . ." (1996b, 265). Bourdieu viewed subjectivity or point of view as embedded in social positions within fields. Fields are composed of social agents (people or institutions) that are positioned in a similar area of the wider social space yet are differentiated within the field. Habitus is a position in social space, but individuals participate in multiple fields in which the value of the different forms of capital they possess will vary and in which they attempt to maintain or enhance their overall position in social space.

Bourdieu increasingly focused on the concept of *champ* or field (to denote particular regions of social space) from the 1980s on, although he first utilized this term much earlier in a publication on the "intellectual field" (1966a). Bourdieu fully developed the concept of "field" in the *Logic of Practice* (1980b/1990),[8] where he also articulated the different aspects of habitus and capital in Kabylia and France. In *The Logic of Practice*, Bourdieu frequently substitutes the term "field" (associated with what he called "institutions" such as the Church or the economy) for "structure." For example, he compared the relationship between habitus and field to that between "incorporated history and an objectified history" (ibid., 66). It was in a field, he suggested, that social agents utilize the "feel for the game" or practical sense. He contrasted the field in a game (as "the pitch or board on which [the game] is played, the rules, the outcome at stake, etc.") with the notion of social fields. These are "the products of a long, slow process of autonomization, and are therefore, so to speak, games 'in themselves' and not 'for themselves,' one does not embark on the game by a conscious act, one is born into the game, with the game . . ." (ibid., 67). Bourdieu further elaborated upon the concept of field in his study of the academic field in *Homo Academicus* (1984b/1988b), and in his work on art—for instance, with the study of Flaubert and the literary field (1993b and 1992b/1996b).

Bourdieu viewed the field as a concept that was relational rather than "substantialist." He rejected an approach that seeks substances or essences in individuals or groups, and which tends to foreground the individual. Bourdieu described the field as a

> field of forces, whose necessity is imposed on agents who are engaged in it, and a field of struggles within which agents confront each other, with differentiated means and ends according to their position in the structure of the field of forces, thus contributing to conserving or transforming its structure. (1998d, 32)

The concept of field provided Bourdieu with a framework to explain the ways in which power and shared worldviews coalesce in particular realms of society. He identified various types of field (literary, artistic, religious, economic, and academic).

One way to understand the distinction between social space and field is to recall the concept of "orders" used by Lévi-Strauss, which shares some affinities with what Bourdieu called "fields." Lévi-Strauss wrote, "Anthropology considers the whole social fabric as a network of different types of orders" ([1958] 1963, 312), which correspond to kinship, economics, social structure, and so on. Bourdieu did not describe fields as networks within the social fabric, but he did see fields as subregions of social space, and a field is more like a network than a social space in his characterizations of it. For Bourdieu, fields are relatively autonomous and so cannot be viewed, in a structural-functionalist way, as somehow constructing a harmonious "whole." The idea I am proposing is simply that orders are for Lévi-Strauss what fields are for Bourdieu—smaller regions or domains of social space.

Bourdieu frequently referred to fields as subregions of a wider national social space, but this signaled their location in abstract social space and not geographic space. Fields are composed of social agents (people or institutions) positioned in a similar area of social space yet differentiated within the field. What Bourdieu referred to as the "stakes" of the struggle in a field are the forms of capital (economic, cultural, social, and symbolic) possessed by agents within the field and recognized as having value. The "exchange rates" of the different forms of capital will vary and are also regulated to a certain extent by bureaucratic institutions (Bourdieu 1994a/1998d, 34). In Bourdieu's framework, the field of power is an area in social space where the most dominant habituses are positioned. Fields are subspaces in a social space that have some autonomy from each other, and a person can participate in more than one field. Another distinction is that habitus is generated in social space, not in fields.

In his critique of field theory, French sociologist Bernard Lahire argues that it tends to view habitus as too unitary. Lahire, rightly in my view, sees field as inadequate, because not all social agents participate in fields (if understood as "professional worlds") and also because "field theory cannot cover all possible cases of relevant contexts of action" (Lahire 2010, 447). He goes on to remark that in the social world, people may act, think, and feel differently in different situations. Although this aspect of what is sometimes referred to as "situational identity" may be taken for granted in ethnographic research, Lahire is pointing to the dangers of an overreliance on field theory to understand social life. His remarks are particularly aimed at those who utilize Bourdieu's theory of field in a very strict and narrow sense. This leads to a focus on "relatively autonomous microcosms" (ibid., 449) that miss what may take place outside of a given field.

Lahire's ([2001] 2011) solution to the problem has been to retain Bourdieu's focus on the interactions of habitus and social world, while also stretching the concept of habitus to include the idea of a "plural actor." Bourdieu acknowledged that habitus acquired in the family can be modified through schooling and other experiences, particularly in more differentiated societies, and that a person can acquire a secondary habitus or have a "split" habitus. My own view is that social space is a concept more amenable than field to understanding the ways in which particular social situations in particular physical locations may lead to different expressions of a person's habitus. This is why I believe that field alone is not adequate for an understanding of the relationship between mobility and habitus.

Although field became an increasingly dominant focus of Bourdieu's work over the years, he also returned to the interest in physical space in relationship to social space that marked the earlier ethnographic work I will discuss in Chapter Two. We can see this, in particular, through the concept of *lieu* or place/location associated with his work in the project *The Weight of the World* (1993c/1999b)—to which I have referred earlier in this chapter—and in his work on the real estate market (2000d/2005)—to be discussed in Chapter Four.

Capital

For Bourdieu, "the immanent structure of the social world" is composed of the distribution of various forms of capital. Capital refers to a form of power. During the 1980s, Bourdieu deployed the concept of social space to articulate the context in which power in the form of capital (economic, cultural, social, and symbolic) is transmitted and circulated or exchanged by social actors. Each habitus, with its associated cultural and symbolic capital, occupies a position in social space and in what Bourdieu called the field of power. The field of power is a region of social space occupied by those who hold the most dominant positions within it. It is what he referred to as the "gaming space" in which people and institutions use "strategies aimed at preserving or transforming these relations of power" (1989a/1996c, 264–65). A person's movement across time and space, and up or down in the social hierarchy, is a product of habitus (including inherited and acquired cultural capital).

In the foundational essay "The Forms of Capital" (1979c/1986a), Bourdieu described capital as both "accumulated labor" and as power in class-based, "differentiated" societies. According to Bourdieu, different forms of capital represent different "guises" of power and they can "change into one another" (ibid., 243) through modes of institutionalization at the level of smaller groups (such as those based on kinship or affinity) or at the level of the state. Bourdieu was interested in the questions of how capital is transmitted and inherited in families, and how it is exchanged (and has relative value) in social space. The ability of a person to accumulate capital beyond what they inherit from their family is constrained, according to this model, by the distribution of various forms of capital that come into play in a particular field and its wider social space.

One of Bourdieu's main contributions to social theory is his idea that there is not a simple correlation between economic capital and cultural capital—you can have a high amount of cultural capital or social capital, which can be beneficial, even when you may have relatively little economic capital and vice versa. In what Bourdieu labeled undifferentiated societies, using the example of rural Algeria, there was little variation among habituses, except for those of gender. In differentiated, class-based societies—such as France and other more urbanized settings, the habitus is connected to social class position. In a "differentiated" social space, the orientations and dispositions of the habitus take on differing amounts of value based on the forms of capital associated with that habitus. Therefore, in a class-based and stratified society, features such as ways of speaking; tastes in food, music, or art; aspirations regarding education and career; ideas about how to decorate a house; and ways of moving the body are all aspects of habitus that have more or less value in a particular social space. That value is influenced by the ways in which it is either legitimized or degraded by those who dominate the social space.

A person who inherits a great deal of capital in all three forms (economic, cultural, and social) will, according to Bourdieu, be better positioned to accumulate additional capital, and someone with less inherited capital will only be able to accumulate additional capital if they have sufficient skills to take advantage of opportunities presented to them. Even maintaining one's inherited capital is partly based on skill in making the best of it. This was a subject addressed by Bourdieu in his discussion of the characters in Flaubert's novel *L'Education Sentimentale*, to which I will turn in Chapter Three. It was also how he explained his own social position and trajectory as an intellectual and academic with high cultural capital, despite his modest social origins and relative lack of inherited capital (Bourdieu 2004a/2007).

Cultural capital is associated exclusively with the particular person who possesses it and, therefore, "it declines and dies with its bearer (with his biological capacity, his memory, etc.)" (ibid., 245). Bourdieu viewed cultural capital as having three states: embodied, objectified, and institutionalized. The first state refers to mental and bodily dispositions or habitus, the second to cultural goods (frequently materialized, as in books or paintings), and the third to educational qualifications or other forms of competence legitimized by institutions. Habitus as embodied culture in undifferentiated societies differs from habitus as cultural capital in class-based societies. Habitus as embodied culture is not, Bourdieu noted, to be viewed as cultural capital in a relatively undifferentiated society, such as the peasant societies he studied in Algeria and rural France. In undifferentiated societies, according to Bourdieu, "access to the means of appropriating the cultural heritage is very equally distributed" (ibid., 255, fn6). Cultural capital confers "exclusive advantages" to certain habituses and thereby is associated with class differentiation in class-based societies. The embodied state of cultural capital, or habitus (in a differentiated society), can be viewed as the product of the conversion of wealth "into an integral part of the person" (ibid., 245).

Cultural capital can become symbolic capital when it appears to be an intrinsic attribute (like talent) of the person with it. Bourdieu explained that he hit upon the notion of cultural capital while researching academic success and finding that although the commonsense view is that it is due to natural talent, the link between social class and school achievement suggests that these are related. He stressed that because cultural capital has both inherited and acquired properties, the part that is inherited is not always recognized as such and frequently appears to be invisible. When it is not recognized as a form of capital (e.g., wealth and power), cultural capital is "symbolic" capital and is viewed instead as a form of authority and "legitimate competence." Those with significant amounts of cultural capital receive profits that are both material and symbolic because of the relative scarcity of their competencies. Because educational qualifications provide an institutional legitimacy to forms of knowledge that may also be acquired outside of schooling, the cultural capital of the autodidact "may be called into question at any time" because it was not conferred by seemingly "objective" educational institutions (ibid., 248).

Here, we can make a comparison with the migrant, who brings knowledge to their host society that may not be valued because it is not sufficiently credentialed. In my fieldwork among former Vietnamese refugees in Texas, it was common for me to encounter men (most of whom were former soldiers in the South Vietnamese army) with university degrees and training in law, medicine, and other professions who worked in menial jobs in the United States because they had neither the language skills nor the credentials to have their "cultural capital" valued as symbolic capital.

Social capital differs from cultural capital in Bourdieu's framework in that, whereas the latter is attached to a person, social capital refers to the possession of resources in the form of relationships of "mutual acquaintance and recognition" that come from "membership in a group" (1979c/1986a, 249). These relationships are based on material and symbolic exchange. Social capital can also include behaviors of bearing, ways of speaking, and pronunciation associated with manners when these are indicative of the prestige of a group. In addition, as Bourdieu wrote, "They are partially irreducible to objective relations of proximity in physical (geographical) space or even in economic and social space" (ibid., 249). Social capital, therefore, is about proximity in physical and social space with others in the group. Any member of the group can mobilize its resources and connections, as well as the cultural capital associated with other people in the group. These groups must be maintained and reproduced through what Bourdieu called "rites of institution," which will be addressed at greater length in Chapter Four. This involves both naming the participants in the group in terms of their relationship to others (i.e., sister, cousin, elder) and exchanges (verbal and material) that simultaneously encourage and produce "mutual knowledge and recognition" (ibid., 250).

Of particular interest to migration studies in relationship to social capital and social space is what Bourdieu had to say about the limits of social groups being the limits of exchange among their members. He viewed each member as "a custodian of the limits of the group," meaning that when a person engages with a form of exchange through trade, marriage, or the sharing of a meal, they might stretch or alter the limits of the group through what might be considered a "misalliance." Bourdieu wrote that "through the introduction of new members into a family, a clan, or a club, the whole definition of the group, i.e., its fines, its boundaries, and its identity, is put at stake, exposed to redefinition, alteration, adulteration" (ibid., 250). Families, the example Bourdieu used to illustrate this point, may have less formal control over the types of exchanges that lead to marriage or other forms of lasting relationship, but they still try to steer their members toward "legitimate" exchanges so as to produce a fairly homogeneous group characterized by social proximity. They do so through occasions they host (such as parties or receptions), places in which they dwell (such as neighborhoods or schools), and practices in which they participate (such as sports or ceremonies). Migrants stretch the limits of a social group when they enter it in ways that may be considered more or less legitimate among those who seek to maintain boundaries.

Bourdieu concluded that labor (time and energy) as well as economic capital are spent in reproducing social capital. This reproduction, he wrote, "presupposes the unceasing effort of sociability, a continuous series of exchanges in which recognition is endlessly affirmed and reaffirmed" (ibid., 250). By understanding the processes involved in the acquisition and reproduction of cultural and social capital, we can better grasp the ways in which individual lives are constrained by the social space in which forms of capital receive various levels of value. Bourdieu's point about the "exposure" of a group posed by "the introduction of new members" has implications for the exclusion of newcomers such as migrants, particularly at the local level of neighborhoods, towns, and cities. Being able to fully participate, and be recognized as legitimately doing so, in such everyday forms of sociality as those parties and receptions Bourdieu mentions, can be an important aspect for what is commonly considered as migrant incorporation.

Social Space and Symbolic Power

For Bourdieu, having symbolic power means being able to name, classify, and describe the social world in ways that "produce" the existence of a recognized group in social space. He maintained that "symbolic struggles over the perception of the social world" (1989c, 17) take place through attempts to make groups visible and to make claims about their size, strength, and cohesiveness. This is enacted through the strategies used by social actors to manipulate their own position in social space (through "presentation of self" in Goffman's terms), and through symbolic manipulations of language—naming, vocabulary used, and so on to identify groups as social realities.

In his essays "Social Space and the Genesis of Groups" (1985b) and "Social Space and Symbolic Power" (1989c), Bourdieu addressed the ways in which groups form and become visible in social space, arguing that both place-making and group-making are projects aimed at creating ideas of fixity in social space related to struggles for power. Bourdieu not only described the positioning of individuals as embodied habituses in social space but also the visibility and positioning of groups in social space. He maintained that a group's position in society is connected to its position in geographic space in concrete places. In turning to groups and how they are socially constructed, Bourdieu had to think about the physical and geographical locations of people in addition to their social positioning.

The social construction of groups entails modes of representation of a collectivity through "demonstrations whose goal is to exhibit a group, its size, its strength, its cohesiveness, to make it exist visibly" (1989c, 20). Social space is structured according to the distribution of various forms of capital and their value in that space. In everyday life, it "tends to function as a symbolic space, a space of lifestyles and status groups characterized by different lifestyles" (ibid., 20). People are distinguished in social space through noticeable contrasts in lifestyle, which are connected to the dispositions of habitus. For example, "those who drink champagne are opposed to those who drink whiskey" (ibid., 20). Bourdieu privileged social space as the "the first and last reality, since it still commands the representations that the social agents can have of it" (1996a, 22).

Bourdieu was particularly interested in challenging Marxist theories of social class. He argued that social classes are not groups, because they are not perceived as such by the "representations" of social agents. They are only groups "on paper," as understood objectively by the social analyst. Social classes could be mobilized, and thereby have a social existence, but this has to be accomplished and is not a given. Bourdieu claimed, "Constructing a theory of social space presupposes a series of breaks with Marxist theory" (1985b, 723). There were three main points to this argument. Bourdieu charged, first, that the Marxist theory of social class seeks to define groups rather than relationships and therefore overlooks the distinction between an "effectively mobilized group" and a theoretical class. The second problem is that Marxism understands the "social field" primarily in terms of the relations of economic production and therefore overlooks forms of symbolic production that also affect social inequality and are connected to the question of why groups do or do not mobilize. This led to Bourdieu's final point that, due to "intellectualism and objectivism," Marxist theory overlooks the "symbolic struggles" regarding representations of social reality. These occur in various social fields that are constituted by internal hierarchies and placed in a hierarchical relationship to each other in wider social space.

Adopting the view that social classes acting as mobilized groups are not the same as theoretical ones, Bourdieu wrote that because workers are closer in social space than are workers and bosses, and may also live in neighborhoods in closer physical proximity to each other, it is easier to mobilize workers among themselves than it is to mobilize the two different categories of people together. He did, however, suggest that in the event of an "international crisis," it would be possible to mobilize a group based on links of national identity and that this is "partly because, by virtue of its specific history, each national social space has its specific structure—e.g. as regards hierarchical distances within the economic field" (1985b, 725). While closeness in social space may be a factor in the formation of groups, ethnic or national divisions may also form. Bourdieu noted that ethnic groups may be placed in a hierarchical relationship to each other within national social space—using the example of the US, where older immigrant groups enjoy higher status than more recent ones.

The Divisions of the Social World

For Bourdieu, world-making is an operation of symbolic power. Symbolic capital has power because it is supported by institutional arrangements and groups that are represented in social space as having legitimacy. This chapter has outlined the ways in which Bourdieu theorized the operation of habitus, forms of capital, social fields, and symbolic power to create a *doxic* representation of the divisions of the social world. Bourdieu's theory of social space is one that seeks to provide a conceptual framework for understanding how this occurs. He posited that social space is an underlying structure of power that is also structured by the operation of habitus. In the next three chapters, I show how Bourdieu put the concepts I have discussed in this chapter into practice in his ethnographic and sociological studies.

NOTES

1. The point that Bourdieu's work cannot be understood without understanding the relationships between field, habitus, and capital has been very eloquently made by Jean-Louis Fabiani (2016). I have benefitted in my own understanding of these concepts from his discussion of them. However, he pays less attention to the mega-concept of social space that concerns me in this book.

2. My view of Bourdieu's world-making recalls the idea of "invention of culture" proposed by Roy Wagner in his 1975 book. Wagner described this as "the anthropologists use of meanings known to him [sic] in constructing an understandable representation of his [sic] subject matter" ([1975] 2016, 9). He emphasized that the "natives" are inventing their own understandings of their culture at the same time that the anthropologist is constructing their understanding. As Tim Ingold recently remarked in his preface to a new edition of Wagner's book, it would be a mistake to see Wagner as "complicit" in the enterprise through which academic world-making participates in "banishing the creativity of other life-worlds" ([1975] 2016, xiv). World-making is going on among those we study as well as among anthropologists. Bourdieu understood this, which is why he emphasized that social space was his own analytic construct.

3. As Fabiani (2016, 38) has perceptively commented, it is difficult to imagine, in Bourdieu's use of the metaphor of "game," that he would identify any truly cooperative games in social life.

4. I have emphasized this point elsewhere (see Reed-Danahay 2005b; 2009; and 2013).

5. See Reed-Danahay (2005b, 15–16 and 52–60) for more detailed discussions of various readings of Bourdieu related to issues of social agency. See also my own earlier critiques of Bourdieu's thought in Reed-Danahay (1993; 1995; and 1996).

6. There is an often-repeated claim (e.g., Johnson [1993, 5] and Fogle [2011, 39]) that Bourdieu's first use of the term "habitus" was in the Postface he added to his French translation of Panofsky's *Gothic Architecture* (Bourdieu 1967). Bourdieu himself claimed that he "introduced" habitus in his writings on Panofsky (Bourdieu 1985a), but I assume he means by this that Panofsky's perspective brought a new dimension to his understanding of habitus. This is because he used habitus earlier, as I will show in Chapter Two when turning to his ethnographic research among French peasants in Béarn where he also first began to develop his concept of social space. Bourdieu's writing on Panofsky is also not the first appearance of his con-

cept of "social space," as claimed by Fogle (2011, 1), and the term does not appear in Bourdieu's article on Weber and the religious field (Bourdieu 1971).

7. For two excellent critical appraisals of Bourdieu's theory of fields, see Hilgers and Mangez (2015) and Fabiani (2016).

8. As Fabiani has observed (2016, 27), the word "field" is scarcely mentioned or utilized as a concept in *Outline of a Theory of Practice* (1972a/1977c), but gained more prominence in the expansion of that project that became *The Logic of Practice* (1980b/1990).

A Sense of One's Place

> Each agent has a practical, bodily knowledge of her present
> and potential position in the social space, a "sense of one's
> place" as Goffman puts it.
> —*Pascalian Meditations* (1997/2000c, 184)

The title of this chapter borrows a phrase from Erving Goffman that Bourdieu cited frequently in his writings on social space and habitus, as illustrated in the above epigraph. What does it mean to have a sense of one's
place (both in terms of physical location and in terms of social positioning
and emplacement), and how can this change when social space expands or
shifts in other ways, or when a person moves to a different social space?
How does the "sense of one's place" affect mobility practices and their consequences? Bourdieu's early ethnographic research in rural France and Algeria explored the relationships between spatiality, temporality, and habitus.
It was in these contexts, based on ethnographic research conducted in the
late 1950s and early 1960s, that Bourdieu first developed his concepts of
social space and habitus. In this chapter, I explore Bourdieu's work in three
different settings: a rural French township, a traditional Kabyle house, and
Algerian resettlement camps.[1] By not only reviewing this early work but also
following its influence over time in Bourdieu's oeuvre, we see the endurance
of a focus on the relationship between embodied habitus, social space,
physical space, and habitat (as both physical and emotional "home").

Social Distance and Proximity in Rural France

Bourdieu effectively conveyed the idea of embodied habitus as location
in both physical space and social space in his article "Célibat et Condi-

tion Paysanne" ["Bachelorhood and the Peasant Condition"] (1962).[2] The analysis focuses on changes in the marriage system in Lesquire, a French township[3] in the region of Béarn where Bourdieu had undertaken ethnographic fieldwork in 1959–60. It was also his natal village and where he spent his childhood. The article's title ties the status of bachelorhood to circumstances in peasant society more generally in mid-twentieth century France. Bourdieu's use of the word "condition" signals its dual meaning in French to denote both social position or rank (which we might refer to as one's "situation" in English) and destiny (as in the "human condition"). The linking of these two meanings, social rank and destiny, has implications for Bourdieu's developing theory of habitus and social space. As I will show in subsequent chapters, Bourdieu later came to view habitus in terms of both trajectory (destiny) and social position or rank in social space. He used the concept of "destiny" not as a predetermined outcome, but rather as a combination of aspirations (based on the dispositions of habitus) and the social expectations and limitations also attached to that habitus and its position in social space.

Bourdieu's study of peasant bachelors in Lesquire was based not on migration but on a changing social space for those who stayed in place. However, his focus on distance and proximity in both social and geographical space is valuable in the context of mobility. We can draw from it ideas about how geographic boundaries relevant to social relationships can shift—expanding or possibly even contracting over time. When the boundaries of social space are connected to shared, commonsense understandings of the world, rather than to physical borders, this leaves open the possibility to explore how the social space of entities such as the nation-state might not depend entirely on geographic territory, and how they are also connected to understandings of social boundaries.

During his fieldwork in Lesquire, Bourdieu was puzzled by nostalgic complaints among residents (particularly older males) that there was a marriage crisis in the township because farmers were finding it difficult to attract a wife. He began the article with the following question: "By what paradox can men's failure to marry appear to those men themselves and to all around them as the most striking symptom of the crisis of a society which has traditionally condemned its younger sons to emigration or bachelorhood?" (1962/2008a, 9). How this had happened was what Bourdieu set out to explain. Because historical records showed little change in the marriage rate for rural men since the late nineteenth century, Bourdieu posited that this perception of a rise in bachelorhood was based not on the statistical frequency of marriages but, rather, on the fact that the type of man who remained unmarried had changed. In the recent past, with the system of primogeniture, younger sons of farm families frequently remained unmarried, and the eldest son enjoyed the most favorable position for a good marriage. Everyone accepted this as a necessary sacrifice for the good of the family. Now (circa 1960), the bachelor had increasingly come to be the eldest, rather than a younger, son.

Changing understandings of social proximity and distance had influenced what Bourdieu referred to as "the marriage market" or "marriage system."[4] Marriage patterns reflected a growing social differentiation within the township of Lesquire. Like other rural French townships, Lesquire had one major village (*le bourg*), also called Lesquire, surrounded by smaller hamlets (*les hameaux*). Its total population, based on the 1954 census, was 1,354 (1962/2008a, 42). The village, which had the largest concentration of population (264), served as the administrative and commercial center and housed the mayor's office, church, school, shops, and cafés. Whereas social distance in the past had been based primarily on the "rank" of the different families (or *maisons*/houses) in Lesquire and its neighboring townships, social distance was now based on geographic distance—that between the remote hamlet and the village, and between the township (which included the village and its surrounding hamlets) and the town or city.

Bourdieu argued that the encroachment of urban life was causing an exodus[5] from Lesquire of young women who had adopted urban values and sought urban husbands. There had been a breakdown of patriarchal society and family socioeconomic relations, accompanied by an ethos based more on free choice and individualism among younger generations (male and female). Such ideas replaced those based on family obligations and traditional values. Not only had rural girls become more attracted to urban men (and this included younger sons from farm households who were more "urbanized" than were their older brothers), many of them were also repulsed by farmers from the remote hamlets. Their tastes had changed because urban influences and increased access to higher levels of public education had contributed to the breakdown of traditional values. Foreshadowing *Distinction*, Bourdieu wrote that girls now held "the monopoly on the judgment of taste" (1962, 104—my translation).

Bourdieu's argument rested, in large part, on the idea of attachment to the farm. He argued that women and youngest sons had always been less attracted to farm life than were the heirs. Due to socialization practices and structural expectations, the habitus of the eldest son (who Bourdieu described as now "em-peasanted") was the one most attached to the farm and family (the *maison*, the patrimony). It was, therefore, the one slowest to change in the face of an expanding social space (constituting a new social hierarchy). Those eldest sons who embodied "good peasant values" had not accepted the newer ethos of individualism adopted more easily by their younger brothers and sisters. When Bourdieu (1972b/2008a) revisited this case in a later article, he wrote that, in the traditional system, young men and women who were considered by their parents (and the logic of the matrimonial system) to be a "good match" felt a "natural affinity" or attraction to each other based on their habitus. Most of the time, therefore, farm girls would be attracted to a farm heir. As Bourdieu put it in a later reworking of the material, "the closed world in which people felt themselves to be among like-minded people has gradually opened up" (1989bc/2008a, 183).

The social distance between farm girls and farm boys grew, and geographic distance widened as rural girls left to marry men living in towns and cities or departed for those places with younger sons in farm families. Rural women, Bourdieu argued, could now more easily find husbands outside of the township and, since they had come to prefer urban men, this explained the "extension of their matrimonial area." Bourdieu viewed what he called the "matrimonial area" (*aire*)[6] as a geographic space in which young people in Lesquire found spouses, and he referred to the social system in which marriage takes place as the "social hierarchy." Although he was not explicit about this in his writing, I interpret these two terms as referring to social space in a geographic sense (area) and in a more abstract sense (social hierarchy). In the traditional marriage system, the geographic and social space of this matrimonial area overlapped. As the social space in which marriages took place expanded to include more urbanized places beyond the township and its villages, perceptions of affinity and feelings of social proximity and distance changed. Farm heirs no longer held positions of high status in the social hierarchy and were now the ones placed lowest and in the most dominated position in this hierarchy. Social space had expanded, leaving the male peasant habitus both "out of place" and "out of time."

Bourdieu based his conclusion that the matrimonial area for residents of Lesquire was enlarging for both men and women on statistics from the late 1800s to the 1960s. He wrote:

> While the radius of 15km within which all marriages formerly took place remains the main area of exchanges (89.5 percent), there is a significant proportion of marriages more than 30km away (10.5 percent). This is evidence that the villagers, whose *social space* is much wider than that of the *hameaux*, have the opportunity of finding wives at a distance and sometimes even in the towns. (1962/2008a, 59—my emphasis)

For rural men from remote hamlets, however, the situation was quite different from that of village men. For them, it had become increasingly difficult to find a young woman who wanted be a farmer's wife. Any enlargement of the matrimonial area for them was based on the difficulty, rather than ease, they faced in attracting a wife.[7] They had to look further afield for a potential spouse, because local girls were looking elsewhere. There was now competition for wives among the men and, as Bourdieu wrote, in this competition, "the peasant from the hamlet is particularly disarmed" (1962/2008a, 65). The social distance between the village and the hamlets had grown, while that between the village and town had lessened. Bourdieu explained: "Whereas, in the older society, bachelorhood was closely linked to the situation of the individual in the social hierarchy, itself the reflection of the distribution of landed property, it is now seen as linked above all, to distribution in *geographical space*" (1962/2008a, 39—my emphasis).

Bourdieu illustrated the growing social distance between the bachelors and the others through his analysis of the Christmas dance in the village of Lesquire. In a later publication (1989b/2008a), Bourdieu cited Goffman's concept of "a sense of one's place" to describe the feeling of being out of place experienced by the bachelors at the dance. The shared physical space of the dance did not reflect social closeness. On the contrary, social distance between the bachelors and their younger peers was keenly visible. Many years after first publishing the article on peasant bachelors, Bourdieu remarked that the Christmas dance was "the visible form of the new logic of the matrimonial market" (2002a/2008a, 10). In the original article, he referred to the dance as the scene of a "clash of civilizations" resulting from what he described as the city "bursting" into peasant life, bringing "its cultural models, its music, its dances, its techniques of the body" (1962/2008a, 83).

Bourdieu vividly described how the bachelor habitus was on display in the physical space of the dance. This dance had been a festive gathering in the past through which the traditional marriage system operated to introduce young men and women (who normally had little contact with each other). Now, Bourdieu observed, it had become a space of exclusion and exile for the peasant bachelors, the farm heirs from remote hamlets. Bourdieu described the scene of the dance, including the dress and social characteristics of those in attendance, in order to illustrate the social distance between the bachelors and the yet unmarried youth of Lesquire. The dance "takes place," he wrote, "in the back room of a café" (1962/2008a, 82). Youthful couples, most of whom were native to Lesquire, took center stage dressed in the newest styles and performing fashionable dance moves. Bourdieu placed this bright and lively scene in sharp relief against another image from the dance: "standing at the edge of the dancing area, forming a dark mass, a group of older men look on in silence" (ibid., 82). They encroached upon the dance floor, hovering. These were the bachelors, out of place in this setting because men of their age who were married did not attend such dances meant for youthful flirtation and courtship. The bachelors were not at ease at the dance and were aware of the social distance between them and the others. They were aware of their place in both physical and social space—on the margins of the dance floor and in increasingly marginal positions in the social hierarchy.

Bourdieu used the term *habitus* to describe the bodily techniques of these bachelors, but his analysis did not just describe the ways they moved their bodies. He also analyzed what he would later come to call the "dispositions" of habitus. Urbanites easily spotted the habitus of the bachelors, embodied in the "*paysanás*, the lumbering peasant" (1962/2008a, 84). The habitus betrays not only the *paysana* himself, but also the position of his habitus in social space (and, in particular, that of the marriage market). Bourdieu emphasized the bodily posture and demeanor of the male peasant *habitus* in order to express the condition of being outside of one's familiar setting—"out of place." This *habitus* exhibited by the bachelors had become a sign of pathology, a stigma. In his descriptions of the *habitus* of the "em-peasanted" peasant, Bourdieu emphasized the connection between the techniques (posture, dress, movement) of the body and the social position of the habitus it embodied. Any attempts on their part to dance with the young women and girls only highlighted the clumsiness of the bachelors. Differences in the affinities of habitus led to the perceived social distance between them and the others in attendance.

Bourdieu pointed to the fatalism among the bachelors in Lesquire regarding their inability to attract a wife. In his later work on education (cf. Bourdieu and Passeron 1970b/1979d), Bourdieu referred to such fatalism as a product of symbolic violence.[8] The bachelors had internalized the devaluation of themselves by others and had become aware of their position and status as unmarriageable. The internalization of the new, more urbanized value system had caused them to feel embarrassed and "out of place" not only at the dance, but also in the village itself where, Bourdieu wrote, they felt "no longer at home" (1962/2008a, 75).[9] Bourdieu also described this as a "misfiring" (ibid., 34) of the traditional system of marriage, which was falling apart. Bourdieu would ultimately conclude that the peasant habitus was participating in its own destruction, a point he reinforced when he revisited this case and reworked his analysis decades later. As Bourdieu later explained (1989b/2008a), he came to see this case in terms of a disjuncture between the habitus acquired by eldest males in traditional farm families, who had been highly prized as husbands, and a changing social space in which the value of that habitus had diminished. The circumstances of their socialization had inculcated a habitus attached to an earlier system of values. Bourdieu wrote of the "*objective attachment* (greatest among the first-born sons of 'great' families) and the *subjective attachment* (inscribed in their habitus and bodily hexis) to the old-style peasant mode of existence" (ibid., 172). The peasant *habitus* had come to be a position of anomaly, a "structured structure" that was no longer also a "structuring structure," to use the vocabulary Bourdieu introduced in *Outline of a Theory of Practice* (1972a/1977c, 72) to describe the habitus.

In his subsequent reflection upon this material, Bourdieu concluded that the peasant bachelor essay contained "the seeds of several major developments in my subsequent research" (Bourdieu 1989b/2008a, 67). He cited habitus, strategy, symbolic domination, and reflexivity as examples. I believe that the reason he neglected to include social space among the other concepts was that it was so central to his focus, so much a part of his approach, that it did not occur to him to list it along with the other terms. The terms "social space" and "habitus" appear in the 1962 article, but Bourdieu had further developed these concepts by the time he returned to this material and argued that peasants occupy, as a whole, a dominated position in "larger social space" (ibid., 179). By then, he had incorporated this concept into other work, most notably in *Distinction* (1979b/1984a). Bourdieu also wrote in his recasting of this case that it illustrated "the overall transformation of the *social space* and, more precisely, of the new unification of the market in symbolic goods" (1989b/2008a, 172—my emphasis). There had been an "opening up of isolates," he argued, due to a unification of the "social field . . . around dominant urban realities" (ibid., 172). Although Bourdieu refers here to the matrimonial market as a social field, he continued to use the phrase social space to refer to the wider sphere of sociality and social positions in which fields are located.

In addition to his references to geographic space in the region, Bourdieu included in the original 1962 article aerial photographs of the village of Lesquire and photographs he took of a village street, of people engaged in farm labor, and of people socializing at the annual agricultural fair (*comice*) and its dance. This shows his interest in material and physical space. He also included a diagram of a house in the village, which showed the layout of space, rooms, and its orientation to the street—with an inner courtyard and back garden. There was no extended commentary on the house, but it provided a backdrop to the discussion of the traditional importance of *la maison* (referring to not only the physical household but also the members of the household) in Lesquire. In Bourdieu's analysis of the traditional Kabyle house, to which I now turn, the house itself was the central focus of an elaborate analysis of social position, social space, and point of view.

The Kabyle House: A Space of Points of View

My second example of Bourdieu's early work is the essay "La Maison Kabyle ou le monde renversé" ("The Kabyle House or the World Reversed"), written in 1963[10] but first published in 1970 in a volume dedicated to Lévi-

Strauss on his sixtieth birthday. In this essay, Bourdieu was beginning to shape his theory of how physical space and social space are inseparable from the position and positioning of the habitus. Although he did not use the term "habitus" in this essay, as he had done in the article on the peasants of Lesquire, he did use the phrase "social space." In this analysis, he placed more emphasis on social structure and less emphasis on social practices. Bourdieu did not include any interviews with Kabyle peasants, as he had done in the article on Lesquire. He described the village and house in ideal-typical terms, rather than refer to a particular place and a particular group of people.[11]

Bourdieu used the layout and spatial position of a typical peasant dwelling, the Kabyle or Berber house (*akham*), to examine the relationship between the body, physical space, and social space. Strongly influenced by both Lévi-Strauss and Bachelard, this essay shows how the physical structure of the house reflects (but does not mirror) the social structure. Key themes in his analysis related to social and physical space include a hierarchy of values expressed through spatial configurations, different points of view among those in the social structure, and homologies in systems of classification in different realms.

Bourdieu began the Kabyle house essay with an evocative portrait of the physical space and its contents. After explaining that the rectangular house had two parts, one for humans and a smaller one for animals, he identified objects placed along the wall running between the two halves: "Upon the dividing wall are kept, at one end, the small clay jars or esparto-grass baskets in which provisions awaiting immediate consumption, such as figs, flour and leguminous plants, are conserved, at the other end, near the door, the water-jars" (1970a/1970c, 151). He described rooms, door, windows, and the arrangement of objects in the house; the spatial locations and movements of men and women in and through the house; and the physical orientation of the house in a wider space of the region, in relationship to the village, and in terms of its placement relative to the cardinal directions.

Bourdieu related physical space to points of view in social space through his analysis of the house and its physical location in the village. He insisted that the layout of the house reflected the mythico-ritual system and, therefore, could not be understood as based solely on technical requirements associated with the household economy. Bourdieu iterated the connections between geographical and social space in the house's spatial layout, connected to "a whole cluster of parallel oppositions" (ibid., 153), in this way: "The situating of the house in geographical and *social space*, and also its internal organization, form one of the 'places' in which are joined together symbolic or social necessity and technical necessity" (ibid., 153, fn5—my emphasis).[12] The subtitle of the essay, "the world reversed," refers to the ways in which the space inside the house is oriented in the opposite way to its external positioning vis-à-vis cardinal directions and their symbolic meanings. For example, what is east outside of the house is west inside of the house. Influenced by Bachelard, Bourdieu took the threshold of the house as a key to this orientation. When entering the house, there was an inversion related to such oppositions as that between male and female spaces in the house; spaces for intimate social relations versus open spaces of sociality; and that between inside and outside.

Bourdieu's analysis of the house connects the physical space and its spatial orientation to Kabyle "mythico-religious" classifications of the world. He later wrote that the house was a "microcosm organized by the same oppositions and homologies that order the whole universe" (1980b/1990, 277). In this way, the house is, as Lévi-Strauss wrote when describing the relationship between what he called "spatial structure and social structure" (using examples from indigenous societies in North and South America), a projection into physical space of "a schema of their institutions" (1963, 331). Bourdieu argued that the spatial orientation and organization of the house was linked to Kabyle social structure/organization (especially gender differences) and social hierarchy. He posited a relationship between proverbs and sayings about the meanings of activities and objects in the house and rules of comportment, moral values, and forms of sociability.

Bourdieu used the house not only as a focal point for a discussion of Kabyle social organization and cosmology, which shows the influence of Lévi-Strauss on the analysis, but also as a site for developing ideas of the embodied habitus and social practice. According to Bourdieu, the Kabyles understood the house as a system of oppositions based on age and gender. Because traditional Kabyle society was "undifferentiated" in Bourdieu's terms, meaning that there were no stark socioeconomic divisions or social classes, the main contrast in point of view was between males and females. In contrast to households in Béarn, Kabyle households were not based around the principle of primogeniture. There was more of a group attachment to the family unit in Kabylia, and the opposition between elder and younger son had less valiance. Therefore, Bourdieu argued, the ethnographer's understanding of the oppositions that structure the Kabyle classificatory system depends "on whether the house is considered from the male or the female point of view" (1980b/1990, 280). The house was implicated in fertility (both of the family and the farm) and connected to notions of male honor (*nif*) and female honor (*h'urma*). Fertility and honor could be affected by following (or not following) certain rules about how to conduct oneself and one's activities in and around the house. Bourdieu claimed that males and females had differing points of view on both the space of the house and social organization, which expressed notions of honor. For example, he observed:

> Whereas, for the man the house is less a place one goes into than a place from which one goes out, the woman can only confer upon these two movements and the different definitions of the house which form an integral part with them, an inverse importance and meaning, since movement towards the outside consists above all for her acts of expulsion, and it is her special role to be responsible for all movements towards the inside, that is to say, from the threshold towards the fireplace. (1970a/1970c, 165)

Although he acknowledged these two points of view, Bourdieu maintained that the male point of view was dominant and that it shaped the female point of view in relationship to it. This is a result of what Bourdieu later came to refer to as *doxa*, or commonsense understandings of the world that appear to be natural but are socially produced. In a relatively stable, undifferentiated society that is not undergoing rapid change, he argued, the *doxa* is accepted and expresses the various positions that people have in the social hierarchy.

Bourdieu included diagrams of the rectangular house structure in his essay. One diagram depicts the different zones of the typical house. He interpreted the symbolic meaning of these zones in terms of the gendered positions in society of men and women. Bourdieu's diagram shows the orientation of the house in physical space, according to the cardinal directions, which are inverted inside the house. This image also indicates the correct positioning of the body when entering the house, reinforcing the embodied aspects of habitus and the articulation of physical and social space through it. When returning to this case in *Outline of a Theory of Practice*, Bourdieu emphasized the body in relationship to the Kabyle house even more than he had in the original essay, arguing:

> It is in the dialectical relationship between the body and a space structured according to the mythico-ritual oppositions that one finds the form par excellence of the structural apprenticeship which leads to the em-bodying of the structures of the world, that is, the appropriating by the world of a body thus enabled to appropriate the world. (1972a/1977c, 89)

It was in the context of his work among the Kabyles that Bourdieu first integrated his theory of *habitus* with the idea of "learning through the body," or the body as "memory pad." Bourdieu argued in several later publications that the Kabyle house served as a form of apprenticeship for the body, writing that children learn about their position in social space through movements in this house. According to Bourdieu, physical spaces orient positionings in social space, but are also reflective of them.

Although the original essay on the Kabyle house uses an ideal-typical approach and does not consider in any detail social practices associated with movement through the house, Bourdieu addressed social practices more fully in later versions of this analysis (1972a and 1980b). In other essays that Bourdieu published in the early to mid-1960s on traditional Kabyle society (e.g., Bourdieu 1966b), he examined aspects of social distance and proximity through practices of gift exchange. He also addressed social "closeness and proximity" in his analysis of Kabyle cross-cousin marriage. This theme of proximity or distance in social space echoes the work on bachelors in Lesquire, and Bourdieu elsewhere (1972b) described a social practice of *"cousinage"* among Béarnaise peasants through which some relatives who were structurally more distant than others could be perceived as socially more close. Bourdieu's work on the Kabyle house used the metaphor of an "enclosed world," and he wrote that the house was an "empire within an empire" (1970a/1970c, 169), so that space is hierarchical and, even if the house is an empire for the men who dominate there, it is subordinate to the wider empire outside of it (the village and region).

Bourdieu started out with a very similar perspective on social space to that of Lévi-Strauss. He remarked in later years that he first wrote about bachelorhood and the peasant condition in rural Béarn during the period in which he was "fascinated" with structuralist constructions (2002a/2008a, 2). In his analysis of the Kabyle house, particularly as articulated in subsequent work (e.g., 1972a), Bourdieu focused attention on homologies of habitus across different realms, even if he did not use the term "habitus" in the original essay. The idea of harmony between habitus and social space relies upon the model of an enclosed social space as a container for this harmony—a somewhat stable "coexistence of points of view," as Bourdieu would later describe social space (1997/2000c, 183). The architecture of the house was in harmony with the habituses of both men and women in rural Kabylia, as he would later claim in subsequent work. The operation of habitus reproduced the house structure, which in turn molded the habituses of subsequent generations who inhabited it. There is a correspondence between the cosmology and the house. The situation in Béarn was different. There had been a rupture in the harmony between habitus and social space. As social space changed, habituses were positioned differently within it.

In the structuralist anthropological perspective associated with Lévi-Strauss, social space is connected to mythico-religious classifications of the world, and can be thought of as the projection onto physical space of systems of thought. Bourdieu adopted this approach in his essay on the

Kabyle house. In his preface to *The Logic of Practice*, where that essay was reprinted, Bourdieu wrote that the Kabyle house is a miniature version of the cosmos, and that it "constituted an object that was both complete and circumscribed" (1980b/1990, 9). The Kabyle house essay analyses a relatively "intact" traditional society and its belief system. As did Lévi-Strauss, Bourdieu's early ethnographic work constructed analytic tools that inclined him to focus on social space viewed in terms of a "limited area" (Lévi-Strauss quoted in Augé 1990, 7).

Anthropological discussions of "the house" and "house societies" frequently reference Bourdieu's work on the Kabyle house. Carsten and Hugh-Jones (1995) date Lévi-Strauss' development of the idea of "house societies" to his 1979 book *La Voie des Masques* ("The Way of the Masks"), which was published after Bourdieu's Kabyle house essay. Bourdieu's interest in domestic spaces was one that endured throughout his career, not only in *Distinction*, but also in his later work on the real estate market (Bourdieu 2000d/2005). Although Bourdieu became increasingly interested in domestic spaces as sites for consumption practices and positionings in social space, he retained an interest in feelings of being "at home" associated with the dispositions of habitus and its placement in both social and physical space. This was a central theme of his research and writing on Algerian resettlement campus to which I now turn.

Uprooted Peasants: Habitus and Habitat[13]

In their 1964 article "Paysans déracinés: Bouleversements morphologiques et changements culturels en Algérie" ("Uprooted Peasants: Morphological Upheavals and Cultural Changes in Algeria"),[14] Bourdieu and his collaborator Abdelmalek Sayad painted a grim picture of resettlement camps created during the Algerian war and into which many Kabyles (among other Algerian ethnic groups), forced to leave their villages, had moved. Although published before the essay on the Kabyle house, Bourdieu and Sayad wrote it around the same time. A key theme of the work on "uprooted" (*déracinés*) peasants is the implication of the new spatial configuration of the camps for sociality and for the peasant habitus. As was the case in his writings on rural France, Bourdieu viewed social space as expanding for those of rural origin. The "quasiurban" camps brought people together who had previously been very distant in both social and physical space. Bourdieu's writings on the camps illustrate his developing ideas about relationships between physical (or geographical) and social space.

Bourdieu and Sayad placed the space of the camps in contrast to that of traditional Kabyle villages. In his earlier monograph *Sociologie de l'Algérie*

(1958),[15] Bourdieu had described the traditional social structures of various different ethnic groups in Algeria and then turned to the effects of colonialism and war on Algerian society. He also included a diagram of the traditional Kabyle village and another of the house. Although the analysis in Bourdieu's 1958 study did not include the symbolic analysis of the house that was so central to the essay on the Kabyle house written later, it developed the argument that the Kabyles had already shifted from a clan-based society to one based on the extended family, expressed through "the house." Among the Kabyles, Bourdieu and Sayad asserted, villages had become less clan-based (since around 1950) than in the past and were organized instead around family units. Resettlement accelerated the erosion of tradition, and the family unit was giving way to a new individualism and the decline of paternal authority. The physical layout or shape of the camps, their morphology, was also very different from that of villages.

Bourdieu and Sayad observed that the "change of habitat" (from village to resettlement camp) was "facilitating the crumbling of traditional social unities" (1964b, 66—my translation). They described arrangements of physical and social space in the resettlement camp that led to melancholy and anxiety, and wrote of the effects of this on habitus:

> Because the familiar world for him is his natal world, because his whole bodily habitus is "made" for the space of his customary movements, the uprooted peasant is touched in the deepest part of his being, so profoundly that he is unable to formulate his disarray, and still less to define the reason for it. (Ibid., 87—my translation)

In a footnote related to this statement, Bourdieu and Sayad referenced Bachelard and quoted his evocative words from the *Poetics of Space* (Bachelard [1958] 1964) about the ways in which our natal house is physically "inscribed" in us. For Bachelard, they note, "the word habit is too worn a word to express this passionate liaison of our bodies, which do not forget, with an unforgettable house" (Bourdieu and Sayad 1964b, 15—my translation). The authors also wrote that Bachelard had cited the French author Noël Arnaud's line: "I am the space where I am" (*Je suis l'espace où je suis*). Although Bourdieu and Sayad do not explain this, Bachelard used the Arnaud quote in his discussion of the metaphor of the corner as a space of solitude, a space of immobility (Bachelard [1958] 1964, 137). In this context, the state of immobility is privileged by both Bachelard and Bourdieu, in that geographic mobility can be emotionally painful, can cause "disarray."

We could rephrase Arnaud's statement in light of Bourdieu's subsequent iterations of habitus as a position in social space. It is illuminating to see that Bourdieu chose to focus on that line by Arnaud, albeit in a footnote, as he was developing his theory of space (physical and social) and habitus. Bourdieu portrayed the em-peasanted men in the camps as immobile, as "stuck" in their position (as in a corner) and not moving toward the urban-oriented values like the younger generations. He subsequently developed a more dynamic view of habitus as a position in social space by incorporating the notion of trajectory (a topic to be addressed more fully in Chapter Three).

Bourdieu and Sayad also described what they called the "cultural contagion"[16] that had occurred as a result of peasant groups from the mountains being resettled among other groups with whom they would not normally have had contact. In the resettlement camps, entire villages of people who had been removed from their land were placed together with people from other mountain communities. Those who had previously been distant in social space and distant in geographical space were now in physical proximity. Bourdieu and Sayad wrote: "The convergence of groups that were previously separated in space, the increase in size of the social unit, the new organization of habitat and the network of displacements—these are the most important and most constant features of the upheaval affecting the morphological substratum of the groups" (1964b, 118—my translation).

The authors drew an analogy between these resettlement camps and cities, positioning both in contrast to traditional social organization. Many people in the camps no longer felt attached to the family or clan. This was due to circumstances in the resettlement camps and, for some, because they took the opportunity of being in the camp to leave for the city. There were disruptions of traditional forms of sociality. The authors noted that women, who had not previously done so, began to veil themselves due to changing spatial arrangements. In the resettlement camps, each social unit (family group) did not have its own "space" and the space of men and women overlapped, leading women to be less protected "from the eyes of strangers" than they had been in more isolated villages. Bourdieu and Sayad emphasized the relationship between disruptions of social space and those of physical space: "Indeed, because of the interdependence that unites the organization of space, the structure of social groups, and the type of sociability, the upheaval in the morphological foundations affects and alters every level of social reality" (Ibid., 57—my translation). The design of the resettlement camps modeled French villages, which had a "spatial basis" to their collectivity, rather than designed on the "genealogical basis" of clans and households that was more traditional in Kabylia. The design incorporated an orderly grid pattern, depicted in diagrams included in the article.

In these camps, peasants mixed with those having had more contact with the city, leading Bourdieu and Sayad to observe a "devaluation of peasant virtues, the breakdown of 'collective controls'" (Ibid., 79—my translation) on behavior, including generational conflicts and changes in women's roles.

Occasions at which the peasant felt ill at ease included the offering of interpersonal greetings, café behavior, food, and eating habits. The authors observed that traditional peasants were now "in continuous contact with those peasants who have already taken certain liberties with tradition" (ibid., 60—my translation). Those "de-peasanted" peasants, Bourdieu and Sayad wrote, were "the only ones capable of adapting as well as can be expected, in opposition to the 'em-peasanted' peasants who, committed to perpetuating their peasant values, appear lost and ridiculous" (ibid., 79—my translation). As the em-peasanted peasant moved through the new streets and new spaces in the resettlement camp, he felt ill at ease in similar ways to the Béarnaise bachelor at the village dance.

The narrative of a decline of communal sentiment, attachment to the family unit, and parental authority in this article is similar to the one Bourdieu crafted in his discussion of changes in the Béarnaise township of Lesquire. As in the article on rural French bachelors, it was the traditional male peasant (*paysan empaysanné*) who was left most emotionally displaced by an expanding social space, no longer feeling comfortable in his bodily habitus (ibid., 87). The French peasant bachelors had not physically moved from their home, but the world around them had changed. For the Kabyles, it was geographical displacement ("uprooting") that caused this feeling. Bourdieu and Sayad used the phrase "local emigration" to signal that the resettlement camps made "the em-peasanted peasant an exile in his own land . . . an émigré at home" (ibid., 79—my translation). Here, they were referring to the ways in which this immigration had not been an international one, but had occurred within Algerian borders.

Bourdieu deployed the notion of bodily habitus to express the condition of being outside of one's familiar setting. As Bourdieu and Sayad noted for the Algerian peasants, "It is no doubt the language of the body, the way of standing, of holding the head and walking, that expresses better than words, the aberration and disorientation" (ibid., 90—my translation). Just as Bourdieu wrote that "the peasant from the hamlet is particularly disarmed" (1962/2004b, 65), in reference to the bachelors in Lesquire, he used similar language (*désarmés*) to write about the older Algerian peasants in resettlement camps. Their peasant "virtues" were no longer valued: "Particularly ill-prepared to adapt to unusual situations, due to their age and their attachment to the traditional order, they are particularly disarmed" (1964b, 79—my translation).

For both the em-peasanted peasants and unemployed Algerian youth (cf. Bourdieu et al. 1963b)[17] subject to changing economic conditions and urbanization, Bourdieu focused on the plight of males who suffer from a breakdown of traditional patriarchal society. The social space in which they were now located had become unfamiliar, and they no longer felt at home.

An enlargement of social space had led to the lack of fit between the habitus of the traditional male peasant and the social space in which he dwelled.

Home, Habitus, and (Social) Space

Bourdieu's ethnographic writings during the early 1960s explored relationships between social space, forms of sociality, values and belief systems, and social hierarchies based on both economic and cultural disparities. An expanding social space, produced by new systems of economic and cultural exchange, created new forms of habitus. This expanded social space left men who had previously occupied dominant positions in social space, those "good peasants" whose habitus was socialized to embody all the peasant virtues, now "disarmed" in the face of a changing social hierarchy. Bourdieu developed connections between physical and social space in these examples through the concept of the embodied habitus, acquired not only via social learning that was mental but also by way of movements in and through space.

Social space in this early work has both an objective and a subjective meaning. For Bourdieu, social space in relatively undifferentiated societies— such as the traditional Kabyle village or Lesquire in rural France—is a hierarchical social structure and a system of social relations that has a threshold or limit informed by the harmony of dispositions among those who participate within it. Social space is the system of social relations in an objective sense as analyzed by the anthropologist, but it is also connected to feelings of being at home, at ease in a more subjective sense among those within it. When the social space changes, the perceptions of being at home can change among those whose habitus is no longer in harmony with new social arrangements, new dispositions, tastes, and affinities.

Bourdieu described traditional Béarnaise and Kabyle societies as enclosed worlds, and was interested in charting the changes associated with the opening up of these worlds. He viewed this opening up as a crisis for traditional society and the habituses it had produced—ways of operating in the world that were not suited for urban society. This is an important limitation in Bourdieu's rural ethnography, which recalls both Lévi-Strauss's emphasis on cultural isolates to which I referred in the Introduction, as well as the structural functionalism of rural ethnography during this period. We can see evidence of the influence of structuralism in Bourdieu's analysis not only in his depiction of the Kabyle house, the township of Lesquire, and the traditional Kabyle village as each being an "isolate" and a "self-enclosed world," but also in his emphasis on structural oppositions within these social units.

Bourdieu's work in the early 1960s emphasized the expansion of social space as a result of processes of urbanization and economic changes related to a capitalist economy. He referred to the traditional Kabyle society as an "enclosed microcosm" (1966b, 212) and to Lesquire as "an enclosed world" (Bourdieu and Bourdieu 1965b, 172). Bourdieu described Lesquire in 2002 as "a world that is breaking up" (2002a/2008a, 4), echoing his earlier observation that "perhaps the essential fact is that this society, once relatively self-enclosed, has now resolutely opened up to the external world" (1962/2008a, 47). The dichotomy between urban versus rural societies in Mediterranean studies at mid-twentieth century that reflected wider historical ideas central to European social thought, as noted by Raymond Williams (1973), influenced Bourdieu's emphasis on "self-enclosed worlds." This was based in part on Ferdinand Tönnies's Gemeinschaft-Gesellschaft ideal-type dichotomy ([1887] 1957) in which the "community" of the village was privileged over the anonymity and anomie of the city. This prevalent assumption led Bourdieu and Sayad to portray resettlement camps as producing an extreme version of anomie among the em-peasanted peasants now residing in them. The theme of urban dystopia was also present in the work of Emile Durkheim (see [1897] 1951) and in the work of Frédéric Le Play (1884), whose work on the stem family in rural France influenced Bourdieu's analysis of marriage strategies (see Bourdieu 2002a/2008a, 161).

Bourdieu made a revealing comment (which I see as a very crucial commentary on the limits as well as potential contributions of his approach) when he remarked that there is inertia in the structures of social space because they are inscribed in physical space. They can, he wrote, "only be modified at the cost of a painful work of transplantation, by moving things and by uprooting or deporting persons" (1996a, 13; see also 1993c/1999b, 124). This appears to be a direct reference to the situation of the displaced and "uprooted" Algerians in the resettlement camps. It implies, moreover, a stable structure of overlap between geographic and social space that existed prior to this "transplantation." On the one hand, Bourdieu's observation that social space may be difficult to change because it is reified in physical space is a useful reminder of the correspondences between the two. On the other hand, however, it risks implying that social space will only change through a painful disruption moving things or people out of their place. The lens adopted by Bourdieu in ethnographic work discussed in this chapter does not sufficiently examine the ways in which social spaces may change in gradual or incremental ways. There is a contradiction in his work during this early period between the idea that boundaries are socially constructed and his tendency to reify those boundaries in his own approach.

As I have previously pointed out (Reed-Danahay 1995; 2004; 2005b), there is a disturbing tone of nostalgia in Bourdieu's early writings about

Béarn and Kabylia (see also Silverstein 2009) whereby he expresses his sympathy for the displaced male peasants in the midst of social transformations. His focus on immobility (also expressed, especially, in the Kabyle case as a form of rootedness) is complicated in that it encompasses both an ideal state of happiness and a feeling of being at home, as well as being a cause for distress when the wider world is changing around the immobile person. Immobility leads to positive feelings when the habitus is in harmony with the wider social space, but to feelings of distress when it is not.

Although Bourdieu uses the metaphors of roots and home, he very much sees these as commonsense notions that have been socially produced, so that the desire for them must be understood as part of the dispositions of habitus. As Jan Willem Duyvendak (2011, 28) has rightly pointed out, Bourdieu "wants to understand why people experience places as natural—as 'home'—and criticizes scholars who fail to reflect on this 'naturalizing' effect of the familiar." Although I will not abandon my concerns regarding Bourdieu's tendencies to contrast undifferentiated and differentiated societies, and to theorize social space at times as an "enclosed world" in the chapters to follow, I do want to balance those concerns with my view that there are some enduring contributions in this early work that are worth remembering.

The idea of social space as expanding (or potentially contracting) over time is a lasting one worth pursuing, and I will take this up more fully in subsequent chapters. However, Bourdieu's perspective must be adapted so that it does not depend upon a static and fixed "before," but rather on a perspective that understands social boundaries as flexible, expanding, and contracting more or less continually over time—albeit at different paces. Another contribution of this work is the focus on habitus as related to the emotions of feeling either at home or out of place. This linking of habitus, social space, and emotion draws attention to the body and its relationship to the physical and social spaces it inhabits and mediates. Bourdieu's concept of habitus as a position in social space encourages attention to the emotional experiences of people who experience a changing social space either through their own geographic movement to a new social space or because the social space in which they dwell has changed.

The example of the bachelors in Lesquire resonates with Bourdieu's later discussions of social distance and proximity in such works as *Distinction*. In the example of the Kabyle house, we see glimpses of Bourdieu's later view of social space as a space of points of view and positioning (and not directly corresponding to physical space). There are echoes in Bourdieu's subsequent work on social space of this earlier analysis of the different regions or locations within the house and the points of view, related to their positions in social space, of those who inhabit the house. Bourdieu showed that the social and economic changes occurring in rural France and in colonial and post-colonial Algeria led to new points of view among formerly rural people who came into contact through processes of urbanization. This led to the contrast between the "em-peasanted" peasants and those who were able to adapt better to urban life. As the social space of rural societies had expanded, new positions in social space, new habituses, arose.

Point of view is an idea that would become more central, especially in Bourdieu's work published after mid-1970, to which I turn in Chapter Three.

NOTES

1. I have analyzed and compared Bourdieu's writings on rural France and on Algerian resettlement elsewhere (Reed-Danahay 1995; 2004, 2005b, and 2009), but not with a specific focus on social space. I take a different approach to this material here.

2. This article appeared in French and in English translation in a volume called *The Bachelor's Ball* (2002a/2008a), which includes three essays (Bourdieu 1962, 1972b, and 1989b) dealing with Béarnaise marriage strategies. The 2008 volume includes the first published English translation, although excerpts appear in Bourdieu (2004b). In his introduction to *The Bachelor's Ball*, Bourdieu indicated that this collection of essays represented a sort of intellectual biography for him. I draw upon the 2008 translation in my use of quotes and other citations of the work discussed in this chapter, but cite also the original French date of publication in order to be clear about which essay in the 2008 collection I am referring to. Bourdieu drew from his research in rural Béarnaise society in several other publications throughout his career.

   This phrase, "the bachelor's ball," was not used in the original article, where the dance was referred to as the Christmas dance (*"le bal de Noël"*), and "dance" is a better translation of *"bal"* into English than is "ball." Although the more picturesque phrase was adopted for the title of the 2002 collection of writings on the marriage system in Lesquire (*Le Bal des Célibataires*), this little county dance was not a grand affair (as the English "ball" connotes).

3. Bourdieu used Lesquire as a pseudonym to refer to this township. I translate the French term *commune* here as township rather than village. In Lesquire, like many rural *communes*, most farms were located in small hamlets rather than in the major village.

4. The significance of this research for kinship studies is worth noting, but my focus here is on the overall development of a theory of social space. See the critical appraisals of this aspect of the Béarnaise ethnography by Tim Jenkins (2006 and 2010), who has undertaken ethnographic research in this region.

5. As I have previously argued in relationship to a study of the published life narratives of rural French women (Reed-Danahay 2002 and 2005a), the discourse of a crisis

in France regarding the exodus of young women was pervasive in the mid-twentieth century. Bourdieu's analysis of the changing social space of Lesquire departs from many popular representations in agrarian novels, which depict women who leave the village for the town as being "corrupt" and weak (Lagrave 1980), in that he emphasizes the pathology of the bachelors, not the women and younger sons who leave. Frédéric Le Play (1865) had earlier blamed the "complicated desires" of youth and women that can only be satisfied in the city for the rural exodus he deplored in the late nineteenth century.

6. I gloss *aire* as area, which is also the translation for this term in Bourdieu 2008a; but the French word *aire* has broader connotations than does the English "area." Beyond the strictly geometric meaning of area (as in surface area), it is used in French to denote a playing field (*aire de jeux*) or a domain of action or influence (*aire d'influence*).

7. Jennifer Cole's (2014) research on Malagasy women who have married French men (some of whom are peasants) in southern France provides an example of an enlarged matrimonial area for rural men who might otherwise remain bachelors. This case similarly represents an expanded social space for the female "marriage migrants" from Madagascar, who are comparable to the young women in Lesquire who seek social mobility through marriage—although Cole does not herself make this link.

8. The argument is that working-class children with dominated habituses exclude themselves from school achievement while their teachers judge them as failures. They accept that they are destined to fail at school, feeling that this is either due to their own "choice" to reject school or due to their lack of ability and inferiority. See Reed-Danahay (2005b, 37–68) for an overview of Bourdieu's work on education and its relationship to his own social trajectory.

9. The original French text reads: "Ainsi, au centre même de son univers, le paysan découvre un monde dans lequel il n'est déjà plus chez lui" (1962, 91).

10. See Bourdieu's statements about its history in Bourdieu (1972a, 59; and 2002a/ 2008a, 2). This essay appeared in English at around the same time it was first published in French (Bourdieu 1970c), so that it has long been available to a wide audience of readers. It is part of a larger body of writings dealing with Kabyle society that Bourdieu published in separate articles during the 1960s and reworked in his subsequent books. The Kabyle house essay appeared in the original 1972 French version (Bourdieu 1972a), but not the English translation of *Outline of a Theory of Practice* (1977c). It was later reprinted, with minor modifications, in *The Logic of Practice* (1980b/1990). It was not included, however, in a recent posthumous compilation of Bourdieu's writings on Algerian societies (Bourdieu 2008b/2013). The three Kabyle ethnographic examples that appeared in the 1972 version of *Outline of a Theory of Practice* were published as a stand-alone set in *Algeria 1960* (Bourdieu 1977a/1979a). His essays on Kabyle honor and sense of time appeared in English in the early 1960s (Bourdieu 1963a and 1966b).

11. Several chapters in Goodman and Silverstein (2009) illuminate the conditions under which Bourdieu conducted his ethnographic research in Algeria. As Silverstein

(2009), Goodman (2009), and Hammoudi (2009) indicate, Bourdieu based his portrait of the Kabyle house on nostalgic reconstructions of an idealized stable society that did not exist, due to the circumstances of the Algerian War, when Bourdieu was in the field. Their insights raise questions about the validity of some of Bourdieu's ethnographic reportage. Goodman (2009), for example, has written an elegant critique of Bourdieu's use of proverbs as a means of identifying characteristics of the Kabyle peasant habitus. In my view, these fine-grained assessments of Bourdieu's work and the ethnographic evidence he used are significant additions to our understanding of his approach, but do not detract from Bourdieu's wider contributions to thinking about the relationships between physical and social space that concern me here.

12. "*l'implantation*" in the original French version (Bourdieu 1970a)

13. The phrase "habitat and habitus" is also used in *Images d'Algérie* (Bourdieu 2003) as the title of a chapter that juxtaposes short excerpts from Bourdieu's writings with photographs he took and diagrams he made of resettlement camps and the "traditional" Kabyle house.

14. See also a recent collection of Bourdieu's Algerian essays collected by Tassadit Yacine (Bourdieu 2008b/2013) in which the 1964 article is reprinted and translated for the first time into English (in the 2013 translation). The book *Le Déracinement* (Bourdieu and Sayad 1964a), which provides a fuller picture of the resettlement camps and their implications for Algerian society, appeared the same year as the shorter article. It has not yet appeared in English translation.

15. This book was written and published before the Kabyle house essay, which had not yet appeared in print when the article and book on the resettlement camps were published.

16. This reference to "cultural contagion" from the 1960s predates a wider use of the term in more recent times to refer to a spreading of ideas or practices that can have a productive impact. For example, see Eriksen (2006). In the nineteenth century, however, cultural contagion was associated with threats to the social order (see Mitchell 2012). It is difficult to know precisely what Bourdieu and Sayad had in mind, but they use the phrase to signal cultural exchanges that were changing ideas and social practices among those settled in the camps.

17. I discuss that work, *Travail et Travailleurs en Algérie,* in more detail in the conclusion of this book.

Landscapes of Mobility

> Who would think to recall a trip without having an idea of the
> landscape in which it took place?
> —*The Biographical Illusion* (1986b/2000a, 302)

In the passage quoted above, Bourdieu used the metaphor of a voyage to make the point that our lives are inextricably connected to the social space that both constitutes the landscapes (social and geographical) in which they enfold and is constituted by the practices and trajectories we enact. In this chapter, I turn to texts in which social space plays a significant role as Bourdieu examined positionings and trajectories across both geographic and social space. These include Bourdieu's analysis of Flaubert's 1869 novel *Sentimental Education* (Bourdieu 1975/1987) and his major works of *Distinction* (1979b/1984a) and *The Social Structures of the Economy* (2000d/ 2005). In these studies Bourdieu conceptualized the social space of what he described as differentiated or class-based societies, such as France. In societies that are more differentiated, neither social space nor individual trajectories are static but are in flux. This is quite different from the perspective Bourdieu adopted in the earlier work, discussed in Chapter Two, in which he characterized social space in relatively undifferentiated societies as undergoing transformation only when external factors (urbanization, colonialism) intervened.

The Biographical Illusion, Mobility, and Social Space

According to Bourdieu, a social analyst cannot use the term "individual" without qualifying that this is a socially constructed notion. This implies that our understanding of mobility practices, including immobilities, should not depend on the idea of an autonomous social actor whose life history is narrated "as if" spatial choices are a matter of free will. Our commonsense understandings of the individual as an autonomous person with unique qualities are bound up, Bourdieu maintained, with both state power and economic power in differentiated class-stratified societies. Such ideas are the result of a process of "individuation," which constitutes the *doxic* individual self and attributes it to biological human beings through symbolic, rhetorical, and institutionalized actions.

In his essay "The Biographical Illusion" (1986b/2000a),[1] Bourdieu argued that a person's life does not unfold as a result of some inherent unity or identity of the individual who follows a particular and unique path, even if this is a common way to tell a life story. Bourdieu stated repeatedly that social scientists must unpack the assumptions that go along with the taken-for-granted idea of the individual. In *Pascalian Meditations* (1997/2000c, 131–32), he drew upon Heidegger to stress that the skin as boundary leads us to posit a separate individual. This seemingly self-evident, commonsense view of the body keeps us from seeing a person as a social agent, as an embodied habitus. That we identify people through their proper names also produces the illusion of continuity: "The proper name is the visible affirmation of the identity of its bearer across time and social space, the basis of the unity of one's successive manifestations, and of the socially accepted possibilities of integrating these manifestations in official records, curriculum vitae, *cursus honorum*, police record, obituary, or biography" (1986b/2000a, 300). The concept of trajectory, unlike that of biography, places the person (or social agent) in social space, and thereby provides an alternative understanding of the life story. A life trajectory must be seen as the outcome of the changing positionings of habitus in a changing social space.

The reason that Bourdieu objected to standard conventions of biography is not that he espoused a postmodern view of the self as fluid. Quite the contrary. Bourdieu viewed the habitus as durable ("the durably installed generative principle of regulated improvisation" [1972a/1977c, 78]) and as a constant when the person as embodied habitus operates within different social fields in social space. The concept of trajectory helps us to understand how habitus interacts with different places and social contexts and may be potentially transformed through mobility practices.

Bourdieu used the concept of trajectory to address issues of temporality, and he adopted the phrase "social aging," to explore mobilities and immobilities over time and within social space. In order to illustrate the relationship between habitus and social space, Bourdieu focused on the position and trajectory of social agents in and across social space in a variety of contexts and social fields. A key element in Bourdieu's concept of social space as articulated in the work described in this chapter is that positions in social space (viewed as physical as well as social) are not static. A person's relationships to others may change, as they may come to feel closer to or more socially distant from others. Habitus is informed by the social position of the person—but also influences the choices they make and their aspirations. The dispositions of habitus inform perceptions of social space and trajectory. Both habitus and social space have a more objective (etic) and a more subjective (emic) aspect to them. The term "trajectory" as used by Bourdieu is more of an objective term that permits the social scientist to articulate the intersections of habitus and social space.[2]

Point of View: Flaubert and *Sentimental Education*

Social and physical space figure very prominently in Bourdieu's analysis of the ways in which Gustav Flaubert depicted French bourgeois society in nineteenth-century Paris in his novel *L'Education sentimentale* (*Sentimental Education*). Not only does Bourdieu examine the social distances and proximities of various characters in the novel, but also the physical space of Paris—which included what Bourdieu referred to as the "triangle" across its space of the business world, the art world, and the student district (1975/ 1987, 99). The ways in which the physical spaces are articulated with social proximities and distances is an important element of Bourdieu's analysis of the novel.

Bourdieu's first publication on *Sentimental Education* appeared in *Actes de la Recherche en Sciences Sociales* in 1975, the inaugural year of that journal.[3] As he did with his earlier ethnographic work in Béarn and Kabylia, Bourdieu returned to Flaubert and to this novel in his writings over the course of several years.[4] In my discussion of Bourdieu's writings on *Sentimental Education*, I will focus primarily on the essay "The Invention of the Artist's Life" (1975/1987), first published not long after *Outline of a Theory of Practice* (1972a) appeared in its original French version. My interest in this work is as an anthropologist, not a literary critic, which means that what is at stake for me is to explore how this work may be useful for anthropologists. My question is that of what insights Bourdieu's analysis of a nineteenth-century novel can lend to anthropologists and other ethnographers about ways to articulate the relationship between social and geographic space. Paying attention to Bourdieu's analysis of *Sentimental Education* enables us to see how he operationalized his theory of habitus and social space through a particular case study, albeit a fictional one—the world Flaubert created.[5] Bourdieu drew upon Flaubert's "world-making," to echo my discussion in Chapter One, in order to craft his own analysis of the social world.

In Flaubert's novel, there are depictions of specific characters acting in specific ways in specific circumstances—details that one rarely finds in Bourdieu's writings. Apart from his analysis of the village dance in Béarn (1962), his description of riposte in Algeria (1966b), and his ethnographic analysis of exchanges between buyers and real estate agents (2000d/2005), Bourdieu rarely described scenes of social interaction in his writings. Even Bourdieu's most ethnographic writings are based primarily on interviews, questionnaires, or examples that are pulled from his observations of everyday life in general. Sociality plays a big role in Flaubert's novel, which leads Bourdieu to focus on the evening "salons" and meals at the homes of the two families that figure prominently within it and reveal the manners, social choices, and world views of a range of people who come into contact at them. This is more akin to what ethnographers describe based on fieldwork.

Bourdieu therefore used *Sentimental Education* as a sort of ethnographic case study from which to draw lessons about social position and social action. He used his analysis of the novel to illustrate the utility of his concepts of habitus, social space, and cultural capital for understanding social hierarchy and domination. Bourdieu wrote (1983/1993b) that he had turned to the study of cultural production in art and literature because this was the realm most laden with the cult of the individual "creator." This was in an article called "The Field of Cultural Production, or: The Economic World Reversed," which recalls the title of his earlier article (1970a/1970c) on the Kabyle house as "the world reversed." Bourdieu suggested that his theory was well suited to intervene and demonstrate that success in artistic production was dependent on the "space of positions" within a literary or artistic field. He wrote that the structure of an artistic field "is nothing other than the structure of the distribution of the capital of specific properties which govern success in the field and the winning of the external or specific profits (such as literary prestige) which are at stake in the field." Therefore, it was important to construct "the space of positions and the space of position-takings [*prises de position*] in which they are expressed" (1983/1993b, 30).

Sentimental Education charts the social trajectories of various university students in Paris at the time of the 1848 Revolution.[6] In his analysis of the novel, Bourdieu focused on the life trajectory of the protagonist, Frédéric Moreau, who is a young man and a student when the action begins. The word "sentimental" in the title refers to Frédéric's emotional education, which takes place at the same time as his formal education. This entails not only his romantic relationships (of which there are several) but also his friendships and the other attachments he forms that shape his ideas about his place in the world (and, more specifically, in Paris). Bourdieu viewed Frédéric's trajectory as the result of the intersections between the dispositions of his habitus and the possibilities or constraints of the social space(s) in which he lived. He wrote, "Frédéric's story is inscribed in the relations between his disposition towards his inheritance—which is tied, as we have seen to the nature of the inheritance, balancing between economic and cultural capital—and the social space in which he is located" (1975/1987, 93). Although his economic circumstances are strained in the beginning of the novel, with his widowed mother hoping he will make a good marriage to stabilize his position in society, Frédéric's fortunes change when he inherits money from a wealthy uncle.

Bourdieu was also interested in Flaubert the novelist, and he wrote extensively about Flaubert's role in shaping the establishment of a literary field as a separate sphere within wider French social space.[7] Flaubert grew up in the provincial city of Rouen in Normandy, where his father was a surgeon. His social position as the child of a provincial bourgeois family is key, according to Bourdieu, to an understanding of his positionings in the literary field of his day and the novels he produced. Bourdieu insisted that *Sentimental Education* is not a mirror of Flaubert's life and should not be taken, as other critics have done, as literally autobiographical; rather, Flaubert depicts the range of possibilities available to him during his own youth through the novel. Frédéric Moreau is not the young Flaubert, but someone who represents an alternative trajectory that Flaubert might have lived, a different possibility and a different sort of positioning and position-takings. Bourdieu later argued, "The novel contains an analysis of the social space in which the author was himself located and thus gives us the instruments we need for an analysis of him" (1993b, 145). Bourdieu also noted that Flaubert objectified "his own position" in social space through his writings (1988b, 559).

Frédéric Moreau is, like Flaubert, from a provincial bourgeois background in Normandy. Frédéric is an "inheritor" of the relative privileges of his social class but refuses many of the choices that his mother desires for him so that he can enhance his position—particularly in the realm of career and marriage. Given the somewhat strained financial situation of his widowed mother, Frédéric is expected to marry someone with an inheritance in order to ensure that he will have "the instruments and distinguishing marks of social existence" (1975/1987, 80). The importance of "social existence" in this milieu is due to the fact that, as Bourdieu writes:

> To exist socially is to be socially situated and dated, to occupy a position in the social structure and to bear its marks, in the form of verbal automatisms or of mental mechanisms and of the entire habitus that the constitutive conditionings of condition produce; it is also to be dependent, to hold and to be held, in short to *belong* and to be forced into the web of social relations that are elicited in the form of obligations, debts, duties, in short of determinations and constraints. (1975/1987, 79–80)[8]

Sentimental Education's plot revolves around Frédéric's coming of age. Frédéric moved to Paris for studies in law yet was also attracted to the arts. He was positioned and positioned himself in a social space characterized by various possible trajectories and points of view illustrated by the different characters he encountered there. Bourdieu compared the social space of the novel to the setting of the types of murder mysteries that take place in old mansions or on deserted islands, where everyone is in a sort of enclosed universe and through which we observe their behaviors for signs of their guilt or innocence.

Much as he did for the social world of French and Algerian peasants, as I discussed in Chapter Two, Bourdieu described the novel as a "closed and finite universe," and he wrote of the "narrowness of the social space in which [the characters] are placed" (1975/1987, 86). The characters in *Sentimental Education* illustrate the realm of possibilities in terms of attitudes and behaviors among the bourgeoisie, the petite bourgeoisie, and those from other social classes with whom they interact. The social space in which Frédéric's geographical and social trajectory unfolds over time can be thought of as a "space of possibilities" constrained to varying degrees by social origins. Bourdieu concluded that over the course of his life, Frédéric fulfills his social destiny, in spite of any illusion of choice, because his course was set by the social milieu in which he grew up and the habitus (with its own particular combination of economic and cultural capital) he acquired in that milieu.

Bourdieu illustrated Frédéric's position in social space through a contrast with the positions of friends he acquires in Paris. This approach reflects the relational approach to social space that is central to Bourdieu's thought. The other students come from different social backgrounds than Frédéric, and have different trajectories. They range from Frédéric (who belongs to "high society" by birth and is also charming and intelligent), to Deslauriers and Hussonnet (who come from a petit-bourgeois background), to Martinon (who is wealthy because his father is a prosperous farmer, but lacks the high social standing based on birth that Frédéric has), and Cisy (who, like Frédéric, was born to "high society," but who is "not very intelligent or ambitious"). Bourdieu analyzed the relationships and movements (social and physical) over time of characters in the novel who include Frédéric, his friends, and key families with whom he is associated. Bourdieu placed less focus on the female characters in the novel, many of whom are at one time or another lovers of Frédéric. His analysis is primarily concerned with the ways that Flaubert depicted the positionings and trajectories in social space of those in both the dominant and dominated sectors of the French bourgeoisie—with a focus on males. This resonates with my discussion of the emphasis on male peasants in Bourdieu's earlier ethnographic work in Chapter Two.

For Bourdieu, *Sentimental Education* illustrates the ways that habitus is a position in social space and in social time, and that the ways in which a person understands their "place" is based on habitus. Flaubert created a social space of possibilities for a young bourgeois male at the end of the nineteenth century in that different characters in the novel represent other habituses and other possibilities. This cast of characters displays the repertoire of habituses that exists among this group of friends; and as Bourdieu describes them, they also display a range of attributes related to what he would later describe as forms of capital (economic, cultural, and social), although he did not use the vocabulary of cultural capital in his 1975 publication.

Frédéric's position in social space is also depicted in relationship to the position of two families in Paris with whom he interacts due to family connections—the Arnoux and the Dambreuses. Bourdieu focused in particular on the differences between the two families, whom he believes Flaubert has invented in order to illustrate conflicts within the bourgeoisie over wealth and status—which Bourdieu later came to view as capital and cultural capital.[9] Arnoux was a prosperous art dealer, and Dambreuse a wealthy banker. They represented different sectors of the bourgeoisie within what Bourdieu referred to as the "field of the dominant class" as depicted in the novel. Foreshadowing *Distinction*, Bourdieu detailed the consumption practices of the two families, including the receptions and dinner parties they held, the ways in which their rooms were decorated, and the types of people who attended social gatherings. In some cases, there is overlap between the attendees at these houses, but the two families do not begin to socialize together until after 1848.

Geographic or physical space and social space come together in Bourdieu's analysis of the novel. He depicts the social space of the characters in *Sentimental Education* as they circulate within Paris and its surrounding region. This is similar to his earlier arguments, discussed in Chapter Two, about the relationship between the *commune* of Lesquire, the setting for his analysis of the habitus of farmer bachelors, and the surrounding social space of the Béarnaise region and the city Pau. As the social space expanded to include urban men as valued marriage partners for young women, eldest sons in farm families, previously the more attractive choice for husband, lost out as more urbanized men attracted wives from farm backgrounds. In the novel *Sentimental Education*, Paris is the dominating social space, an urban pole of attraction for the bourgeoisie, such as the young Frédéric. In many ways, it is the inverse of Lesquire—a dominated social space in rural France.

We see the anthropological roots of Bourdieu's work in his continued attention to questions of inheritance and kinship in this novel. We can also see the influence of Bourdieu's research on education, in which he examined educational success or failure in a number of works by using the concept of the "inheritor." This refers to the child of bourgeois background who inherited their social position and an embodied habitus that was well matched to the expectations of the educational system. School success, Bourdieu argued, was less an outcome of the merits and intelligence of the child, but rather the outcome of their socialization and acquisition of the sort of habitus that was recognized by teachers as one meriting scholastic approval.[10] Frédéric is an "inheritor" who, nonetheless, questioned his social destiny and the path expected of him. However, as Bourdieu maintained, Frédéric eventually fulfilled that destiny. His peers, who had different types and amounts of inherited cultural capital, followed different trajectories.

One of the most important contributions of Bourdieu's work to studies of mobility in his writings on Flaubert and *Sentimental Education* is his attention to the articulations of social space and geographic space. He used diagrams and maps to indicate the positioning of Frédéric, as well as the other characters in the novel, in social and geographic space. In one Venn diagram, Bourdieu represented the different sectors of the bourgeoisie with two opposing but related poles of art and politics in a circle to the left overlapping with that of politics and business to the right. Frédéric is positioned in the center, where these two fields overlap. This diagram characterized the social space and fields in which Frédéric was positioned. Using a geographic map of Paris, Bourdieu illustrated the social space in which Frédéric is positioned and positions himself both in social space that is more abstract and in the physical space of Parisian neighborhoods. On the map indicating streets and neighborhoods, Bourdieu superimposed the location of the main characters in the novel, including Frédéric, and their location in physical space. With lines and arrows, he showed trajectories and movements in social space that are also movements across physical space.[11]

In his attention to the spatial dimensions of the story, Bourdieu noted that these are never explicitly remarked upon in the novel. However, Flaubert depicted the oppositions in space between various neighborhoods of Paris as they were connected to the social divisions both in Paris more broadly and among the characters in the novel. The Latin Quarter is opposed to Montmartre and to St. Germain. Bourdieu observed that as the social fortunes of the characters changed, their physical movements and places of residence changed:

> Thus, ascending and descending social trajectories clearly are distinguished in this structural and hierarchical space: for the former, the movement is from the south towards the north-west (Martinon and, for a while Frédéric); for the latter, it is from west towards east and

north to south (Rosanette, Arnoux). Deslauriers's failure is shown by the fact that he never leaves the point of departure, the students' and artists' section [place des Trois Maries]. (1975/1987, 102-3)

Bourdieu's analysis of Flaubert's novel illustrates the ways in which social space, which he also referred to as "the immanent structure of the social world" (1986a, 242), is composed of the distribution of various forms of capital. This social world (or social space) provides constraints on the efficacy of the social practices of individuals and groups. A person who inherits a great deal of capital in all three forms will, according to Bourdieu, be better positioned to accumulate additional capital, and someone with less inherited capital will only be able to accumulate additional capital if they have sufficient skills to take advantage of opportunities presented to them. Even maintaining one's inherited capital is partly based on skill in making the best of it. As I discussed in the Introduction to this book, it was also how Bourdieu explained his own social position and trajectory as an intellectual and academic with high cultural capital, despite his modest social origins and relative lack of inherited capital. According to Bourdieu, "each individual trajectory must be understood as a particular way of traversing the social space" (1975/1987, 75).

Social Aging

An important concept with implications for mobility that Bourdieu introduced in his analysis of *Sentimental Education* was that of "social aging." This is related to Bourdieu's distinction between the biological individual and the embodied habitus, and describes the ways in which a person ages socially. Over the course of their life, does a person stay in the same location in social space, move to a lower position, or advance via social mobility? Bourdieu wrote:

> Social aging certainly is measured by the number of changes in position within the social structure, and these changes result in restricting the range of initially acceptable possibilities; or, in other words, it is measured by the bifurcations of the tree which, with its innumerable dead branches, represents a career or retrospectively, a curriculum vitae. (1975/1987, 87)

Bourdieu described Frédéric Moreau as someone who, because he refused as a young man to accept the social destiny his mother hoped for him, remains in a social age of adolescence while his peers move on. In a later reflection upon this novel, Bourdieu noted that Flaubert implied the idea of social aging in his use of the phrase "sentimental education" to describe Frédéric's trajectory (1992b/1996b, 10).

Bourdieu later clarified his concept of trajectory and social aging in *Distinction*, emphasizing that family origin is not the only thing that determines the social trajectory of a person. People from the same "class fraction" or same family do not all have the same outcomes in life. There is a relationship between origins, the social practices of the person, and wider conditions of existence (such as the job market or other social factors) in shaping a person's trajectory. Bourdieu maintained that social origin is "merely the starting point of the trajectory" (1979b/1984a, 105). There are collective trajectories (overall trends of the social position of a certain class fraction over time), and there are individual trajectories. These are not entirely homologous. The "decline or fall" of a person's social career will, however, be linked to their social origins. For example, Bourdieu noted that if the children of teachers do not maintain the same social position as their parents, they tend to fall into the "established petite bourgeoisie," whereas the children of professionals are more likely to decline into the "new middle-class fractions" (ibid., 571, fn12).

For Bourdieu, the events in a person's life can be viewed as "just so many investments and moves in social space" (1986b/2000a, 302). Therefore, he continued, "One can understand a trajectory (that is, the social aging which is independent of biological aging, although it inevitably accompanies it) only on condition of having previously constructed the successive states of the field through which the trajectory has progressed" (ibid., 302). A change of one's "place" can result not only from "displacement in the social space," but also by "marching" in place while "peers or competitors" move forward (1975/1987, 87). This comment echoes Bourdieu's concern with the em-peasanted peasants in his earlier work, especially those bachelors in Béarn who stayed in place (socially and geographically) while their brothers and sisters moved on. The concept of social trajectory implied in this notion of social aging has implications for mobility and immobility—helping us to consider the ways in which wider factors of social origin and changes in social space affect the mobilities (social and geographical) of a person. The possibilities available in social space are not the same for all people, and can change over time. Trajectory can be understood as Bourdieu's term for mobility.

Legitimate Culture: Taste and *Distinction*

In *Distinction* (1979b/1984a),[12] Bourdieu's most widely-known book, he depicted a much broader tableau of the French bourgeoisie. Here, he studied his own milieu of contemporary mid-twentieth-century France. Bourdieu explored the relationship between the dominant and dominated sectors of the middle and upper classes, as well as their relationship to dominated groups such as the working class. Although *Distinction* has most often served as the starting point for discussions of habitus and social space in Bourdieu's work,[13] it should not stand as the definitive example of Bourdieu's thinking on this subject. It is best to see *Distinction* as a major contribution standing in the middle of a career that spanned a period from the late 1950s to the early twenty-first century.

Bourdieu's hypothesis guiding the research on which *Distinction* is based was that there is a "unity of tastes" among those with similar habituses and positions in social space. The ethnographic aspects of this study have been overshadowed in many applications of *Distinction* that focus primarily on the statistical mapping of social space. It is important to remember that Bourdieu explained in his discussion of methods that he wanted to be sure to refer to "reality" and concrete objects and people (in the form of photographs, interview extracts, and facsimiles of books) rather than keep the level of analysis very abstract. In his introduction to the English translation of the book, Bourdieu emphasized that this analysis of French social space was meant to be a "sort of ethnography of France" (1984a, xi), which utilized the holistic methods of anthropology (meaning that many aspects of life—culture, home decor, language, education, intellectual thought, and so on—were included). As Bourdieu emphasized, *Distinction* was primarily intended to not only describe the specific case of French social space but to serve, as did other ethnographic monographs, as a case study and method that could potentially be adapted and developed in other contexts.

Although Bourdieu described the book as a "sort of ethnography," it is based primarily on survey questionnaires and statistical data methods—with supporting examples culled from extracts of popular magazines, personal narratives, and photographs. It is not based on ethnographic fieldwork in the traditional sense. The concept of social space as articulated in *Distinction* does not have as much connection to physical or geographical space as do other examples of Bourdieu's work discussed in this book. However, there is recognition of the role that physical proximity plays in the social affinities that help create groups in social space. Bourdieu asserted the importance of geographic region as a factor in the linguistic repertoires available, the stigma of certain "provincial" ways of talking and moving the body (associated with embodied habitus), and the uneven access to cultural goods that reflect cultural capital created by geographic locations.

After *Distinction* was published in English and other languages, Bourdieu felt compelled to clarify the book's broader message in order to respond to early criticisms of the book that it was "very French" and too specific to be of more general interest.[14] For example, in a lecture delivered in Japan regarding *Distinction*, Bourdieu explained, "By presenting the model of social space and symbolic space that I have built up for the particular case of France, I shall still be speaking to you about Japan (just as, speaking elsewhere, I would be still be speaking about Germany or the United States)" (1991a, 627). This is important to bear in mind in order to grasp what Bourdieu meant by social space in *Distinction*, because the book includes many references to specific aspects of French society regarding its centralized state and educational system and assumes the geographic and social division between "Paris and the provinces" that is a common way in France to depict French society.

In *Distinction*, the concept of "taste"—which is a sign of the dispositions of habitus—is added to the repertoire of Bourdieu's concepts (i.e., habitus, social space, field, and trajectory) that were present in his analysis of Flaubert's novel *Sentimental Education*. Bourdieu also used "taste" much earlier, as I noted in Chapter Two, in his 1962 article on changing marriage patterns, when he referred to young rural women as holding "the monopoly on the judgment of taste" (1962, 104—my translation). Tastes, Bourdieu wrote in *Distinction*, "function as markers of class" (1979b/1984a, 2) in class-based societies, because consumption practices and markets are organized in a hierarchy that places higher value on some than on others. Tastes, as "aesthetic stances," are, Bourdieu wrote, "opportunities to experience or assert one's position in social space, as a rank to be upheld or a distance to be kept" (ibid., 57). In his use of the term, Bourdieu played with the dual meanings of taste: as it is used in the normative sense for "refined things" associated with high culture; and taste as viewed in the more anthropological understanding of culture that includes tastes in relation to such things as foods. The former usage refers to tastes for luxuries, and the latter to tastes for necessities. Associated with this is the role of taste in a person's lifestyle, viewed as "a system of classified and classifying practices" (ibid., 171).

According to Bourdieu, taste "functions as a sort of social orientation, a 'sense of one's place,' in guiding the occupants of a given place in social space towards the social positions adjusted to their properties, and towards the practices or good which befit the occupants of that position" (ibid., 466). He had used this idea of a "sense of one's place" earlier in his work on peasant habitus. Bourdieu frequently viewed embodied habitus, across his many writings about it, as connected to a sense of one's place both socially and physically or geographically.

When Bourdieu wrote that "taste is what brings together things and people that go together" (1979b/1984a, 241), he meant that one's position in social space (which is a function of the various types and amounts of capital a person has inherited and accumulated) is both informed and formed by one's tastes. He used the term "elective affinities" to describe the feelings of social closeness that draw people together. Tastes are signs of the dispositions of embodied habitus, and habitus is a position in social space. A person's lifestyle is generated by their habitus. Lifestyle includes the practices associated with tastes (what people like and desire, as well as what disgusts them).[15]

Social space, for Bourdieu, is a differentiated space of lifestyles, of habituses, and of social conditions that entails the workings of social hierarchy. In *Distinction*, he depicted social space visually through the use of diagrams that are oriented with directions (up and down, near and far) and with axes that are not those of cardinal directions, as in the analysis of the Kabyle house or the map of Paris he used in his analysis of *Sentimental Education*, but of capital (economic and cultural, and measured in terms of volume as well as according to whether these are dominating or dominated forms of capital). In his elaborate diagrams illustrating connections between "the space of social positions" and "the space of life-styles" (ibid., 128–29), Bourdieu identified positions in social space according to markers such as type of occupation, consumption tastes, education, and residence on a rural to urban continuum related to population size. The main axes are cultural capital and economic capital—at the top of one diagram are positioned those with high amounts of both; at the bottom, low amounts of both. To the left are those with high cultural capital but lower economic capital, and to the right, those with a lot of economic capital but less cultural capital. The orientations and dispositions of the habitus take on differing amounts of value within social space. Bourdieu referred to these as forms of capital—cultural, symbolic, and social. Therefore, in a class-based society such as France, such features as ways of speaking; tastes in food, music, or art; aspirations regarding education and career; ideas about how to decorate a house; and ways of moving the body are all aspects of habitus that have more or less value in a particular social space. Social space is dominated by the habitus of the dominant social class—those who determine the value of cultural capital.

Bourdieu emphasized that the social space he depicted in *Distinction* must not be understood as actual physical space or social space in which social interaction takes place. It is not meant to refer to "the practical space of everyday life" in which, he wrote, neighbors "may be more remote than strangers" (ibid., 169). Social space in this book should be understood instead as an "abstract representation" of the space of everyday life. Bourdieu intentionally constructed it, "like a map, to give a bird's-eye view, a point of view on the whole set of points from which ordinary agents (including the sociologist and his reader, in their ordinary behavior) see the social world" (ibid., 169). Because of this, the gaps and discontinuities that might be present in what he referred to as the "'travelling space' of ordinary experience" cannot be captured in the abstract diagrams, associated with correspondence analysis, of social positions, tastes, and points of view in social space.

Bourdieu felt that it was necessary to "construct social space as an objective space, a structure of objective relations which determines the possible form of interactions and of the representations the interactors can have of them" (ibid., 244). He took the position in *Distinction* that he was not interested in viewing social space in terms of the subjective representations held by social actors of each other's performances as a way to understand the social world, an approach he attributed to Goffman (ibid., 579, fn32), because this ignored the underlying structure of those performances and interactions. As the examples of Bourdieu's earlier work I have provided in this book illustrate, and as the next example to which I will turn shows, this was not always Bourdieu's position. In some of his work, he did pay attention to the ways in which social actors understood their position in social space. I interpret Bourdieu's distancing himself from Goffman in *Distinction* as not the definitive statement of his approach to social space, but a perspective that he adopted in this particular work in order to underscore his view that social space was an underlying structure and not solely to be understood in terms of visible social interactions.

The appendices to *Distinction* contain details regarding the evidence upon which Bourdieu's analysis of the role of taste in social hierarchy depends. Paying attention to the ways in which Bourdieu described his methods is instructive for understanding what he meant by social space and its implications not only for analysis of the social world "out there" but for understanding the position of the researcher and their point of view on the subject being studied. Bourdieu indicated that *Distinction* was based on two surveys, one conducted in 1963 and another in 1967–68, that included 1,217 respondents evenly divided between Paris and the provinces. More people from the upper and middle classes were surveyed than those of other groups because, as Bourdieu explained, he wanted to investigate the different "fractions" of those more dominant social classes in particular (ibid., 504–5). The survey schedule administered by interviewers is provided in its entirety in the back of the book. It collects basic demographic information (such as age, gender, marital status, income, occupation, education, and place of residence) and includes questions related to what the respondents like, do, and purchase (ranging from leisure activities to home furnishings to art). There is also a section in the questionnaire for the interviewer to record their observations about various attributes of the home in which the interview took place and the person interviewed (physical appearance,

speech). Bourdieu explained that these surveys were conducted after preliminary research that entailed "extended interviews and ethnographic observations" (ibid., 504), but it is unclear if any of this was directly used in
the analysis. When there was need to clarify some of the material from the
surveys, Bourdieu inserted lengthier interview extracts that were from other
published research sources (not his own). For example, personal narratives
about the occupational trajectories of two twentysomething interviewees
were included in one section of the book (ibid., 146–47). *Distinction* also
drew from census data and over fifty surveys conducted between 1965 and
1975 by both INSEE (The French National Institute for Social and Economic Studies), and by private market research and opinion poll companies
in France such as SOFRES and IFOP.

Interestingly, Bourdieu excluded farmers and farm workers from his own
questionnaires, even though they were included in some of the other surveys from which the analysis drew. His justification for this was that the
questions asked seemed inappropriate for identifying "the dispositions of
a population totally excluded from legitimate culture and even, to a large
extent, from 'middle-brow' culture (*la culture moyenne*)" (ibid., 505). In a
footnote (ibid., 602, fn4), Bourdieu noted that by the time he was writing
Distinction in the late 1970s, that might have been less the case than it was
when the surveys were conducted—due to the increased exposure to formal education among this segment of the population that was leading to
more unification of the "market for symbolic goods" (1979b, 589, fn3—my
translation).

It is significant that not only were rural dwellers excluded from the survey, but there is also no mention in *Distinction* of immigrant populations or
non-native French being interviewed or even being present in French social
space. It seems reasonable to assume, based on what he said about his
exclusion of farmers, that Bourdieu felt the questions asked would also not
be pertinent for immigrants. That France included immigrants in this period
of time is not taken into consideration in the book, and the assumption is
that the social space Bourdieu seeks to describe is composed of native-born
French.[16] Bourdieu would have been very aware of the presence of immigrants, especially given his knowledge of the aftermath of the Algerian war,
but his intention in *Distinction* was to depict the social space of "legitimate"
culture—that defined by the bourgeoisie. It is important to recognize this
about *Distinction*, because Bourdieu was interested in mapping the forms of
symbolic power and the field of power in France in that work.

In the next example to which I turn, *The Social Structures of the Economy*,
Bourdieu used the more abstract correspondence analysis methods associated with *Distinction*, but also included ethnographic depictions of social
interaction and individual behavior. In addition, he made his sympathy for

the aspiring petit-bourgeois class quite evident in that work. Another important departure from *Distinction* is that Bourdieu paid more attention to the role of the state in shaping tastes and desires.

Social Space and the Housing Market

In *The Social Structures of the Economy* (2000d/2005), his last major work, Bourdieu used ethnographic descriptions of encounters between buyers and sellers in the domain of real estate, combined with correspondence analysis, to analyze the symbolic power of the state and its relationship to economic capital and social hierarchy. The argument is that buying a single-family house cannot be viewed as a purely economic transaction if both habitus and social space are taken into account. Both taste in house and geographic location of house are connected to the habitus of the buyer. Buying a house is connected to emotions about home and family and can be part of what Bourdieu referred to as a "reproduction project" (ibid., 21) of the family patrimony. Buyers are affected not only by their economic resources, but also by "tastes" associated with the dispositions of their habitus, to which marketing campaigns of housing developers seek to appeal. Advertising does not, however, create demands and desires; rather, it exploits preexisting dispositions. Real estate advertisements seek to make people feel at home (ibid., 24) when they view a particular house model and its location.

The ways in which people are positioned in social space are connected to not only their taste in housing, but also to whether they are renters or homeowners. For example, Bourdieu's research showed that French people with more cultural capital than economic capital tend to rent homes rather than buy them. He warned, however, that viewing desires for "home" and cultural meanings of household and home as a shared phenomenon does not sufficiently focus on the fact that the housing market is a differentiated field in which those desires are based on positioning in social space. Preferences regarding owing or renting a house will "vary according to different factors: economic capital, cultural capital, the structure of overall capital, social trajectory, age, marital status, number of children, position in the family life-cycle, etc." (ibid., 25). The firms building and marketing houses are themselves positioned in a field of real estate production that will correspond in most cases with the position of the buyers. People will gravitate, therefore, to the kinds of firms that produce the kinds of houses that match their own aesthetic preferences and economic constraints. This is the idea of "affinity," which is not conscious but operates as a "spontaneous orchestration of practices" (ibid., 73).

The French state looms larger in this analysis than it did in *Distinction*, as it is shown to shape desires and tastes regarding housing choices. The state and its agents help to produce the market for real estate and then regulate it. The demand for single-family houses is "socially maintained and reactivated" by advertisers through media (Bourdieu mentioned women's magazines; but in today's context, one could also include social media). However, the state "orients" those needs through the production of regulations and standards in the housing market (including both construction and sales). Banks, which have the most to gain from these exchanges, profit from the subsidies the state gives to individuals so that they may buy a house. In this way, Bourdieu argued, the state not only controls the housing market, but also helps to construct it through this financial assistance. He concludes that "the housing market is sustained and controlled, directly and indirectly, by the public authorities" that regulate all aspects of it from property law to controls over credit (ibid., 92). This is how the state is made evident to everyday people—both through its regulations and through the interactions people have with civil servants (bureaucrats) who either enforce (say "no") or provide some leniency with those regulations. Through his analysis of the housing market and real estate field, Bourdieu illustrated the state's presence in the encounters between buyer and seller (real estate agent).

Bourdieu placed a great deal of attention on bureaucrats and bureaucratic organizations that comprise "the bureaucratic field" associated with the state in *The Social Structures of the Economy*. State regulation of the housing market proceeds in large part through decisions and recommendations by commissions that are composed of people with ties to both civil service and industries such as banking. Those who are dominant in social space are part of the system of regulation at the state level (including serving on commissions) and are also connected to economic capital, such as the banks that profit from the real estate market. Bourdieu used the example of the 1976 reform of housing subsidies in France, under President Valéry Giscard d'Estaing, to illustrate the operation of bureaucracy and its connections to the dominant sectors of society. The commission formed to create the new regulations became an arena of struggles around French housing policy between those invested in social policy associated with the Left that would protect more vulnerable homebuyers, and those associated with the Right who advocated a more liberal policy.

Bourdieu viewed the housing reform in terms of the "bureaucratic game" (ibid., 118) in a field where rules can be bent, transgressed, and subverted when the participants are viewed as legitimate "servants of the state" (ibid., 119). These are the people who possess sufficient symbolic capital to legitimately bend rules.[17] Drawing upon Parsons's ideas of ascription versus achievement, Bourdieu argued that "strategies of condescension" were utilized by those more dominant in social space when they crossed symbolic boundaries. In the essay "Rites as Acts of Institution" (1982b/1992c, 87), he observed, "He who is sure of his cultural identity can play with the rules of the cultural game," and those who have been "consecrated" are authorized to "to make transgressions which would otherwise be forbidden."

Bourdieu used struggles around housing regulations to make his point that those who are positioned more highly in the bureaucratic structure have more leeway in transgressing rules. Bureaucrats in lower positions, who in the past frequently come from petit-bourgeois backgrounds, are more invested in following rules due to their aspirations for social mobility and insecurities about their positions. He wrote: "It follows that one cannot establish a mechanical relation between positions and position-taking: position-taking always involves a greater or lesser element of free play, which agents can use to a greater or lesser extent depending on their dispositions, which themselves match their positions more or less closely" (2000d/2005, 129). With this example, Bourdieu connects the territorial space of housing, social space, and the real estate field. Homebuyers enter the real estate field when they apply for a mortgage and look for a house. This field is composed of firms that construct and produce single-family houses (the focus of the study) and the bureaucracy that regulates this and also provides mortgage subsidies to buyers.

Bourdieu argued in *The Social Structures of the Economy* that it is wrong to think of the state as uniform and centralized in contrast to a local level that is more heterogeneous and peripheral. To see the local as a site from which to resist state power makes the state power appear too unitary and distant from everyday life. The formulation of housing policy at the national level is the product of various interactions among social actors that take place within structural constraints. At the more regional or local level, where policy is defined and enacted, there are also "different or antagonistic strategies" among social actors (ibid., 126). Bourdieu argued against seeing the "center" as the site of a universal rule as opposed to the "local" as the site of application of the rule because it tends to support the image of neutrality at the central/national level pitted against more "provincial" or peripheral interests. Bourdieu's point is that there is no neutrality, and there are struggles at all levels.

Bourdieu emphasized that his model of the housing market lends more attention to individuals than do other economic models of choice or decision-making:

> We see, in passing, against the charge of "holism" which one attracts as soon as one pays the slightest attention to the social properties of

agents, that the approach chosen here restores the interest in individuals, and in individuals restored to their full dignity as agents acting by virtue of their embodied social properties—their habitus—and hence different and unequal. (Ibid., 96)

For Bourdieu, the encounters/social interactions between buyers and real estate agents are "actualizations" of structural factors that were, nevertheless, uncertain in terms of course and outcome. He wrote: "Observation and ethnographic description thus offer the only means of apprehending and reconstructing the materialization, in the lived experience of the actors, shaped by the action of factors that can only act by working through it [the materialization]" (2000d, 210— my translation). An important point about ethnographic observation for Bourdieu, however, is that "the truth of the interaction is not to be found in the interaction itself (a two-way relation that is always in fact a three-way relation, between the two agents and the social space in which they are located)" (2000d/2005, 148).

To illustrate this point, Bourdieu described the encounter between a family with two children and a salesman at a housing show as an "actualization at a single point in time" of various, more hidden processes. First, there is the financial power of banks, which provides the sales agent with the means to evaluate the purchasing power of the family; and, second, the relative power of the family/client, who can deploy cultural capital to exploit their purchasing power. Bourdieu described the ritualistic encounter and its tempo whereby the sales agent seeks to establish rapport with the client while also evaluating their purchasing power. Depending upon the linguistic and cultural capital of the clients, they are in a better or worse condition of negotiation regarding the exchange in order to achieve their own goals (related to their economic capital and also their tastes and dispositions regarding a house and its location). Bourdieu concluded that an "economic act" (ibid., 175) has to work through the social form of the exchange between people who bring to it their various dispositions and which can result in either a pleasant outcome of trust or one of hostility.

Bourdieu's analysis of the real estate market draws attention to what he referred to as the "suffering" of the petite bourgeoisie, which he claimed to have not received as much attention as that of the poor or working class. This group seeks the single-family home and therefore goes more into debt with creditors in order to achieve this dream. The petite bourgeoisie suffers an inordinate amount of symbolic violence because they have greater aspirations than do those in other positions (higher and lower) in social space. Their aspirations frequently, however, remain unmet, and this leads to disillusionment and dissatisfaction. Bourdieu felt that social commentators (many of whom have bourgeois origins) criticize this group because it is "both too close to home and too distant" (ibid., 186) from their own position in social space, precisely because the petite bourgeoisie aspire to a bourgeois condition. Criticizing or belittling the aspirations of this segment of the population maintains the symbolic boundary between them and the bourgeoisie.

In his study of the housing market, Bourdieu introduced the concept of a desire for "home" that is aspirational and connected to social mobility. This contrasts with his previous approach in rural societies where he described em-peasanted peasants who wanted to feel at home by staying in place and therefore suffered when they were either geographically displaced (as was the case for the Kabyles in the resettlement camps of post-war Algeria) or displaced because the world around them had changed (as was the case among the bachelors in Béarn).

Taste, Emotion, Position

The work I have discussed in this chapter shows Bourdieu turning his attention to the positions and trajectories in social space of the bourgeoisie and, especially, the aspiring petite bourgeoisie. In earlier work, Bourdieu deployed the concept of social space to depict various local settings—a house in a Kabyle village, a settlement camp in post-war Algeria, a region of rural France, and a city (Paris) in relationship to a nearby Province (Normandy). He turned his attention to the broader scale of national social space in *Distinction*, where he developed that idea in his most systematic way. In *The Social Structures of the Economy*, the state plays a much larger role than in Bourdieu's previous works. Understanding these different contexts in which social space was used to describe the social world leads to an appreciation of how Bourdieu's concept can be applied using either a zoom or wide-angle lens on society.

Bourdieu posited a relationship between time, physical space, and social space that emphasized how social practices generated from habitus are influenced both by the other habituses in a particular social space, and the possibilities (in terms of both "objective" opportunities and "subjective" aspirations) available to each habitus. These possibilities are, according to Bourdieu, shaped by state power through its agents (bureaucrats) and policies. Social space became an increasingly central concept in Bourdieu's work as he came to see habitus in a differentiated society as responding to these possibilities while also generating the universe of what was considered possible—the "space of possibilities" that is social space. The work discussed in this chapter makes use of the concept of point of view in a social space related to social position and positionings.

Movement in social space and mobility across geographic space are frequently connected to aspirations (except in cases of forced migration). More specifically, aspirations are influenced by perceptions of possibility and by objective structures and structurings that can be identified with the concepts of social space and field. Aspirations are also linked to "taste," interpreted both as an affinity to certain people, particular things, and particular geographic locations (including neighborhoods and specific houses). In Bourdieu's conceptual framework, habitus entails the dispositions that include emotional responses to people, places, and things. Whether or not a person feels at home, may be related to either mobility or immobility. The ability to be mobile (socially and geographically) is affected by one's habitus and all of the capital associated with it. Choices about location in space and in society are related to the emotional aspects of taste and affinity.

As I read Bourdieu's work, especially the studies with which I have been concerned in this chapter, two questions about his approach arise for me that call for further exploration. First, is social space a closed system? Sometimes, Bourdieu wrote about it as if it were, but he also acknowledged (as is apparent in the earlier ethnographic work discussed in the last chapter) that social space can expand, contract, and change over time. This is relevant for studies of mobility in that it prompts additional research on the articulation of territorial space and social space. If social space is closed but people can cross geographical borders, does this mean they necessarily enter a new social space when they do so? Are the limits of geographic borders coterminous with the boundary of a social space? My second question about Bourdieu's approach is how the dominant get to dominate. How does Bourdieu explain the basis for their power? This is a central question in studies of mobility and migration because it calls for further investigation into how geographically mobile persons will be positioned in the hierarchy of social space in new places. Are they able to acquire the symbolic capital needed for social mobility and for social emplacement? How can they acquire power in social space and the fields within it? What are the barriers to the recognition of their "social existence"? These questions are critical to my focus in the remaining chapters of this book. In the next chapter, I address them by turning in more detail to Bourdieu's writings on the state and state power.

NOTES

1. See Lipstadt (2008) for a comparison of three works by Bourdieu, including this essay and his analysis of Flaubert's novel *Sentimental Education*, from the perspectives of an architectural historian. Lipstadt shows the importance of space in Bour-

dieu's thought through her analysis, which parallels some of my own interests in this work. She does not, however, unpack Bourdieu's concept of social space or its relationship to that of field in her analysis. See also Reed-Danahay (2005b) for an earlier discussion of Bourdieu's writings on the illusions of biography.

2. Although Bourdieu was skeptical of what he called "the biographical illusion," he was nevertheless interested in the ways in which people articulated their experiences and perceptions of social life. See chapter 5 in *Locating Bourdieu* (Reed-Danahay 2005b) for a more extensive discussion of Bourdieu's use of personal narrative, which shows his interest in subjective perspectives.

3. Bourdieu established this journal in 1975 and remained at its head until his death in 2002.

4. The English translation of the original French article appeared in 1987 (Bourdieu 1987). He delivered a series of lectures on this material in 1986 at Princeton (Johnson 1993, vii), subsequently published in the compilation of writings *The Field of Cultural Production* (Bourdieu 1993b). In a volume first published in France in 1992, *The Rules of Art: Genesis and Structure of the Literary Field* (Bourdieu 1996b), Bourdieu further reworked and expanded upon some of the earlier writings on Flaubert.

5. Several anthropologists have examined novels as ethnographic genres, and have discussed the relationships between literary and ethnographic portraits of social life. See Handler and Segal ([1990] 1999), Rapport (1994), Herzfeld (1997), and Cohen (2013).

6. The year 1848 was a time of much social unrest and turmoil in France and throughout Europe. The 1848 Revolution in France refers to the events that led to the establishment of the Second Republic. Much like the student and worker movements in France of May 1968, there were demonstrations in Paris, and Bourdieu drew parallels between the two events.

7. See Bourdieu (1992b/1996b and 1993b). This does not fall within the scope of my focus in this book.

8. The translated version (1987) of the original French "enserré dans des reseaux de relations sociales" (1975, 70) uses the term "forced" to translate *enserré* when "enclosed" or "trapped" better captures Bourdieu's meaning.

9. In a later reanalysis of this example, Bourdieu (1992b) adopted the vocabulary of social space as a field of power and field of struggle, including the important role of economic, cultural, and social capital.

10. The key works to which I refer include Bourdieu and Passeron (1964c and 1970b). I have discussed Bourdieu's work on education at some length elsewhere (Reed-Danahay 2005b; see also Reed-Danahay 1996).

11. Bourdieu's use of the map of Paris is reminiscent of maps used in an earlier text by the French cultural geographer Paul-Henry Chombart de Lauwe (1965), who also used the term "social space" (*l'espace social*) in his work, as I noted in the Introduction to this book. By comparing the two uses of maps of Paris, we can see the differences in approach to the relationship between individuals and their movement over geographic space in the work of these two men. The image included in Bourdieu's

analysis of *Sentimental Education* maps the trajectory of individuals, while Chombart de Lauwe focused more on aggregate data of mobilities across space.

12. *Distinction* was first published in France in 1979, but the background research was conducted earlier (during the 1960s), and a long coauthored article (Bourdieu and de St. Martin 1976) contained much of the material later published in the book. See de St. Martin (2015) for a discussion of the genesis of *Distinction* and the collaborative work upon which it was based, although little of that work was explicitly credited or cited by Bourdieu.

13. As Coulangeon and Duval (2013/2015, 6–7) note, attention to the cultural aspects of *Distinction* (by which they mean art and literature) have tended to overshadow the importance of this work for theories of social class.

14. For example, in her comparison of the upper-middle-classes in the US and in France, Michèle Lamont (1992) charges Bourdieu with transferring the ways in which social distinctions are drawn in the Parisian intellectual milieu to all of France in *Distinction*. Although her study was inspired by Bourdieu's work on social boundaries (she reinterprets his notion of "taste" as symbolic boundary), Lamont criticizes Bourdieu for ignoring morality's role in symbolic boundary-making and also for positing that social actors operate in closed fields in which a zero-sum game operates so that one person's rise in status must infer another person's downward mobility. Lamont does not focus on geographic mobility, except for mentioning that geographic mobility was greater in the US than in France for the upper-middle-class at the time of her study.

15. Bourdieu illustrated this through a diagram showing the direction of influence leading from "conditions of existence" via habitus to "life-style" (1979a/1984a, Figure 8, 171).

16. During the period of this research, approximately 7 percent of the French population was composed of immigrants (defined as someone born a foreigner outside of France who currently resides in France). The number is now over 9 percent, based on the 2015 census (INSEE 2017, 158). When Bourdieu discussed issues of language, he was referring to regional dialects and accents, rather than foreign ones.

17. For an earlier ethnographic study of bureaucrats at the local level and the ways in which they may bend rules or appear "indifferent," see Herzfeld (1992). Herzfeld's analysis also adopts a symbolic approach to the study of bureaucracy, but with more of a focus on rhetorics of familiarity that depend upon kinship metaphors and cut across various levels of nation-states. Bourdieu assumed the acceptance of the legitimacy of bureaucrats, and overstated in some ways their symbolic power, in contrast to the more nuanced analysis offered by Herzfeld.

4

The Nation-State and Thresholds of Social Space

> All those boundaries of inside and outside that are linked with the national character are largely products of the state, by way of the educational system, literature and all kinds of paths for the transmission and inculcation of these deep and unconscious dispositions bound up with the state.
> —*On the State* (2012/2014, 144)[1]

The social space of the nation-state became more of a focus for Bourdieu from the 1980s and onward. Bourdieu questioned monolithic approaches to the state, but also wanted to understand why such views had become so widespread. He sought to articulate the ways in which the state constitutes and maintains the territorial boundaries and social space of the nation. This is highly relevant for contemporary conceptualizations of the boundaries and thresholds of the nation-state, and has implications for studies of migration and mobility. In his approach to the state, Bourdieu gestures toward possibilities of citizen positionings in the social space of their nation even when they do not live within the territory of the state, and, conversely, of immigrants and their children living within a state territory who are not full participants and are marginalized in its national social space.[2] At the same time, Bourdieu's perspective calls into question some of the assumptions associated with the idea of "transnational social space," as I mentioned in the Introduction, which do not sufficiently examine national social space and its relationship to the state when addressing the ways in which mobile people move and communicate across national boundaries.

In this chapter, I examine Bourdieu's attention to the symbolic power of the state as it creates territorial borders and marginality in both geographic and social space through classifications of regions, language, and groups. I turn to several of Bourdieu's key texts regarding the nation-state, including *On the State, Language and Symbolic Power, The State Nobility*, and several related articles.[3]

Nation and State

Well into his lectures from 1989–92 at the Collège de France, published as *On the State* (2012/2014, 144), Bourdieu told the audience that the question of how the state gets people to obey is "really the underlying problem" he sought to address. His approach to answering this question was to view the state as engaged in "the production and canonization of social classifications" (ibid., 9). No doubt in answer to critics who charged him with having a theory only of social reproduction rather than one of transformation or resistances, Bourdieu noted that he found the reproduction of the state, and questions about how it shapes obedience to it, more important than those about resistance or challenges to the state. His approach emphasizes the ways in which the state constitutes and maintains national social space through representations and perceptions of the social world as "natural."

Bourdieu claimed that the reason he did not begin to use the term "the state" in his writing until the late 1980s (ibid., 113), was that he hesitated to use a word whose meaning was unclear. In a reflection upon dictionary definitions of the state, Bourdieu wrote that people most often view it as both a "bureaucratic apparatus that manages collective interests" and "the territory on which the authority of the apparatus is exercised" (ibid., 31). To illustrate this, Bourdieu observed that when people think of the French state, they think of its government, armed forces, and bureaucracy, but also of France as a physical territory.[4] This links both social and physical/geographic space—a key element, as I have asserted throughout this book, in Bourdieu's theory of social space.

Although Bourdieu admitted that he sometimes entered into this phrasing himself, he wanted to avoid statements viewing the state as an actor (i.e., "the state does xyz") and preferred to speak of state institutions, actors, and agents.[5] Bourdieu built upon Weber's approach to the study of religion, which examined the "producers of religious messages" instead of only looking at the symbolic aspects of religious belief and ritual, and adapted this to the study of the state. He thus viewed bureaucrats as "agents of the state who have constituted themselves into a state nobility by instituting the state" and who produce discourse regarding what the state *is* that works to construct and reproduce the state (Bourdieu 1993a/1994b, 16). The state is created and sustained by social agents "who speak in the name of the whole" and who are similar to what Weber called "law prophets" (Bourdieu 2012/2014, 45). The French president is expected to speak officially in terms of what France believes, for example, rather than what he believes. Because the state's viewpoint is presented as disinterested it is not perceived as a point of view, but accepted as universal (ibid., 69). Bourdieu viewed commissions set up by the state to oversee policies as key symbolic mechanisms for conveying the neutral and disinterested nature of the state—as in the banking and real estate policies that influence the housing market discussed in Chapter Three.

As Didier Fassin, following Bourdieu, observed about the state, it includes a variety of institutions that "defend differing ideas and interests" (Fassin [2013] 2015, 6). The state is thereby produced through its institutions and the various social agents who represent it. Central to Bourdieu's perspective was that, through institutions and state agents, the state works to legitimize its sovereignty and unity. Two other scholars have characterized Bourdieu's approach thus: "States profoundly shape the normative order, influencing the very terminology we use to describe them and where we locate their boundaries" (Morgan and Orloff 2017, 10).

What is arbitrary becomes understood as natural. Bourdieu realized that this is a feature of culture in the anthropological sense, and he viewed culture as an "instrument of cohesion, of social unity" by agents of the state. He pointed to the dual meaning of culture as both "legitimate culture" (having to do with being a cultivated person) and culture in the (anthropological) sense of "ways of living" that help to maintain social order. The state intervenes both in sanctioning forms of legitimate culture and by helping to create the national ideas of shared culture that have to do with everyday "ways of living" (Bourdieu 2012/2014, 153).

Nation and state go hand in hand in Bourdieu's later writings. Bourdieu viewed the national as an invention of the state that, in turn, helps constitute and maintain the state. He noted in one of his lectures at the Collège de France that when he had previously written about social space and the genesis of groups/classes (e.g., 1985b and 1989c), he "was in fact referring to the national social space that is constructed at the same time as the state is constructed, that the state constructs as it constructs itself" (2012/2014, 223). Bourdieu contrasted the development of the state in Germany and in France. In Germany, national affiliations and sentiments preceded the construction of the state, whereas in France, the state constructed the nation (ibid., 347). He wrote that "the state expresses the nation" in Germany, but in France, "The French revolutionaries . . . made the universal state, and this state would go on to make the nation through the school, the army, etc." (ibid., 347).

Bourdieu described the ways in which the taken-for-granted divisions and distinctions of national social space depend upon the symbolic power of the state. I use the term "nation-state" here as a shorthand, but must acknowledge that Bourdieu referenced the state more than he did national identity or nationalism in his writings. He rarely used the term "nation-state" (*état-nation*), referring more often either to the state or the nation. However, when he did use that term, it is apparent that it signaled national social space. For example, in his essay on "Rethinking the State" ("Esprits d'Etat"), Bourdieu maintained that the universalization of primary education in France during the nineteenth century was a unifying action of the state, which constructed the nation-state (1993a/1994b). It seems reasonable to assume, therefore, that for Bourdieu, the "nation-state" was the nation that also had a state system of government. Although Bourdieu posited a national social space, he described the state not as a social space but, rather, as a differentiated field within national social space in which power was concentrated. This field is, therefore, a particular region of the national social space in which it is associated and which it works to construct.

Bourdieu was interested in the social construction of the territorial borders of national social space as well as both the construction of social boundaries within it and its limits or thresholds. The state shapes the ways in which identities are represented and classified so as to instill both a national identity and differences based on class, region, ethnicity, and gender. Bourdieu viewed national social space as always differentiated and hierarchical. He disagreed with those who argued that contemporary nation-states such as Japan, France, and the US were becoming increasingly middle-class societies. In the context of remarks he made in Oslo regarding this point, Bourdieu stated, "All my work shows that in a country said to be on the way to becoming homogenized, democratized, and so on, difference is everywhere" (1996a, 20).

The social space of a nation entails a shared "common sense"—that is, a perception of the world, and a way of classifying the social order. As Bourdieu emphasized in *Pascalian Meditations* (1997/2000c, 98), this commonsense view of the world is what permits people to agree to disagree ("agreement in disagreement"), meaning that they agree on the divisions and classifications of social life, but may interpret individual social actions differently depending on their own position in social space. For example, Bourdieu observed, a behavior might be judged as "shameless" by some but as "unpretentious" by others. This national common sense is, according to Bourdieu, transmitted primarily through schooling. The major role of educational institutions is to "construct the nation as a population endowed with the same categories and therefore the same common sense" (ibid., 98). Common sense, which Bourdieu also referred to as *doxa*, is essential to his understanding of habitus as a disposition that informs practices and ways of thinking.[6] Being in another country provokes feelings of strangeness, according to Bourdieu, not only due to language differences, but also to "discrepancies between the world as it presents itself at each moment and the system of dispositions and expectations constituting common sense" (ibid., 98). Bourdieu's idea of the nation-state, therefore, involves not only institutions of the state (including the educational system), but also a national common sense.

Bourdieu made several key claims in his lectures on the state that help illuminate his understanding of the relationship between national identity and the state. First, he explicitly built upon Weber's definition of the state by adding symbolic violence to the role of the state. Second, he argued that insufficient attention has been paid to the concept of logical conformity as part of state power in scholarship regarding Durkheim's work—especially as he articulated this idea in *The Elementary Forms of Religious Life*. By "logical conformity," Bourdieu meant shared understanding of reality and categories of thought and perception. A third aspect of the state is its work of centralization (of the power to classify associated with forms of capital) and unification (of space, social practices, and perceptions of reality), seen most clearly in the realm of language (the imposition of a standardized language). According to Bourdieu,

> This kind of centralization reaches its limits in the French state (although it is also true for the English and American state). This unification of space, the development of which is accompanied by the birth of a central power, implies the unification and uniformatization of both the geographic and social space. (2012/2014, 223)

Bourdieu argued that the formation of state territory was aimed at superseding other forms of belonging. By establishing a unified (territorial) space, the state "makes geographical proximity predominate in relation to social, genealogical proximity." Bourdieu explained that there are two forms of belonging in many kinship-based societies: "belonging to a lineage group and belonging to a place" (ibid., 224). Creating attachments to the nation and the state (as geographic and social space) rather than kin groups has been a central project of the state. Here, Bourdieu linked social and physical space to the ways in which the state undermines pervious forms of affiliation based on lineage, which harkens back to his early work in Béarn. Although he did not make explicit reference to the state in his 1962 essay on Béarnaise bachelorhood, Bourdieu did suggest that the marriage market had been transformed as urbanization led to expanded geographical thresholds for marriage partners—previously limited to a more local level and relationships between lineage groups.

Bourdieu asserted, "One of the major powers of the state is to produce and impose (especially through the school system) categories of thought that we spontaneously apply to all things of the social world—including the state itself" (Bourdieu 1993a/1994b, 1). He proposed a "radical questioning" of our assumptions about the state. This is a difficult task, Bourdieu maintained, because the state is most powerful in the realm of "symbolic production," which is largely hidden and tacitly perceived. Social science is implicated in the construction of the state for two reasons. First, sociological research and writing depicts the reality of the state in certain ways that reinforce the *doxa*; second, social science is dependent upon the state through both the academic certifications that ensure its legitimacy and through research funding. The state works on such deep levels of consciousness, according to Bourdieu, that the modes of seeing the world (what he refers to as "cognitive structures") shaped by the state become embodied dispositions that produce a "doxic submission of the dominated to the structures of the social order" (ibid., 14). Bourdieu departs here from a Marxist vocabulary of "ideology" in order to argue that state power is better explained as a question of "belief." *Doxa* is not imposed from some unitary ideology coming from above; it is created through everyday practices and experiences shaped by state institutions and agents. For Bourdieu, the state is best viewed as "the culmination of a process of concentration of different species of capital," including physical force and instruments of coercion, economic, cultural, and symbolic capital (ibid., 4). During his lectures on the state, Bourdieu described it as "the central bank of symbolic capital" (2012/2014, 217).

The "dominant impose their domination" by way of instilling pre-reflexive acceptance of the legitimacy of the state. This does not mean, however, that the commonsense vision of the world is not one based upon political struggle between the dominant and the dominated. The state exerts its power over its "territorial expanse" through *doxa*; but although that appears to be natural, it is instead "a particular point of view, the point of view of the dominant, when it presents and imposes itself as a universal point of view" (1993a/1994b 15). Through its influence on shaping perceptions of social reality, the state "creates the conditions for a kind of immediate orchestration of habituses which is itself the foundation of a consensus over this set of shared evidences constitutive of (national) common sense" (ibid., 13). To illustrate this, Bourdieu uses the example of the ways in which the state works to coordinate time through the annual calendar in order to produce the "seasonal migrations" of vacation trips by people during times of school vacations or national holidays, which provide shared forms of reference that "make social life possible" (ibid., 14).

For Bourdieu, "the state is a space" (2012/2014, 368) that involves various struggles. It is divided along what he depicted as left-right binaries, somewhat mirroring the political field in terms of the division of France between the Left and the Right, but not completely congruent with that (see ibid., 368–69). One binary involves what he referred to as the left and right sides of state space in an imagination of the geometric composition of social space, following his analyses in *Distinction*. Those social agents positioned on the right side have high economic capital but relatively lower cultural capital. Those positioned on the left side have high cultural capital but relatively lower economic capital. This space also includes what Bourdieu labeled the left and right "hands" of the state, which has more to do with social policies and practices. The left hand is the part of the state involved in service and welfare; the right hand of the state engages in control, discipline, and coercion.[7] Bourdieu departed from Marxist theorists of the state (and such writers as Foucault and Elias who stressed the disciplinary role of the state), by arguing that the state engages in both control and service. As he put it, state institutions "control all the better by serving" (ibid., 142).[8] In his final lecture at the Collège de France on the state, Bourdieu used René Lenoir's analysis of the social space depicted in French crime novels to illustrate the struggles inherent in the state:

> If you give a description of the social space, [the police chief and the judge] are fairly close. But they are nonetheless divided by a set of systematic differences: police chiefs come from a lower social origin, they are more provincial (often from the southwest), first generation; judges are more bourgeois, more Parisian, more Catholic. It is a bit left-right but not completely so. There is a struggle among them and a little "civil war" within the state. (Ibid., 368)

Although the judge and the police chiefs are both agents of the state and are brought into close physical proximity (especially in the courtroom), they are socially very distant and differently positioned in the wider national space.

It must be acknowledged here that Henri Lefebvre also used the phrase "state space." The main difference between the ways in which Bourdieu and Lefebvre understood the relationship between the state and space is that although both used symbolic and material approaches, Bourdieu placed more emphasis on the former. Just as Bourdieu sought to broaden Weber's argument that the state held the monopoly on force within its territory by adding the concept of symbolic violence, he saw the state as influencing our perceptions of and ways of classifying the social world, which, in turn, affect our understandings of the material world and our actions upon it.

This expanded the view of the state as a territorial unit by looking at the ways of thinking about the world that are shaped by the state. For Lefebvre, state space referred to the ways in which the state administered physical space and articulated its power through spatial organization (Brenner and Elden 2009, 353). When Bourdieu used the phrase "state space," he meant the social space of the nation, the commonsense understandings that have been instilled by state institutions such as the school. For Lefebvre, it was the physical territory of the state and its divisions.

Rites of Institution and Social Boundaries

Central to Bourdieu's theory of the nation-state is his analysis of what he termed "rites of institution," in which he offered a new interpretation of "rites of passage."[9] Bourdieu claimed that such rituals are not about separating the initiated from the uninitiated who have not yet undergone the ritual, a major theme in Van Gennep's idea of rites of passage. They are, rather, primarily aimed at distinguishing between those who will never undergo the ritual and attain the status conferred by it from those who are permitted to be so initiated.

For Bourdieu, it is the social division between those who have been initiated and those who will never have that possibility that is important. He renamed rites of passage as "rites of institution" to underscore the ways that they institute or establish social reality and also the ways in which they may serve to appoint (another meaning of institute) select individuals to various positions in social space through the rite. State power, for Bourdieu, is enacted partly through rituals that function to consecrate or legitimize various individuals in ways that make divisions in social life appear to be real and accepted as common sense. Rites of institution, which are also *acts* of institution, confer identity cards, legal names and signatures, educational credentials, and so on. Bourdieu also wrote that what was at stake was the line or boundary, rather than the passage or change in social status (1982b/1992c, 81). This meant that such rituals are not just about crossing thresholds for those permitted to do so; they are also about setting limits to doing so. The social legitimacy that follows from undergoing such a rite of institution works to delineate social boundaries.

Bourdieu contended that rites of institution can be found in both differentiated and less differentiated societies. However, in state (i.e., differentiated) societies, the state "lies at the basis for the symbolic efficacy of all rites of institution" (1993a/1994b, 13). Unique ways of instituting common sense or *doxa* are associated with stratified nation-states. In less differentiated societies, the divisions of social life are "instituted" in minds and bodies "through the whole spatial and temporal organization of social life" (ibid., 13). The process is less diffuse in state societies because, Bourdieu reasoned, the state shapes habitus (as "durable dispositions") and principles of classification (sex, age, competence) primarily through its systems of formal education. Although children may acquire their primary habitus in the family, it is further shaped through the institutions and regulation of practices shaped by the state.

If the habitus is the embodied orientation to the world and to the self that has been shaped through early childhood experiences in a particular social milieu, then it seems Bourdieu is suggesting that rites of institution help to restrain impulses to stray from those dispositions. He wrote that in order to "combat any temptation not to behave according to one's rank," there is a process of naturalizing of difference that turns it "into a second nature through inculcation and incorporation as a set of habits" (1982b/1992c, 85). Only those who have been authorized to do so, by ways of rites of institution, may "make transgressions which would otherwise be forbidden," because their position in social space has been legitimized in ways that imbue them with a sort of "indisputable and permanent essence" (ibid., 87). Those with stigmatized identities due to a lower position in the social hierarchy are not permitted this freedom. Bourdieu wrote that rites of institutions work to keep people in their place. They function to "discourage permanently the temptation to cross over, to transgress the boundary, to desert, to resign" (ibid., 85). This perspective has important implications for social mobility as well as for migration. Spatial practices are connected to positions in social space, so that physical mobility can be blocked when viewed as transgressing a social boundary.

An arbitrary boundary is authorized through each act of institution, although the rite attempts to

> misrepresent the arbitrariness and present the boundary as legitimate and natural; or (and this amounts to the same thing) it effects a solemn, that is to say a licensed and extraordinary transgression of the boundaries which constitute the social and ideational order which is concerned at all costs to protect (as in the separation of the sexes or in the case of marriage rituals). (Bourdieu 1982b/1992c, 81)

Those who undergo a rite of institution acquire a social identity or "social essence" that may be accompanied by a recognition of social status, but which also imposes limits on what a person can and should do. One example offered by Bourdieu from his research among the Kabyles is that circumcision differentiates the circumcised child (male) from the child who will never be circumcised (female) and is therefore more about the social boundaries between masculine and feminine than about the passage from one stage of life to another for a male.

The example *par excellence* from the French state, according to Bourdieu, is the competition (*concours*) undergone by those who seek entrance to the elite institutions known as the *grandes écoles*.[10] A diploma, the symbol of having undergone a subsequent rite of institution after graduation, is a "piece of magic" (1982b/1992c, 84), as much as are the amulets of other types of societies. In a recent use of Bourdieu's concept of rites of institution, which has particular relevance for the theme of this book, Fassin and Mazouz (2009) offered an ethnographic analysis of the process of French naturalization, including the final ceremony to confer citizenship, as a rite of institution that serves to differentiate not only between citizens and noncitizens, but more significantly between native-born and naturalized citizens.

Language and State Power

For Bourdieu, language is a vehicle for solidifying the uniform common sense of the state—through the institution of national and official languages, and also by making the divisions of social life appear natural.[11] This entails distinctions between regional and local languages, considered inferior and associated with dominated groups, and the ways of speaking and linguistic repertoires of more dominant groups in social space. When he commented disapprovingly that "we do not investigate the notion of national borders" (2012/2014, 114), Bourdieu was referring primarily to what it means to be French in terms of language. That is, how is the frontier of national identity associated with speakers of the national language? Algerian independence, he notes (ibid., 115), provoked questions such as, "Do you need to speak French to be French? And if you don't speak French, are you still French? Is it enough to speak French in order to be French?"[12]

Bourdieu focused primarily on France in his considerations of language and symbolic power. Due to his own rural origins in southwestern France, Bourdieu's native tongue was a regional one; he acquired more prestigious ways of speaking through formal education. Bourdieu's interest in the relationship between language and habitus derives in part, therefore, from his personal life trajectory. Because he viewed habitus as embodied, Bourdieu also viewed language as not just a form of verbal and written expression, but also as embodied through acts of speaking that are bodily acts of posture and ways of moving the body. These signal, as in the case of the bachelors in rural Béarn at the village dance (Bourdieu 1962), one's position in both social and physical space.

As the editor of Bourdieu's writings compiled in the volume *Language and Symbolic Power* observed, Bourdieu viewed the emergence of dominant languages in particular geographic locations as associated with the construction of nation-states (Thompson 1991, 5). The social space of the nation is thereby associated with the territorial limits of the nation (its geographic or physical space) through the institution of an official language associated with national identity. This was particularly marked in France, where the *langue d'oeil* of French became the official language and was spread through the universalization of primary education throughout France in the late nineteenth century. Historian Eric Hobsbawm argued that the standardization of law and administration throughout Europe in the nineteenth century was associated with the formation of the nation-state and its associated "mass-production" of traditions, including education. According to Hobsbawm, it was state education in particular that "transformed people into citizens of a particular country" (1983, 264). One popular schoolbook in France, *La Tour de la France Par Deux Enfants* (Bruno 1877), written as the French nation-state was solidifying its existence, helped to shape the geographic and social space of the nation of France through a fictional trip by two youngsters throughout the French territory.[13] Although Bourdieu did not make reference to this book in his writings, it illustrates his view that mechanisms for constructing the shared sense of belonging to the nation were largely produced by educational institutions.

Bourdieu drew upon Ferdinand de Saussure's remark that language defines space, rather than the inverse, in order to underscore that there are no "natural limits" to dialects or languages (Bourdieu 1991b, 44). He was, however, critical of Saussure's distinction between *langue* (language) and *parole* (speech), on the basis that it does not interrogate the "institutional conditions" that produce an official language. Linguists, Bourdieu argued, implicitly accept the official definitions of official language associated with a political unit, which, "within the territorial limits of that unit, imposes itself on the whole population as the only legitimate language" (ibid., 45). For Bourdieu, both the origins and the social uses of the official language are deeply connected to state power. Official occasions and official places in which the state-sanctioned language dominates work to reinforce state power. Moreover, the state works to unify what Bourdieu referred to as the "linguistic market" in ways that cause the official language to be recognized as legitimate and regional dialects and other ways of speaking to be devalued. Although he did not discuss immigrants in this context, Bourdieu's perspective has implications for understanding the ways in which the linguistic practices of mobile people who enter a new national social space can be valued or devalued.

Standardization is key to the symbolic power of the dominant language. Because the nation-state is "an entirely abstract group based on law" (ibid., 48),[14] it needs to establish an impersonal and anonymous standard language in order to fulfill its functions. This language can operate without reference to particular contextual circumstances and can be efficiently used by people who do not know each other in order to communicate. As I noted above, Bourdieu associated this with "the demands of bureaucratic predictability" wherein both civil servants and their clients are perceived as operating in a standard and universal realm (ibid., 48).

Although he posited that the educational system acts to devalue vernacular forms of speech, Bourdieu also argued that this was not strictly tied to the imposition of a dominant language by schools and teachers. It was, in a more complicated process, the outcome of the interaction between the system of education and a changing labor market. Because educational qualifications have validity across the nation, especially in a centralized system such as France, this works to create a unification of labor markets that depend on these credentials. Bourdieu noted that for rural regions where regional dialects were spoken, when the school system came to be perceived as crucial to gaining access to highly-prized civil service jobs that were the primary employment opportunities available in less industrialized areas of France, parents became more willing to encourage children to increase their chances in the school system by speaking French at home rather than the regional language or dialect.[15] The state thus created the need for educational credentials in the labor market while simultaneously controlling the conferral of those qualifications. In this way, the official language became necessary in turn for the acquisition of those qualifications that could lead to particular sorts of jobs.

Bourdieu acknowledged that there continues to be differentiation among speakers (associated with class, region, and/or ethnicity), despite institutions and practices that work to unify and standardize language. This is because there is a crucial difference between *knowledge* of the official language and *recognition* of its legitimacy. The acceptance or recognition of the legitimacy of the dominant language is more widespread than competence in using it. Bourdieu is essentially arguing here that the nation-state has imposed an official language that is associated with higher prestige, and that this is accepted as common sense so that people who do not have a high level of competence in this language accept that they speak a vulgar dialect or language. Through the process of symbolic violence, they internalize the devaluation of the linguistic capital associated with their habitus.

Bourdieu interjected an important temporal aspect to this argument. He noted that social agents are positioned in both social space and social time, with awareness of who is above/ahead or below/behind them in terms of competence in the legitimate language. This means "the sense of the value of one's own linguistic products is a fundamental dimension of the sense of knowing the place which one occupies in social space" (1991b, 82). Therefore, the state fosters a universalizing of the standards for judgment about linguistic worth, but does not universalize behaviors conforming those standards. Those who are more socially aspirant, especially the group Bourdieu referred to as the petite bourgeoisie, place most emphasis on speaking "correctly" and try to enhance their linguistic competence.

Regional Languages and Boundaries

Bourdieu was particularly interested in the relationship between regional languages and national social space. In addressing this issue, he focused on struggles among scholars of various disciplines involved in describing regions—including geographers, economists, and ethnographers; as well as among those associated with regional movements. For Bourdieu, the important thing to observe is less the content of the region but, rather, the ways that political and administrative borders of a region come into being.

Bourdieu referenced the work of Emile Benveniste on the history of the concept of the region in order to demonstrate that it originates in the authority vested in the king that permitted him to delineate domains of national territory and foreign territory associated with both the interior and the exterior and also the sacred and the profane (Bourdieu 1980a/1991b, 221). Bourdieu used the example of what is "known" as the Occitan region of France, which encompasses several smaller geographically-identified subregions—including that of his natal region of Béarn. The formation of an idea of "Occitanie" in France, associated with the Occitan language, should not, however, be viewed as arising from local ways of speaking, according to Bourdieu. This has more to do, Bourdieu claimed, with the division creating a distinction between the Occitan language and "legitimate" French. The differences in syntax, vocabulary, and pronunciation between these two ways of speaking underlie what Bourdieu refers to as the "systematic devaluation" of uses of Occitan. Moreover, this occurs independently of social class and should be considered as a "masked form of racism (founded on the mythic opposition between the north and the south)" (1980a, 70—my translation),[16] referring to the geographical division in France between the north and what is referred to as "*le midi*" or the south. Through this process, the region becomes a stigmatized place and those living there and speaking the regional dialect are also devalued by association. A geographical area ("*province*") defined by its economic and social distance from the center of France, in that it lacks both the material and symbolic capital concentrated in the center (i.e., Paris), comes to be viewed as peripheral through this double distance (in social and geographical space). The idea of a region as a geographic unit defined by its "soil" masks, according to Bourdieu, the fact that its regions are historically produced as social units.

The stigmatization of regions and those who live in them has a parallel with the stigmas associated with ethnic groups and migrants. For Bourdieu, boundaries (social and geographic) produce "cultural difference," rather than the other way around, due to the effects of symbolic power producing commonsense ways of classifying the world's divisions. Bourdieu nuanced this perspective by explaining that cultural difference is most likely "the product of a historical dialectic of cumulative differentiation" (1980a, 66, fn10—my translation). The subjective feeling of belonging (*appartenance*) is connected, according to Bourdieu, to the more objective criteria for belonging in a certain category or to a group ("such as ancestry, territory, language, religion, economic activity" [1980a/1991b, 226]). Both the objective criteria for and subjective feelings of belonging arise from representations of the way the world is divided. Social practices that are informed by those representations also contribute to their construction. For those seen to belong to regional and ethnic groups, who have a stigma associated with their "place of origin," there are what Bourdieu called "durable marks, such as accent," that work to "make and unmake groups." He wrote:

> What is at stake here is the power of imposing a vision of the social world through principles of di-vision which, when they are imposed on a whole group, establish meaning and a consensus about meaning, and in particular about identity and unity of the group, which creates the reality of the unity and the identity of the group. (Ibid., 221)

Geographic frontiers are thus equated with these social frontiers and boundaries. For Bourdieu, social space is a theoretical concept that helps to illuminate relationships and divisions in social life. In his understanding of the state's role in reinforcing commonsense understanding of these divisions, Bourdieu addressed not only the differences between the habituses of social agents, but also the ways in which groups were made to seem real and regions within state territory perceived as natural.

Before he wrote about the representation of regions and languages in France, Bourdieu addressed the idea of the peasantry as a social class (1977b; 2008a).[17] His aim was to illustrate the struggle implicated in understandings of social reality between the representations that people make of themselves and those constructed by others within the same social space. As a person who grew up in a rural region of southwestern France, and who had experienced the stigma associated with social and geographic proximity to peasants and to local ways of speaking as a result, Bourdieu was sensitive to the constructions of center and periphery that inform ways of approaching local regions spatially and socially. He was also interested in the ways that the peasantry as a group was constructed as an object and how social classes in general come to be viewed as part of reality. These processes are connected to the imposition of common sense about the divisions of the social world.

In a statement that seems to posit little social agency among peasants, Bourdieu remarked that "the dominated classes, dominated even in the production of their self-image and therefore their social identity, do not speak, they are spoken" (ibid., 197). Another way of interpreting this is that Bourdieu is referring to the pervasive view of peasants that lends them little voice to articulate their own view of themselves. The peasant class, according to Bourdieu, is the "example par excellence of the class as object" (ibid., 198), because it must confront so many ways in which it is objectified by those who are dominant. Peasants are viewed as uncouth, clumsy, ignorant, and described through derogatory terms (such as *plouc*). The only recourse for peasants was to be reactive and at times seemingly reactionary in the face of this domination and representation of them. Peasants are the subject of contradictory images that can either exalt their rural life and its virtues or condemn them as backward. In this analysis, Bourdieu made scant reference to the state and identified the dominant as the "urban bourgeoisie" (ibid., 199). His main aim was to argue against the Marxist view of the peasantry as a conservative force by insisting that this class is never viewed for itself, but always shaped by more dominant visions of it. Even when peasants may engage in revolutionary acts, Bourdieu asserted, their domination prohibits their ability to be seen as a "revolutionary force," and they continue to be represented as "reactionary" (ibid., 200).

Bourdieu began a 1980 article,[18] in which he drew upon his natal region of Béarn to discuss divisions in geographic space, with a saying in the Béarnaise dialect, translated into French in an accompanying footnote. The quoted text states, "Things will go badly for the Béarnais when their sons speak French" (1980a, 63—my translation). By using this quote, Bourdieu seems to suggest that the imposition of the dominant language was not accepted or adopted without some questioning of the results of doing so. However, Bourdieu did feel that peasants had little choice about whether or not to accept the dominant language, even if they were aware of the effects it would have.

Education, Social Space, and the Field of Power

As can be seen in his critique of dominant languages, Bourdieu placed a great deal of emphasis on the role of national education systems in sustaining the state's power. He viewed educational systems and practices as key to understanding the relationship between the state and national identity. Although he admitted that this was a position he came to gradually, rather than one he started with in his earlier studies of education, Bourdieu contended in his lectures on the state at the Collège de France: "All analyses of the school are in fact analyses of the state and the reproduction of the state" (2012/2014, 346). Although he distinguished between formal education and less formal means of socialization, Bourdieu viewed education very broadly—to include forms of inculcation that are associated with family upbringing and modes of training outside of schools. His theory of habitus rests, after all, upon a view of inculcation in childhood that shapes the worldviews and dispositions of habitus. As I noted in Chapter Two, Bourdieu's analysis of the Kabyle house addressed how its spatial layout taught children about social roles and identities, including gender identity, as they moved in and through the house.

Schools help constitute what Bourdieu referred to as "national emotions": ideas about "those things 'that only we can feel,' or 'that you have to be born in the country in order to feel,' things for which people are prepared to die, like spelling" (2012/2014, 158).[19] The school shapes habitus and is instrumental in shaping memory so that, as Bourdieu wrote, following Halbwachs, "Our memory is largely structured by our school career" (ibid., 177). Bourdieu saw the work of the educational system also as one that "involves the making of normalized individuals, who are homogenized in terms of writing, spelling, their way of speaking" (ibid., 121). As with much of Bourdieu's writing on what Laura Nader (1977) referred to as "controlling processes," it must not, in my view, be taken too literally that Bourdieu believed the state actually accomplishes this homogenization. Rather, the educational system seeks to create the *doxa* of "normalized individuals" who then become the standard against which those who are viewed as having less-valued cultural and symbolic capital are measured.

The relationship between literacy and education is another aspect to Bourdieu's argument about the state because, following Jack Goody, he understood writing as crucial to the development of the state. Bourdieu noted that writing is "the state instrument par excellence, the instrument of totalization" (2012/2014, 215), and that the viewpoint of both the state and writing are similar (ibid., 214–15). Both objectify and are thus able to transcend time, by which Bourdieu meant recording action and thus freezing it in time. He used the example of ethnographers who, in the act of writing about the people they study, separate themselves from the "natives" and thereby totalize their experience in ways that those people would not do themselves (especially if they are not literate).

Bourdieu's book *The State Nobility*, which I view as the partner to *Distinction*, placed more emphasis on the state in its discussion of the social space of France, and those social agents who are "chosen" to reproduce it. In it, he investigated the ways in which the French educational system consecrates a "state nobility" who work to construct and maintain the contemporary state. This consecration operates through rites of institution in the most prestigious institutions of higher education in France through the educational titles they confer, which constitute a form of academic capital. This symbolic capital legitimizes the power and domination of elites in French society. Bourdieu's earlier and best-known work on education (i.e., Bourdieu and Passeron 1970b) focused on the social reproduction of hierarchical divisions in France between the bourgeoisie, petite bourgeoisie, working class, and so on, rather than on national identity or the state per se.

The State Nobility encapsulates Bourdieu's view that education is a major vehicle through which the symbolic power of the state is instituted. It is a sociological and ethnographic study that focuses on the École Normale Supérieure (ENS) in Paris, notably also Bourdieu's alma mater. In it, Bourdieu analyzes how schools shape national identity and contribute to the processes of centralization, unification, and standardization that are elements of the contemporary nation-state. He explained his interest in studying academic institutions by positing that "the sociology of education lies at the foundation of a general anthropology of power and legitimacy" (1989a/1996c, 5). In his foreword to the English edition of *The State Nobility*, Loïc Wacquant wrote "one of Bourdieu's key arguments is that the state is not necessarily where we look for it" and that for Bourdieu, "the school is the state's most potent conduit and servant" (1996, xvii–xviii).[20]

A distinctive feature of France, in contrast to other countries like the United States, is that its elite educational institutions are public and state-funded. France has a system of higher education that is divided between the large public universities and the more elite and selective so-called *"grandes écoles."* These institutions have traditionally served as the training grounds for the nation's elite in both the private and public sectors. Most can only be entered after a program of preparatory classes following high school (*lycée*) and obtaining a high score on the entrance exams. The presence of the highly centralized state in French education, both in terms of funding and in awarding diplomas, led Bourdieu to focus on the relationship between the state and the *grandes écoles*. Bourdieu was interested in the differences among the student bodies and traditions between the *grandes écoles*—which specialize in training in such areas as political science, public administration, business, engineering, science, and social science. Each school recruits students of particular family backgrounds with affinities of habitus.

Bourdieu emphasized in *The State Nobility* that he considered social space to be a "structure of domination" (1989a/1996c, 186). In the prologue, he made a comment that helps illuminate his understanding of social space. He wrote that social space is the "objective structure," and habitus is the "subjective consciousness of the positions in this space" (ibid., 38). When he wrote that social agents "are only effective and efficient because they are not reduced to what is ordinarily meant by the notion of the individual" (ibid., 38), Bourdieu meant that their actions are informed by both social space as structure and the embodied dispositions of habitus. Bourdieu described the educational system as an "immense cognitive machine" (ibid., 53) that must not, however, be viewed as the product of a "state ideological apparatus" with agents who were outside the game (ibid., 53). Here, we can see him distinguishing himself from Althusser and other Marxist writers who did not pay sufficient attention to the social practices associated with state power and who tended to reify the state. Bourdieu wanted to understand how the social judgments about each other held by teachers and students, as well as their social practices, were expressions of internalized mental or cognitive structures.

The importance of the *grandes écoles* for Bourdieu was that they occupy a particular region in social space that he called the "field of power." He mentioned that "different national traditions" have different structural characteristics of the field of power—providing an example of the cult of team sports during the Victorian era in England (ibid., 74). This leads me to conclude that Bourdieu envisioned the field of power in which the state is located as existing within national social space. Bourdieu viewed academic institutions as constituting an "academic field" in which there is a structural opposition between the *grandes écoles* and less prestigious institutions, and, within the subfield of the *grandes écoles* themselves, a differentiation based on the social positions of those who attend them. These fields and subfields are located within what he considered to be "social space as a whole" (ibid., 136), by which he presumably meant the nation. Bourdieu wrote that the *grandes écoles* constitute "a field whose functioning as a structure contributes to the reproduction of the structure of social space and the structure of the field of power" (ibid., 139).

Fundamental to Bourdieu's idea of the "field of power" is that power must be justified and legitimized:

> No power can be satisfied with existing just as power, that is, as brute force, entirely devoid of justification—in a word, arbitrary—and it must justify its existence, as well as the form it takes, or at least ensure that the arbitrary nature of its foundations will be misrecognized and thus that it will be recognized as legitimate. (Ibid., 263)

In *The State Nobility*, Bourdieu defined the field of power as "a gaming space" in which agents and institutions that occupy dominant positions and "different forms of power" in social space deploy strategies "aimed at preserving or transforming these relations of power" (ibid., 264–65). Those with different forms of capital (which can support their power) engage in symbolic strategies to legitimize their domination and thereby "maintain or better their position in social space" (ibid., 263).

Bourdieu referred to the *grandes écoles* as a "space of differences" (ibid., 161) and wrote that each of these institutions foster a unique "esprit de corps" in that they are "miniature closed societies that, like the insular universes so dear to ethnologists, share a single lifestyle, visible not only in coherent and distinctive systems of cultural references and ethical or political values, but also in bodily hexis, clothing, ways of speaking, and even sexual habits" (ibid., 180).[21] Bourdieu's point was not so much that elite institutions inculcated particular forms of habitus in their students, but rather that they recruited students from similar backgrounds who would feel an affinity for each other due to shared habitus. Bourdieu concluded that elite educational institutions attract and recruit students who already have the habitus and dispositions that the schools purport to instill in them, and that "a high proportion of [them] have already been brought up in families located in the very region of the field of power fed by the institution" (ibid., 139). Many of the teachers were also themselves products of these same institutions, with the result that, as Bourdieu wrote, each school will "recognize their own" (ibid., 181).

For Bourdieu, the notion of "esprit de corps" should be understood both in terms of biological and social bodies. It is through selecting students of similar embodied habitus and creating groups of "socially homogenous classmates" that each school "fosters togetherness among like-minded people and, above all, tends to exclude the 'undesirable' company" of less suitable people (ibid., 183). This also leads the students to acquire more social capital through the acquaintances they make at school with like-minded classmates. Bourdieu described habitus in this context as the "social positions embodied in bodily dispositions" (ibid., 182) that lead students to gravitate toward others in similar positions. This process of group formation is structured through an institutional basis that creates a legitimate and consecrated group whose dominant position in social space is accepted as natural.

The *grandes écoles* also perpetuate distinctions in social space by way of their own different niches. Different *grandes écoles*, such as the École Normale Supérieure (EN) or the École National d'Administration (ENA), attract and recruit students who are from "different regions of social space and the field of power" (ibid., 140). Bourdieu argued that although it appears to be a "choice" to apply for admission to one of the *grandes écoles* and also a mark of intelligence, such decisions are a product of the "structured habitus" of both the selected and the selectors operating within the field of educational institutions. A homology links this field to the fundamental structures of social space and the field of power. Bourdieu argued that we can observe this not only by how often it works that the children of those in certain positions in the field of power within the structure of social space wind up attending the *grandes écoles* and entering careers leading to elite forms of power and influence, but also by noting that there are also "misfirings," when positions and dispositions do not have a smooth relationship (ibid., 183). Such "deviant trajectories," which would also include that of Bourdieu himself given his own modest origins, can lead to feelings of displacement. The gap between the trajectory of an individual and what Bourdieu referred to as the "modal trajectory" of their group of origin can lead to feeling "out of place" (ibid., 185). In this discussion of the students at the *grandes écoles*, Bourdieu drew upon earlier ideas of trajectory and habitus that I have discussed in the previous two chapters. The alternative view to misfiring is that of "social destiny," which Bourdieu applied to the protagonist of Flaubert's novel *Sentimental Education*.

Bourdieu drew upon Paul Nizan's autobiography *Aden Arabie*, which he later referred to as a book that personally struck a chord with him as a former student at the École Normale Supérieure (Bourdieu 1997/2000c, 34). Nizan related his experiences as a *normalien* who, like Bourdieu, had modest social origins. Bourdieu wrote with reference to this autobiography:

> The more or less autobiographical narratives of writers from the dominated regions of social and geographical space constitute incomparable sociological documents as first-hand accounts of the subjective experiences related to these social trajectories (and not of the corresponding "realities") that are in fact more reliable, being more naïve, than we think. (1989a/1996c, 408, fn14)

It is significant that Bourdieu relied upon Nizan's personal narrative here to explore the subjective experiences of a mobile person, which shows that he did not (as he is sometimes charged) ignore that power can be questioned. Nor did he view habitus as creating docile bodies having no consciousness. For Bourdieu, the upwardly socially mobile person transgresses symbolic boundaries when writing about their experiences. He referred to people like Nizan (and himself) as "transplants" from rural life. He articulated his view that subordinate peoples (or those from marginal backgrounds) may be keen observers of structures of power. The geographical and social mobility experienced by Nizan demonstrates, for Bourdieu, the emotional costs of such a transplantation. When writing about their experiences, those who have been socially mobile are "giving away the game" (ibid., 108) in ways that the dominant (the "inheritors") do not, and this can result in their continued marginalization. This is a prime example of violating what Michael Herzfeld ([2005] 2016, 7) calls "cultural intimacy"—self-stereotypes that create a sense of shared sociality within a nation-state but are viewed as embarrassing when shared with outsiders. It follows from Herzfeld that nation-states would be careful not only to police their territorial borders but also the social borders that permit risky newcomers to enter into spaces of cultural intimacy. Bourdieu was using Nizan to illustrate insider knowledge in the *grandes ecoles*, but we can certainly extend this to the nation-state in which they are key institutions.

Nation as Social and Territorial Space

Although Bourdieu did not address the reach of state space outside of the borders of the nation in his writings on the state, if we take into account his earlier work on geographic area and social space as something that can expand and contract, I propose that his concept of social space may be extended beyond the nation state.[22] Through his focus on social space as entailing positionings of habitus as well as locations in physical space and territory, Bourdieu's approach helps ask the right questions about how people can inhabit a national social space even when they are not living within the territory of that nation. Migrants who are living within the physical territory of a nation to which they have relocated may be quite marginal to the social space of that nation because they do not possess the appropriate forms of social, cultural, and symbolic capital that "place" a person in social space. Bourdieu's observations about the formation of groups in social space also has potential to help understand the ways that various categories of immigrants are positioned both in geographic space and social space (the space of power relations) in relationship both to other immigrant groups and those perceived as "mainstream."

Bourdieu's concept of social space has implications for understanding what influences feelings of being "at home" in national social space and in a more localized place. When the social space changes, as for the migrant who moves across a national border or anyone for whom social space has expanded, the perceptions of being at home can change among those whose habitus is ill-equipped to operate within new social arrangements. New dispositions, tastes, and affinities can be useful to acquire, but a person's position in any social space depends on the relative value of their habitus. The role of the state in facilitating or hindering the ability of migrants to adopt "national feelings" (Simon 2012) or share "cultural intimacy" (Herzfeld [2005] 2016) in the countries to which they move is a key question for future research that is usefully complemented by Bourdieu's concepts of social space and habitus. Migrant belongings and migrant positionings in social space are closely connected.

In the following chapter, I explore ways to apply Bourdieu's concept of social space to the supranational level of the European Union—which is a polity still in the making that places mobility (rather than rootedness) at the center of its project.

NOTES

1. Bourdieu's use of the phrase "national character" in this passage should not be taken at face value to mean he adheres to the ideas of national character associated with the "culture and personality" school in anthropology. He is referring to commonsense understandings of national identity that have been socially constructed.

2. This latter point is amply illustrated by Jean Beamon in her book *Citizen Outsiders* (2017).

3. See Loyal (2017) and Swartz (2013) for more sociological approaches to Bourdieu and state power, which are less concerned with social space and the ethnographic perspectives through which I approach his work.

4. France as a nation is commonly referred to with the metonym *"l'hexagone"* (hexagon), a term that symbolizes the nation with reference to the geographic shape of continental France. This association between the geographic territory and government is perhaps more striking in the French case than in others, even though the French nation-state includes overseas departments such as Martinique.

5. This point has been taken up in two recent edited volumes on the state: Fassin ([2013] 2015) and Morgan and Orloff (2017). This perspective is different from the one adopted by James Scott (1998), who views the state as a more monolithic entity.

6. Bourdieu's references to habitus and national forms of common sense imply that he was referring to a secondary habitus acquired through educational inculcation. Although he never specifically addressed this question of the relationship between national *doxa* and the *doxa* of the primary habitus, I assume that he intended for us to understand that national habitus is layered upon or incorporated into the primary habitus.

7. See also the discussion of the state's left and right hands in Bourdieu et al. (1993c/ 1999b, 183–84).

8. In his political interventions (e.g., Bourdieu 1998a and 1998c), Bourdieu advocated for a state that would, along with other types of collectivities (such as labor unions), place limits on capitalism and its effects.

9. See Van Gennep (1909) and Turner (1969).

10. Although Bourdieu focused on the French *grandes écoles*, he also noted that institutions in other societies aimed at training those "destined to become members of the dominant class" operate in similar ways through initiation and consecration (1992c, 79).

11. In his discussion of the imposition of a national language in France, James Scott (1998, 72) takes a different approach. For him, this is about the imposition of state

power and the unification of the state by dissolving any forms of communication that would not be "legible" to the state. For Bourdieu, it is more about creating social divisions that become accepted as natural and thereby enact a form of symbolic violence against those who do not speak the legitimate language.

12. French citizenship is granted through both *jus soli* and *jus sanguinis*. As a colony of France, Algeria was considered to be a French territory and therefore citizenship was granted to those born in Algeria before Independence in 1962. When Algerians fled to France after the war and sought to reaffirm their French nationality, however, there was controversy over who could be considered truly French. See Shepherd (2006).

13. See Ozouf and Ozouf (1984) for further discussion of the importance of this book in the history of the construction of the French state and French national identity.

14. Here, Bourdieu's description of the nation resonates with the idea of the "imagined community" (Anderson [1983] 1991).

15. This is something that I also observed during my research on the primary school in a dairy farming *commune* in central France. Local people were aware that Auvergnat, the local language, was spoken less at home in the latter half of the twentieth century. Local memories of teachers demeaning children at school when they spoke the local language there were common, and many parents told me that they did not want their children to face this same linguistic discrimination. However, the expansion of the local "social space" of the *commune* in which I conducted my ethnographic research must have also played a part, as farmers needed French language skills in order to be competitive in a shrinking market for their products. They also realized that educational credentials, which required French language skills, had become increasingly important for those who entered farming careers as well as for their siblings who would pursue other occupations. See Reed-Danahay (1996).

16. In the original French version : "une forme douce et larvée de racisme (fondé sur l'opposition mythique du Nord et du Midi)."

17. Bourdieu's 1977 article "Une Classe Objet," about the peasantry, was reprinted as the Postscript to his collection of writings about rural France (2002a/2008a).

18. This essay was also published in modified form in *Ce Que Parler Veut Dire* (1982a) and then translated into English, with other modifications, for the volume *Language and Symbolic Power* (1991b).

19. Bourdieu cast much scorn on the French obsession with spelling and grammar (see 2012/2014, 119–21). His reference to being willing to die for spelling is based on what erupted as "la guerre de l'orthographe" in 1989–90 over proposed changes to French spelling.

20. Although I previously discussed *The State Nobility* primarily in terms of Bourdieu's theories of education and social reproduction (Reed-Danahay 2005b), here my interest is in how we can read *The State Nobility* as an articulation of Bourdieu's ideas about social space and the state. I should also note here that my ethnographic study of education in rural France (Reed-Danahay 1996), although critical of Bourdieu's reproduction model in his earlier writings on schooling, was also aimed at seeing the state through the lens of education.

21. As I have repeatedly pointed out in this book, Bourdieu frequently referred to "enclosed" (*enserré*) worlds or spaces when discussing the subjects of his research, who were somehow living in these "insular universes." He used this vocabulary in early studies of peasants and to describe the setting of Flaubert's novel *Sentimental Education*. Here, we see him referring to institutions of higher education in the same way. It is unclear, however, if Bourdieu meant they are closed systems or that those within them are immersed in the doxic understandings of the world that prevail in those social spaces. The term *enserré* can be translated as enclosed, immersed, or surrounded. It can also mean imprisoned.

22. Sapiro (2018) has made a similar suggestion that Bourdieu's concept of field can be extended beyond a national level. See also Go and Krause (2010) and Kauppi (2018).

The European Union as Social Space

> One still needs to rethink the question of the status of the foreigner in modern democracies, in other words the frontiers which can legitimately be imposed on the movements of persons in worlds which, like our own, derive so much advantage from the circulation of persons and goods.
>
> —*Acts of Resistance* (1998a, 17)

In this chapter, I consider the potential applications of Bourdieu's concept of social space for an understanding of contemporary mobility and immobility within the European Union (EU). Though social space was frequently used by Bourdieu to refer to national space, as discussed in Chapter Four, I can find no reference to the European Union as a social space in Bourdieu's writings that describes it in comparable terms to the way he described France as a social space. As Niilo Kauppi has pointed out, "Bourdieu never studied the European Union as a sociological object, but in its current, neoliberal form, he condemned it" (2003, 782–83). In spite of Kauppi's claim, it seems to me that even when Bourdieu was writing in a more public and politically engaged way, as with his criticisms of the EU's neoliberalism and his advocacy for a "Social Europe," we can glean insights from the social analyses that lay behind his point of view.

By placing Bourdieu's criticisms of the EU alongside his writings on social space, I will explore the possible applications of his approach to social space in the context of the EU as supranational social space. Spatial mobility in Europe entails crossing both social and geographic boundaries. The EU is engaged in constructing not only a European political entity, but also a European social space that fosters "we-feelings" of shared belonging. Critical ethnographic research, informed by Bourdieu's concept of social space (alongside habitus, capital, field, and symbolic power), can help us understand to what degree it is accomplishing these goals and the spatial choices and aspirations (informed by the dispositions of habitus) that lead to mobility and immobility among people living within the borders of the EU.

As Pullano (2014) points out, it is essential to consider the territorial as well as social aspects of the European Union and not to separate them. Bourdieu's theory of social space, which brings together both territorial space and social relations, has many potential applications for understanding the European Union from this perspective. In considering the EU as a social space in Bourdieu's terms, which involves considering the relationship between its territorial space and social relationships and hierarchies within it, it is necessary to take into account, at the same time, that the territorial regions within Europe are perceived not only in terms of national boundaries but in terms of a hierarchy in which regions are considered more socially and economically vulnerable as well as more or less "European" within the EU. This chapter considers how an idea Bourdieu developed at smaller-scale levels (region, nation-state) can be applied to the supranational level—taking into account the links between social and geographical space that are central to his concept of social space.

Mobility and Immobility in the EU

Beginning with the establishment of the European Economic Community with the Treaty of Rome in 1957, what later came to be known as the European Union has espoused the values of what it refers to as the "four freedoms." These are the free movement of goods, services, people, and capital/money. Although the original driving force for mobility in the EU was labor mobility, there is a prevailing hope that geographic mobility will enhance feelings of attachment to the EU among its citizens. Over the course of its history and the different treaties of the EU, free movement developed through the Single Market and later the Schengen Agreement,[1] expanding to include not just workers but all citizens and all people legally visiting or residing in any EU country. Mobility is, therefore, central to the European Union project.

During the time that I worked on this book, the European Union was frequently described as being in a fragile state, with its future threatened on several fronts. A headline in the *New York Times* in the summer of 2018, for example, proclaimed: "Europe could melt down over a simple question of borders" (Fisher 2018). A special report of *The Economist* published on the occasion of the EU's sixtieth anniversary in March 2017 led with the statement: "The European Project has sometimes given the impression of being in perpetual crisis."[2] The EU is a body that grew from a postwar set of agreements among six nations regarding economic cooperation (The European Coal and Steel Community) to a twenty-eight-member organization (although this will drop to twenty-seven following the exit of the UK) with a huge bureaucracy and several key institutions.[3] It expanded greatly following the end of the cold war and the accession of several post-Soviet nations. A language of catastrophe emerged during the financial crisis of 2008, when austerity measures were imposed on member states of Spain, Italy, and Greece. A decade later, there was a "migration crisis," at its height in 2016—the same year that the United Kingdom voted on a referendum in favor of its exit from the EU ("Brexit"). Although migratory flows across the Mediterranean have slowed considerably, the aftermath of what was perceived as a "crisis" for Europe (although it was more accurately a crisis for the migrants fleeing horrible conditions of war, violence, and political repression) and the austerity measures associated with the financial crisis have led to the increase of nationalist and populist political movements across Europe. Following the UK Referendum in June 2016 to withdraw its membership in the EU, there followed a period of turmoil as the proposed deadline by which the UK would leave the EU (initially at the end of March 2019) loomed over a chaotic and contentious process of composing a Withdrawal Agreement that would be acceptable to the EU and the majority of members of the UK Parliament.[4]

In the context of these recent challenges, EU efforts to create a sense of shared citizenship and belonging among its citizens have been promoted through various programs involving geographic mobility. In the summer of 2018, the European Commission launched a program called DiscoverEU for European citizens who were aged eighteen. It promised to distribute fifteen thousand free travel passes based on a competitive process via applications submitted online.[5] The program was to continue at least through the summer of 2019. The website for the program's launch asked, "Why not seize this chance to experience freedom of movement, better understand Europe's diversity, enjoy its cultural richness, make new friends and ultimately, discover yourself?" A Facebook group encouraged the travelers to post about their experiences and to add photos. In a 2016 document describing plans to undertake this initiative, the rationale was described thus:

> Providing travelling and mobility opportunities around Europe for young people turning 18 has an educational and cultural value, and it is consistent with the new EU policy framework for young people outlined in the 2016 Commission Communication "Investing in Europe's youth." The project seeks to offer all young people, regardless of

their background and including young people with reduced mobility, a chance to travel abroad. Their trip should be connected to a place with a specific value in terms of European cultural heritage, European sites, places of historic interest, specific social or cultural values and traditions. The project should especially promote the opportunity towards young people with the least chance to travel.[6]

This program coincided with a related initiative for geographic mobility, this time in the form of eurotourism both within one's own country and throughout the rest of Europe. It was the declaration of 2018 as "The European Year of Cultural Heritage."[7] As described on the website, the aim was "to encourage people to discover and engage with Europe's cultural heritage, and to reinforce a sense of belonging to a common European space." A new EU slogan was associated with this initiative: "Our heritage: Where the past meets the future." The website never specified the nature of this "common" cultural heritage, and each member state (and associated states such as Iceland and Switzerland) had a national coordinator to arrange events at the national level. A glance at some of the activities indicates that there were events related to museums, to gardens, to celebrating women's contributions, and to religious heritage. It seems that celebrating cultural heritage in each national context via events labeled as "European" was aimed at creating a common "space" of belonging. In this initiative, Europe is expressed as composed of nations with particular heritages of their own, not as a "transnational" space that somehow supersedes these member states. In this initiative, those who experience European cultural heritage do so through the lens of the national contexts in which it is displayed.

These are just two illustrations of the ways in which the EU tries to connect the territorial boundaries of the European Union and the sense of social affiliation within it. Like the schoolbook I mentioned in Chapter Four that taught French geography and identity through a fictional tour of the country, these initiatives encourage travel to help foster feelings of belonging. As anthropologists (e.g., MacDonald 1993; Demossier 2007; Stacul, Moutsou, and Kopnina 2006) studying the European Union "from below" have observed, belonging in a diverse Europe of states and regions poses challenges for the construction of a united European space that is free of social or territorial borders (see also Balibar [2001] 2004 and Reed-Danahay 2007). The EU's website, Europa.eu, characterizes "United in diversity" as the motto of the European Union, and states that it first came into use in 2000. The website explains that the EU motto "signifies how Europeans have come together, in the form of the EU, to work for peace and prosperity, while at the same time being enriched by the continent's many different cultures, traditions and languages."[8] There is no recognition in that statement of the social class divisions in Europe or of the challenges facing the integration of a growing number of migrants. There is also no mention of different "regions" in Europe that are positioned differently vis-à-vis each other (East versus West, North versus South, and the EU 15 versus postaccession states). In the two recent EU initiatives described above, geographic mobility is advanced as a pleasurable mode of both self-discovery and discovery of common EU identity.

But who benefits from the EU's mobility projects? Elizabeth Murphy-Lejeune has pointed to the discrepancy between the rights of travel within the EU for its citizens and the reality of immobility for the vast majority who "remain settled in their national borders which they leave only for short trips" (2002, 2). There are also asylum-seekers, noncitizens, currently being held in refugee camps throughout Europe. The Erasmus (Erasmus+ from 2014–2020) program of the EU, which organizes exchanges at the university level through which youth move to undertake a program of study in cities outside of their own nation, has been highly touted as having produced an entire generation of EU citizens who are committed to the European project. The phenomenon of Erasmus marriages (those between partners who are citizens of different EU member states) and even Erasmus babies (resulting from these partnerships) have been viewed as a sign of hope toward a socially integrated Europe. For some critics, however, Erasmus may be in the process of "becoming a symbol of inequality within the EU as opposed to being a beacon of hope" (Cairns et al. 2017, 68). This program tends, these authors argue, to enhance the forms of economic, cultural, and symbolic capital already possessed by the students who participate, rather than providing opportunities for others. This recalls Bourdieu's point about the *grandes écoles* in *The State Nobility* that I discussed in Chapter Four. These French institutions are among those elite European institutions of higher education that have a strong presence in the Erasmus+ exchanges.

Recchi (2015, 7) has stressed that mobility within the European Union for EU citizens is more about "supranational" than "transnational" processes. He points out that few mobile Europeans adopt the citizenship of the countries in which they reside. Favell and Recchi provide an alternative view to that of mobile Europeans as elites and note that their research indicates "mobile Europeans are often provincial, upwardly mobile, middle- and lower-middle-class individuals with high education" (2011, 74). I would characterize them as "middling migrants" (Conradson and Latham 2005). In Pierre Bourdieu's terms, these are members of the aspiring petite bourgeoisie. What is not clear, however, is how much this is creating denationalized Europeans and more ethnographic research on this topic is greatly needed. Although Favell and Recchi do not utilize Bourdieu's thought in this way, it seems to me that from a Bourdieusian perspective, it is unlikely that the primary habitus acquired in a context of a nation-state would disappear even as alterations would occur during the lifetime of a person following a mobile trajectory. It is more likely that those whose habituses are more disposed to travel would be those who move, which would explain why the aspiring middle-classes compose the majority of EU movers.

Toward a Social Europe as Social Space

One way to approach the European Union as a social space is by looking at the vocabulary used by earlier politicians, contemporaries of Bourdieu, who referred to a European social space. The term *espace social européen* (literally "European social space," but translated into English in official documents as European social "area")[9] was used beginning in the 1980s to refer to a "social Europe" that would accompany the economic cooperation among member states. For François Mitterrand and Jacques Delors, who promoted this concept, a European social space was a concept meant to complement the idea of Europe as an economic space for the flow of goods, labor, and services. The social space of Europe would be one of human rights and protections for workers and other residents. This meaning of the phrase "European social space" continues to be used in the field of social service provisions.[10] Delors, who was a decade older than Bourdieu, was also a major proponent of a "social Europe" during his term as President of the European Commission. As Gisèle Sapiro has pointed out, Bourdieu began an effort "to impel a European social movement and to create a European public space" in the mid-1990s (2010, xiii).[11] Bourdieu believed, however, that the EU was undemocratic, and did not provide sufficient protections for workers.[12] He promoted the idea of "social Europe" as a vigorous civil society in which dialogue between intellectuals and workers could take place.

Writing about Mitterrand's legacy toward the end of his presidency (1981–95), Elizabeth Haywood asserted that "Mitterrand's first European initiative following his election in 1981 was the European social area" (Haywood 1993, 274). Linda Hantrais has observed that although Mitterrand advocated the creation of a "social space" (*espace social*), this was later "taken up by Jacques Delors when he became President of the Commission in 1985" (Hantrais 2007, 5). The idea of a social Europe was one promoted by Mitterrand, a socialist, to soften the neo-liberal economic policies of the EU criticized by the PCF (French communist party) and PS (French socialist party) by seeking to ensure social protections for workers and have this included in EU regulations. Before Mitterrand's call for a European social space, the social protections of the EU were limited. The assumption of the early architects of the EEC was that economic integration would lead to social improvements, but this was, for the most part, however, left to the member states. The Treaty of Rome in 1957, which established the European Economic Community (EEC), did not include any social provisions (Hantrais 2007).

Jacques Delors, a French politician with long-standing connections to Catholic trade unionism, viewed Social Europe and the European social space (area) (*espace social*) as crucial to developing a European version of capitalism that would differ from the Anglo-Saxon model espoused by Ronald Reagan and Margaret Thatcher. In her analysis of the social Europe proposed by Delors, Alessandra Butimi writes that his "objective was indeed a moral order to be established within the old Continent, but progressively attained at the global level" (2018, 206). For Delors, social space was the social dimension accompanying European economic integration. This social space would be one of dialogue between workers (represented by trade unions) and employers, aimed at ensuring social protections for workers across Europe.

As Hantrais (2007) argues, the EU was founded upon a model of economic cooperation and integration, and most of its institutions support that goal. The social dimensions of European economic integration, however, still take a secondary role in EU policy. In her account of the development of "social Europe" in the twentieth century, Hantrais shows that although there were significant agreements reached about social dimensions, few were legally binding. The UK objected repeatedly to the insertion of wording to protect workers and would not sign the Charter for the Fundamental Social Rights of Workers in 1989, leaving the other eleven member states to develop a more informal mode of cooperation. The UK again objected to a chapter on social dimensions of Europe being included in the Maastricht Treaty establishing the European Union and European citizenship in 1992. Several social protections were ensured with the Treaty of Amsterdam (1997), which prohibited various forms of employment discrimination based on age, gender, religion, and ethnic origins. The Treaty of Nice (2000) included the Charter of the Fundamental Rights of EU citizens, which ensured human rights protections (and was signed by the UK).

As explained in the influential Venturini report (1989, 34) produced while Delors was President of the European Commission, Europe was "an area of mobility" (with "area" being the translation of "*espace*") with its social dimension of freedom of movement for all "persons within the Community." The report called for more coordination and conformity among member states in order to ensure equal treatment of nationals and workers from other member states. Venturini also noted that the labor market was not just one of business but also includes those in finance and in research. He referred to a new initiative to encourage mobility among students and researchers, stating, "The increasingly European dimensions of work stem from the increasingly European dimension of students and diplomas" (ibid., 38). In that pre-Schengen Europe of 1989, Venturini also concluded, "The possibility of moving about and taking up residence without checks, a tangible sign of belonging to a single entity, does not exist at the present time" (ibid., 38).

On the sixtieth anniversary of the EU in March 2017, the Rome Declaration reaffirmed the commitment of the EU to a "social Europe."[13] The declaration defined this as:

> A social Europe: a Union which, based on sustainable growth, promotes economic and social progress as well as cohesion and convergence, while upholding the integrity of the internal market; a Union taking into account the diversity of national systems and the key role of social partners; a Union which promotes equality between women and men as well as rights and equal opportunities for all; a Union which fights unemployment, discrimination, social exclusion and poverty; a Union where young people receive the best education and training and can study and find jobs across the continent; a Union which preserves our cultural heritage and promotes cultural diversity.[14]

This hopeful message is, however, a blueprint that must be enacted in order to assure social protections for European citizens and others living within EU borders.

Social Europe and Neoliberalism

In the early 1980s, when Francois Mitterrand came to power as President of France, Bourdieu spoke publicly about such matters as the French government's refusal to condemn the crackdown in Poland of the Solidarity movement. He believed that the strong connections between intellectuals and workers in Poland associated with that movement could be a model for developing a more equal and just society in France and in Europe more generally. In an interview with Didier Eribon in 1981, Bourdieu defended his position about the need for intellectuals to become involved in social struggles, but cautioned against what he characterized as "the Leninist dream of the intellectual giving discipline to the working-class apparatus." Intellectuals had to also be "fellow-travelers" who retained a critical perspective on these social struggles (Eribon and Pierre 1981/Bourdieu 2008c, 130).

The term "neoliberalism" appears as an entry associated with Giscard d'Estaing in the 1976 *Encyclopedie des Idées Reçues* ("Encyclopedia of Conventional Wisdom") that Bourdieu compiled with Luc Boltanski, (Bourdieu and Boltanski 1976a, 23).[15] In the course of their critique of the relationship between the intellectual field and holders of political power in France, Bourdieu and Boltanski quote Giscard using this term in a published conversation with Louis Armand[16] about the future of Europe (Armand and d'Estaing 1969). The future President of France argued in the passage cited by Bourdieu and Boltanski that liberal thought was the best modern approach to the economy and deserved a new label: neoliberalism. Although Bourdieu had not made much reference to what was then the European Community in his other writings in the 1970s, we see that his engagement with a critique of the neoliberal tendencies of Europe had already begun over a decade before he began to write more frequently about the EU.

Bourdieu felt that it was important to work at a broader level than the nation-state to fight systems of inequality—that of Europe. The European Union should lead to universalization, to a "universal state" in which people could be mobilized to participate in ways that did not lead to "mystifying their consciousness" (1998a, 9). Bourdieu asserted, however, "We will certainly not have gained much if eurocentrism is substituted for the wounded nationalisms of the old imperial nations" (ibid., 9). In an interview originally published in *Le Monde* in 1992, Bourdieu argued that "the state has withdrawn, or is withdrawing, from a number of sectors of social life for which it was previously responsible: social housing, public service broadcasting, schools, hospitals, etc." (ibid., 2). In a later address, to trade unionists in Greece in 1996, Bourdieu spoke of an "economics of happiness" (ibid., 40–41) that would measure profits against the costs of precarity. Bourdieu believed that by developing the "social dimension" of Europe, and applying standards regarding such issues as the length of the workweek that would be enforced in each member state, there would be less structural violence associated with financial markets.

For Bourdieu, the policies of neoliberalism reinforced and constructed notions of individualism and rational action that were creating Darwinian struggles and undermining conditions for collective struggle among those suffering from those policies. Bourdieu's theory of habitus thus came to intersect with his politics, as he saw the concept of the individual not just as a modern notion related to the modern economy as opposed to a precapitalist economy (that is, in terms of theory). He viewed the concept of "the autonomous individual" as dangerous and prohibitive of political actions that could protect the poor and working class. Bourdieu's criticisms of neoliberalism were mainly that it was breaking down collective structures that would lead people to mobilize to improve their lot and achieve happiness. The economic world it had created was one that was becoming self-evident (*doxic*) to people, with concepts of globalization taken to be facts rather than seen as the imposition of a worldview.[17] The policies of the IMF (International Monetary Fund) and the OECD (Organization for Economic Co-operation and Development) were "reducing labor costs, reducing public expenditures and making work more flexible" (1998c, 1). Bourdieu pointed to the symbolic and structural violence inherent in management practices relying upon metaphors whereby "organizational discourse has never talked as much of trust, co-operation, loyalty, and organizational culture as in an era when adherence to the organization is obtained at each moment by eliminating all temporal guarantee of employment" (ibid., 4).

Bourdieu further cautioned that "the market" had become more powerful than the nation-state, and that any intervention by the state was being discredited. He suggested the bleak prospect that whatever mechanisms were keeping chaos at bay, by what little survival of state intervention existed, would soon be dismantled. The solution was to appear to support the disintegrating state while working to construct a new social order, the "supranational state" of Europe: "One that will not have as its only law the pursuit of egoistic interest and the individual passion for profit and that will make room for collectives oriented toward the rational pursuit of ends collectively arrived at and collectively ratified" (ibid., 6).

Bourdieu was concerned that the media had painted the European question in terms that portrayed those in favor of the EU's neoliberal policies as progressive and modern, and those against them as archaic or even anti-Semitic. This was too clear-cut a division, according to Bourdieu. He felt that the Social Democrats who were the most visible leaders in the EU were undermining collective struggles of the past. He feared that their neoliberal policies would contribute

> In the name of monetary stability and budgetary rigor, to the liquidation of the most admirable profits of the social struggles of the last two centuries: universalism, egalitarianism . . . or internationalism; and to the destruction of the very essence of the idea or socialist ideal, that is to say, broadly, the ambition to protect solidarities menaced by economic forces through collective action. (1999a, 2)

Even though he had concerns about the neoliberal directions of the EU, Bourdieu also felt that Europe had to come together collectively in order to keep the United States from dictating much of the global economic and diplomatic policy. He critiqued an Anglo-Saxon approach underlying neoliberalism.

Bourdieu suggested that those who want to promote a "social Europe" that would protect workers in opposition to what he called a "Europe of banks and money," a "police and prison Europe," and a "military Europe" needed to find ways of mobilization. One model he advocated was that of worker unions organized at the European level, and he wrote that syndicalism in Europe could be "the motor of a social Europe" that broke with the nationalism associated with nationally organized unions, the discourse on the inevitability of globalization of the economy, neoliberalism, and "social liberalism" that supports deregulation favoring corporations while appearing to be social policies (1999a, 4). Bourdieu painted a utopia that included hopes of an "*internationale*" of immigrants in Europe, but also admitted that creating a social Europe would entail changing the dispositions of millions of people. Referring to E. P. Thompson's *The Making of the English Working Class*, Bourdieu suggested that the nineteenth-century model of a worker's movement could be a model for the present since the conditions facing workers today are comparable. This movement, he suggested, would be one of contestation and negotiation.

Europe as Supranational Social Space?

In what ways can the European Union be constituted as a supranational "state space" in Bourdieu's terms? How do the national spaces within it persist in institutionalizing and perpetuating forms of national common sense? Is a European habitus necessarily present in a European social space?

Although Bourdieu did not write about the European Union specifically as a social space, we can understand how he might approach this. First, he indicated that his model of France as a social space could be adapted to other nations, even though it had its own particular features.[18] Therefore, it is possible that he could envision ways to adapt this to European constructions of a social space that was not national but supranational and associated with a European state. The EU as a social space, in Bourdieu's terms, would be viewed as a structured space, with inequalities related to modes and amounts of capital associated with places and people being more or less dominant in the social hierarchy. This space would be viewed as containing fields, including the field of power, which would entail the institutions of the EU such as the European Central Bank, Court of Justice, and also the EU's security apparatus—Frontex. The main challenge for the EU's field of power would be how to establish its legitimacy, which Bourdieu felt was accomplished in France primarily through the educational system, which granted credentials and forms of symbolic capital. National attachments are also, according to Bourdieu, promoted through the educational system. Bourdieu did not discuss everyday or banal forms of nationalism (Billig 1995), however, which provide restraints on Europeanization as a process entailing feelings of belonging as citizens of the EU. Europe needs to construct banal forms of Europeanization in everyday life to construct a European social space. In France, there are conflicts between regional and national attachments, just as there are between national and EU attachments; but there is a large difference between these two cases in that nation-states are more powerful than regions. In the centralized government of France, regions have limited autonomy and the educational system is still a national-level institution. Creating an EU social space presents a great challenge, and the main avenue to success in the geopolitical space of Europe has been achieved by relatively elite mobile Europeans.

Recent scholarship on the European Union, particularly in the fields of political sociology and international relations, has turned to Bourdieu's vocabulary of social space and field. Studies of European security professionals (e.g., Bigo, Bonditti, and Olsson [2010] 2016) have described a security field within a wider social space of Europe, and they focus on ways to understand the borders and various levels of jurisdiction in this complicated structure. Most of these approaches focus primarily, however, on EU institutions rather than on the lives of people living within the EU's borders, including not only citizens but also migrants and refugees who are subject to its border regimes.

Although he does not pose the question of whether or not the European Union can be understood as a social space, Kauppi (2018) has applied Bourdieu's social field theory to understanding the European Parliament (EP) as a transnational social field. Noting that the "state nobility" have become increasingly transnational, Kauppi examines the ways in which social actors, the elected MEPs (Members of the European Parliament), draw upon a variety of resources at different scalar levels (national as well as European) to seek power and influence within this field. Adopting the perspective that the transnational can fuse both the national and the supranational, Kauppi argues that a transnational social field should not be viewed as surpassing or minimizing the nation. In a few examples, such as that of the National Front (known since June 2018 as the Rassemblement National or National Rally) and its leader Marine Le Pen (a former MEP), he shows how politicians in the EP mobilize resources at various levels. He concludes both that those who work toward European integration in the EP are not to be seen as "swapping" a European identity for a national one (these can be mobilized at different times for different purposes) and that caution is needed regarding the question of whether or not a uniform European political class is forming. As his research and that of others he cites show, these social actors draw upon resources specific to the social fields in which they operate (the European Parliament as opposed, for example, to the European Commission), making this unlikely in the near future. However, as I noted in Chapter Four, Bourdieu's concept of the state was not one of a monolithic entity, and he recognized that it had a Left hand and a Right hand, and that there are different interests at stake among members of the "state nobility."

The European Union has been referred to as a "transnational social space" by several scholars. Rumford makes two important points about this: first, that it does not imply the weakening of the nation-state, and second, that it entails a different view of territoriality in that "transnational space is not necessarily bounded, cohesive or geographically contiguous" (2003, 36). He mentions that the EU has been variously conceived of as a public sphere, a civil society, and a social space. When viewed as a civil society, the EU appears as if patterned on the nation-state, but the other two terms signify a broader and different conceptualization.

Pernicka and Lahusen (2018) draw upon Bourdieu's theories of social space and field to demonstrate how this approach, originally based upon national social space, can be useful in understanding what they describe as "horizontal Europeanisation"—meaning transnational institutions and social networks that organize at the European-wide level. These authors write that they "intend to emphasize that a nation-state's borders no longer contain this social space, but it is now reorganized within transnational, European and/or global spaces" (ibid., 3). They do so even as they acknowledge that European elites derive their symbolic capital primarily from the national "frames of reference" even as they compete on a European stage, which is also a major conclusion of Kauppi's research cited above. Pernicka and Lahusen make the important point that migrants must enter this European social space, geographically bounded by the external frontiers of the EU, and that any forms of capital (economic, cultural, social, symbolic) that they bring with them will have a different value within this space as a whole (even within different nation-states). They write that "the possession of economic, cultural and social capital and, more importantly, the perception and recognition of its legitimacy therefore essentially determines one's (power) position and room for manoeuvre within European social space" (ibid., 4).[19]

Based on their analysis, Pernicka and Lahusen call for more research on the ways in which social actors can increase their social capital across national boundaries through relationships of friendship and collegiality. This is a relevant consideration for migration scholars. I am not, however, persuaded by their claim that social space is no longer contained within the nation because of a larger social space created in the EU. National social space continues to be a factor, particularly for those who do not cross borders and stay "at home." The social spaces of member states may also extend beyond their territorial boundaries within the EU as EU movers continue to participate in national frames of reference while living outside national borders. It may be more accurate to view this in terms of overlapping social spaces associated with national belonging and supranational belonging. Creating the EU as a social space must be viewed as a project in the making in the same way that the nation-state was historically imagined and constructed. The cosmopolitan habitus of the mobile European professional who can deftly participate in multiple social spaces and utilize forms of capital to their benefit has some advantages in the emerging supranational social space of Europe. For others, however, this is not the case.

Two other recent approaches to European social space, both influenced by Bourdieu's approach to social space in *Distinction* (1979b), employ contrasting models of how to construct an analysis of this social space. Brousse (2017) examines economic and cultural capital in European nation-states in order to investigate how the social divisions within each of them can be seen as part of a pan-European social structure. She begins her article by stating that those who engage in comparative studies of social inequality rarely consider "if Europe in its entirety could be described as a social space" (ibid., 13). Brousse draws upon statistical data, following Bourdieu's use of French national survey data in *Distinction*, to first compile the social space of twenty-four European nations and then to see what comparisons can be made. This research asks if Europe can be considered as a unified social space. There is both a spatial and social aspect to Brousse's analysis in that the findings of the study show that there are center-periphery regions of the European Union, and that the northern countries tend, on the whole, to have less structural inequality than those in the southern part.

Brousse finds that three social divisions can be found across all of the nations examined—a dominant class, a middle class, and a working class. She points out, however, that each of these was created within the context of a particular nation-state. She also writes that, given that the European Union is not a state with the same degree of jurisdiction as the nation-states, people orient themselves primarily within the social space of their nation. In almost all of the cases considered in her study, the gap between the dominant class and middle class is large, while the boundary between the middle class and working class is more variable across different nation-states. Brousse concludes that several factors hinder the creation of a more unified European social space. First, the lack of a strong supranational state that could do more to regulate common working conditions, protections for workers, and mediate against structural inequality continues to result in the center-periphery relations of different regions in Europe. Second, she sees that even though the parallel conditions of workers in the different nations could result in more "professional solidarity across frontiers" (ibid., 141—my translation), as occurred during the international worker movements of the early twentieth century, there has been an increasing trend to mobilize instead at the national level and to only see common cause among conationals.

A different approach "maps" the social space of French citizens in Berlin. Duchêne-Lacroix and Koukoutsaki-Monnier (2016) elicited (through questionnaires and interviews) the self-identifications of these citizens as variously French, German, European, cosmopolitan, or some combination of these. They then constructed a diagram with the two axes of "integration capital" and "French-German" to plot the respondents in terms of their "full affinity" with Germany at one end of the continuum to "no affinity" with Germany at the other. Those who felt more European than French could express both cosmopolitan self-identity and a more or less stronger affinity with Germany or France. The attempt here is to investigate "the feelings of (supra/trans/bi/non . . .) national belonging through the position of the ego in a 'social space'" and the "multilocal attachments" they express (ibid., 139). These authors assume that such self-identification is a product of habitus. A main conclusion of this research is that European identity can be claimed "alongside national identifications as their natural extensions" (ibid., 141). This study is not based on observable behaviors, but on a questionnaire and follow up interviews regarding such activities as what newspapers the research participants read (German or French language), their level of French and level of German language proficiency, their frequency of travel to France, their friendships in France and Germany, and where they received their education. The authors are particularly interested in the question of "integration" in Berlin for the French citizens questioned, and one measure of this for them is whether or not the respondent plans to retire in Germany (it was 16 percent).

Taken together, these studies of the French in Berlin and the configurations of social inequality at national and European levels use Bourdieu's concept of social space in ways that complement each other and bring the potential value of his approach to the fore. One looks primarily at social inequality while the other looks at national or supranational identity with less attention to social class. Both shed light on how mobile EU citizens come to adopt more or less cosmopolitan or European outlooks. Ongoing questions regarding European social space include how European people feel, as well as how much they see themselves as sharing common ground with conationals as opposed to citizens of other European nations.

In addition to this work on European social space, several other scholars have applied Bourdieu's concept of social space to the study of mobile Europeans and migrants to Europe. This work draws upon the concepts of habitus and capital to discuss mobile lives and practices.[20] For example, in their study of so-called British "lifestyle migrants" living in Spain, Oliver and O'Reilly (2010) apply several of Bourdieu's concepts to the question of how class position is reproduced in a new social space, but they conflate social space and social field. They propose, "These people are essentially placed within two social spaces—the British and the Spanish" (ibid., 51). The authors argue that the Costa del Sol is a social field in which the migrants are engaged in the stakes of the "game" of attaining what they view as the good life, thereby maintaining their social-class position in British social space. It is unclear, however, to what degree these migrants are positioned in the wider national social space of Spain, as they seem to be interacting primarily with other lifestyle migrants in what the authors describe as the social field.

In a use of Bourdieu's concept of social space in the context of migration studies that I feel most closely captures Bourdieu's approach, Jiménez Zunino (2014) offers a study of middle-class migrants from Argentina to Spain. As in the study of lifestyle migrants in Spain, this study uses social space to examine how migrants are positioned in two social spaces. Jiménez Zunino notes the "dissonance between two classification systems with different socio-historical configurations: the one existing in a person's social space at origin, and the one operating in the social space at destination" (ibid., 41). She makes the important point that a migrant can feign naïveté and "play" with classifications in the social space of destination for a period of time upon arrival, but then must eventually find strategies for insertion that are more lasting. There are also classifications in the country of destination that affect migrant positionings having to do with positive or negative stereotypes. The case of the middle-class Argentinians in Spain shows how the concept of social space can be used in mobility studies, alongside that of habitus and capital, without positing that migrants participate in a transnational social space. They are best viewed, using Bourdieu's approach, as navigating two social spaces and exploiting the capital they bring with them to their best advantage in the social space of destination.

Bourdieu's concept of social space suggests that it is important to understand the articulations of national social space within the supranational space of the EU. Most attention to the EU as a supranational space has been among scholars in political science, political sociology, and international relations who are primarily focused on governance and EU integration. Bourdieu's approach to the nation-state took into consideration the state and also national social space (connected to feelings of belonging and also commonsense understandings of the social world and divisions within it). A more ethnographic perspective on the EU would view the state and the nation as both social and territorial spaces. In applying this perspective to the EU, there is more need of ethnographic research on those aspects of belonging that are also part of the construction of a European state or supranational social space.

For the conclusion of this book, I turn to examples of Bourdieu's ethnographic writings that are most relevant for studies of mobility and migration, and I explore the concept of emplacement. I point toward an ethnography of social space that might lead to new approaches for understanding mobility and immobility in the contemporary world.

NOTES

1. The Schengen Agreement, first implemented in 1995, permits freedom of movement without border control, regardless of nationality, across most EU member states (one notable exception has been the UK) and a few nonmember states that have also signed the agreement (i.e., Switzerland). There are provisions in the agreement for temporarily establishing border checks in times of threat to public safety. The geographical territory covered by the Agreement is known as The Schengen Area.

2. https://www.economist.com/special-report/2017/03/25/the-future-of-the-euro pean-union.

3. What is now known as the European Union began in 1950 as the European Coal and Steel Community (including Belgium, France, Germany, Italy, Luxembourg, and the Netherlands). The Treaty of Rome in 1957 established the Common Market, known as the European Economic Community (EEC) or less formally as the European Community. It was not until 1993 that the European Union was established with the Maastricht Treaty, which also established European citizenship for citizens of all member states of the EU.

4. The UK exit from the EU has been delayed several times because the UK Parliament has failed to ratify the Withdrawal Agreement. As I complete final edits on this book, the new date for departure is the end of October 2019, although quite a lot of uncertainty now surrounds the process following the resignation of Prime Minister Theresa May and the ascension of Boris Johnson as Prime Minister. Discussions regarding a second referendum and the possibility of a "no-deal" Brexit are currently on the table.

5. https://europa.eu/youth/discovereu_en.

6. https://ec.europa.eu/transparency/regdoc/rep/3/2018/EN/C-2018-1187-F1-EN-ANNEX-1-PART-1.PDF.

7. https://europa.eu/cultural-heritage/.

8. https://europa.eu/european-union/about-eu/symbols/motto_en.

9. In general, *espace* is translated in English as "area" in EU documents that refer both to physical space and social space. The Schengen area is, thus, *l'espace Schengen* in French.

10. The periodical *Espace social Européen*, established in 1989, is aimed at French policy makers in areas of health and human services, and has a pro-EU orientation. http://www.espace-social.com/.

11. Bourdieu's political interventions regarding Europe are included in two volumes that collect his writings and speeches as a public intellectual. The first, *Interventions 1961–2001: Science Sociale et Action Politique* (2002b) appeared in English translation

as *Political Interventions: Social Science and Political Action* (2008c). A more recent volume with the English translations of fewer but the most well-known texts is *Sociology as a Martial Art: Political Writings by Pierre Bourdieu* (Sapiro 2010). My discussion of Bourdieu's thought on the European Union and social space will draw both upon these volumes and upon the original sources that I consulted before these collections appeared.

12. I previously discussed Bourdieu's criticisms of neoliberalism and the EU in *Locating Bourdieu* (Reed-Danahay 2005b). Here, I expand upon those earlier observations and broaden the scope of my discussion.

13. I attended events in Rome that month organized by the EU, in my capacity as a Jean Monnet Chair. I was one of only a handful of US citizens, including the former US Ambassador to the EU, at the meetings in which I participated. The dilemmas of creating a sense of belonging and commitment to the EU were much discussed at these meetings, as were varying points of view regarding what type of Europe should be constructed in the aftermath of Brexit and the growing right-wing opposition to the EU among nationalist movements throughout Europe. Much hope was pinned on the younger generation.

14. http://www.consilium.europa.eu/en/press/press-releases/2017/03/25/rome-declaration/pdf.

15. This title is adapted from Flaubert's satiric *Dictionnaire des Idées Reçues* (Dictionary of Conventional Wisdom [or Received Ideas]), published posthumously in 1913.

16. Louis Armand, a French engineer and former Resistance officer, was involved in several European initiatives and had served as the first Director of Eurotom, the nuclear energy organization founded in 1957.

17. See also Tsing (2000) for a critical discussion of metaphors of circulation associated with an accepted reality of globalization that are widely used in contemporary scholarship.

18. Several scholars, most notably Atkinson (2017) who has applied this model to the UK, have adapted it to just this purpose.

19. As Rogers (2004, 174) points out, in another indication of the relevance of a wider European social space for migrants, studies have shown that Chinese migrants generally see themselves as moving to "Europe" rather than a particular country, and organize through family organizations at the European level. It is unclear from this, however, what happens when they interact with agents of the nation-states in which they settle or citizenship regimes that enact national language and cultural literacy requirements.

20. Though not utilizing Bourdieu's concepts or addressing European social space, Umut Erel (2010) has developed the notion of "migration specific cultural capital" in a study of female Turkish migrants to Germany and the UK that points in the direction of how Bourdieu's thought can be adapted to mobility studies. The idea proposed is that these women generate new forms of cultural capital that have value in the host societies, and also that they are able to optimize the cultural capital they have acquired in Turkey to a better advantage in Germany and the UK.

Toward an Ethnography of Social Space

> All social destinies, positive or negative, consecration or stigma, are equally *fatal*—I want to say deadly—because they confine those whom they distinguish within fixed limits and make them recognize those limits.
> —"Les Rites comme Actes d'Institution"
> (1982b, 61—my translation)

For Bourdieu, mobility is to be understood through the concept of trajectory in and across social and geographic space(s). His approach underscores the relations of power that affect spatial choices within the "space of possibilities" available to a social actor. These are the possibilities perceived by the social actor as well as those less evident structures of the social space. Social and geographic boundaries, as referenced in the epigraph to this conclusion, come to be recognized as natural. A person's ability to cross or even transgress such limits is constrained by the "social destiny" that is influenced by the dispositions of their habitus and relative position in social space. Those who are more privileged (and possess valued forms of capital) are also freer to cross social and geographic boundaries, while others face obstacles to mobility, and still others are forced to relocate. Bourdieu's vision of the social world as a social space is not static, but one in which people change positions and relationships to each other. Maintaining one's position in social space, and location in geographic space, is not straightforward any more than are aspirations for mobility. The vast majority of people do not migrate and not all people seek social or geographic mobility.

This book has provided a sort of blueprint for understanding Bourdieu's theory of practice through his concept of social space and the related concepts of habitus, capital, field, and symbolic power. As I have shown, Bourdieu's approach addressed both social and physical or geographic space. The dilemmas of how to view the relationship between bounded territories and social spaces of affinity and belonging continue to be debated among a wide range of scholars in different disciplines. Is it all about global flows and transnational movement, or is it also about people seeking emplacement where they find themselves? What role does the nation-state continue to play in mobilities, migrations, and moorings?

In this conclusion, I propose that we develop ethnographic approaches, using insights offered by Bourdieu, which incorporate the study of "migrant belongings" (Fortier 2000) in two types of space: the physical/geographic places where migrants dwell, and more abstract social spaces that may transcend geographic boundaries. To the idea of belonging, I would add consideration of migrant positionings, drawing upon Bourdieu's focus on trajectories of habitus within social space. Paying attention to perceptions of distance and proximity in both social and geographical space is a fruitful tactic for better conceptualizing social practices associated with mobility and immobility.

Ethnographic approaches to mobility can build upon Bourdieu's concept of social space in order to better grasp the processes through which mobilities, immobilities, and emplacements are shaped by institutional structures, everyday practices, emotions, and commonsense understandings of social life. For example, taking into consideration affinities of habitus in social space may lead to better understandings of mobility practices (why, when, and where people move), social processes of inclusion and exclusion, and feelings of belonging.

Mobility Stories, Autoethnography, and "Spontaneous Sociology"

An ethnography of social space, influenced by Bourdieu's approach, can usefully incorporate the study of personal narratives viewed as autoethnographies of mobility.[1] Ethnographic studies of mobile people are rarely conducted in "real time," with the observer literally travelling alongside those being studied. We more often interact with people in some physical location or place even when they may be engaged in circular forms of mobility or are in more temporary locations between movements. In addition to participant observation research in those physical places, ethnographers frequently collect personal narratives and life histories from their research participants in order to understand subjective experiences and feelings related to mobility.[2] Another source for understanding migration and mobility is that of published memoirs and fiction produced by former migrants.[3]

We can view migration stories as autoethnographic narratives that place the self within a social context (Reed-Danahay 1997; 2017a; 2019). Using a Bourdieusian vocabulary, this means viewing the life trajectory within the social space(s) in which it unfolds as a person moves across geographic and social spaces. Bourdieu did not use the term "autoethnography" and no doubt would have mistakenly associated all of its deployments with a certain form of narcissism that he abhorred. He delineated an intellectual stance that he called "anti-autobiography" (Bourdieu and Wacquant 1992a, 213) and, as I have discussed in Chapter Three, criticized the illusions of biography that depended on the myth of the autonomous individual. Bourdieu maintained that genres of biography and autobiography frequently ignore the social space in which a life was lived, which entails the constraints and possibilities afforded to a person due to their position within it. The "space of possibilities" (Bourdieu 2008a, 4) in which a person is situated in life and which forms the basis of the choices they make must, he argued, be taken into account.

When understood not as an ethnography of the self but as that of a trajectory, however, autoethnography is a similar concept to that of "spontaneous sociology" used by Bourdieu. As Tassadit Yacine has noted, Bourdieu learned a great deal from Kabyle intellectuals "who practiced ethnology without knowing it in the form of 'ethnographic stories'" (2008, 24). And as Bourdieu told Mouloud Mammeri during an interview, he also learned a lot from what he called the "spontaneous literature" that was produced by schoolteachers in Béarn, who composed the local monographs that constituted the only form of ethnology of that region available when he began his own research there (Bourdieu 2008b, 205).[4]

In addressing the possibilities for and consequences of mobility, Bourdieu used autoethnographic methods both in writing related to his own life trajectory and in writing that drew upon the personal narratives he collected during fieldwork.[5] For example, in the volume *Weight of the World*, Bourdieu used the concept of testimony (*temoignage*) to refer to interviews collected among working-class and immigrant French people and the teachers and social workers who interacted with them. Through his juxtaposition of these various personal narratives, Bourdieu illustrated a wider picture of the social space in which less privileged children struggle to position themselves or accept their "place." As in his analysis of the characters in *Sentimental Education* that I discussed in Chapter Three, Bourdieu provides the range of possibilities available to, in this case, children of immigrant backgrounds living in late twentieth century France. These stories show differences in habitus among the various people who shared their life experiences with Bourdieu.

Bourdieu later wrote that he borrowed the method of juxtaposing interviews not from social science, but from the novels of Virginia Woolf and James Joyce, in which various points of view were juxtaposed in order to provide a plurality of perspectives rather than one unified and omniscient narrator. He noted that this reflected not just a literary device but was also "in the very reality of the social world," where there are "colliding interests, different dispositions and lifestyles" (1993b, 15—my translation) in work or living situations where people of different backgrounds are thrown together. These narratives thus derive, in other words, from those distant in social space being placed in physical proximity.

For the project that resulted in *Weight of the World*, Bourdieu interviewed a child of Algerian immigrants who was twenty years old at the time of the interview. This youth had pursued more education than his peers in a housing project north of Paris. Bourdieu was interested in this young man's own commentary on his life, which reveals his subjective understanding of his positionings in social space, at the same time that Bourdieu the sociologist was interpreting this in terms of the conditions that made this desire for education possible. The youth was insecure about his chances for school success, constantly worrying about failure. He had the sense that his own experience was disconnected from the neighborhood in which he grew up. This boy's father earned a decent wage, and the parents encouraged him to succeed in school (Bourdieu et al. 1993c/1999b, 60–61). For Bourdieu, those who have aspirations for mobility, like this young man, are in the most precarious position because their desires face the constraints of social classifications and boundaries that work to keep them "in their place."

Bourdieu followed his discussion of this young man with the transcript of an interview he conducted with two adolescent males who had dropped out of school and were therefore stigmatized as "delinquents"—one whose parents were Moroccan and the other from a poor French family. Their failures in school were, according to Bourdieu, connected to the dispositions of their habituses. The Moroccan youth had entered school without sufficient French skills, and was thus doomed from the start. Bourdieu suggested that his situation was just an extreme case of that of the French youth who dropped out of school before getting his diploma (BEP). During the interview, these young men told Bourdieu, "Oh, the teachers don't give a shit," and "In our project no one goes to school" (ibid., 66). For Bourdieu, their rejection of school can be interpreted as their having made a "virtue out of necessity," and of accepting their social destiny. Bourdieu labeled this section of the book "The Order of Things," referring not only to the classification of the social world that keeps people in their place, but also to the fatalistic worldview of these youths who accept their place.

These narratives speak to processes related to mobility and immobility. The dispositions of habitus lead some, like the child of Algerian immigrants who desired more education, to move in social space, but not without the emotional costs of feeling estranged from those who are near to them physically. Others, like the two adolescents who had rejected school, experience immobility because of their dominated position in social space. They accept their "social destiny." Although the parents of the Moroccan youth had been geographically mobile, he did not acquire the linguistic capital that would enable him to advance socially. For the young man from a poor French family, the dispositions of his habitus were in line with the dominated position he had in social space, leading him to "choose" immobility when it is more like a social destiny for him.

During a much earlier period of his career, Bourdieu collected the labor narratives of young men displaced by the Algerian war as part of the collaborative study of postcolonial Algeria that resulted in the book *Travail et Travailleurs en Algérie* (Bourdieu et al. 1963b). Many of these men were unemployed, displaced workers who had moved from rural to urban areas. Bourdieu was particularly interested in analyzing their transition from participating in a precapitalist economic system to that of being inserted into an emerging capitalist economy. In describing his interest in subjective experiences, Bourdieu wrote: "In the course of analyzing these interviews, I had the feeling that the differences between individuals in the same category were due much more to the degree of consciousness that they had about their situation and their ability to explain it, than to the differences objectively inscribed in their comportment and attitudes" (Bourdieu et al. 1963b, 266–67—my translation). This statement illustrates the ways in which Bourdieu came to view habitus in terms of a structuring practice. Some people will have more of an understanding of their situation and possibilities, and this has to do with the position of their habitus in social space. Those who have experienced mobility (geographic and social) will be more able to articulate their position and trajectory than those who stay in their place. And this can entail either downward or upward social mobility, recalling the fall in social fortunes of the Béarnaise bachelors discussed in Chapter Two who had a keen sense of displacement.

Bourdieu labeled one of his interviewees, an Algerian cook, as a "spontaneous sociologist" (Bourdieu et al. 1963b, 508—my translation)—a term that I believe is closely related to the idea of autoethnography. Because he had travelled widely both geographically and among different social circles, this cook had developed a sensibility that permitted him to have a perspective of both distance and familiarity regarding his life trajectory—like that of an ethnologist. He could, therefore, articulate his understanding of the capitalist (European) and precapitalist (Algerian) worlds and his own economic marginality within the new postcolonial economy.

When he returned to this material many year later (2000b), Bourdieu argued that this man's narrative was useful in conveying the "practical economic sense" that guided his actions and also served as a biographical document revealing details of the acquisition of a "modern" economic habitus as an experience shared collectively among members of that generation. Bourdieu suggested that the cook's point of view was "taken from a point in objective social space at once central—unlike the vast majority of manual workers and clerks, he had seen the world of the Europeans from the inside—and yet marginal, because he had never broken his ties to his companions in misfortune" (ibid., 29). Here, Bourdieu used the concept of social space to explain the man's position as someone with a habitus that had altered due to his social and geographic mobility. The Algerian cook was positioned in the social space of France due to his experiences working among the representatives of France in Algiers, yet retained a position of marginality due to his social origins and through which he was able to see his own trajectory more explicitly.

Bourdieu's attention to the narratives of migrants and displaced workers that can be traced from earlier ethnographic work in Algeria to later research in late twentieth-century France has affinities both with his own socioanalysis and description of his life trajectory that I discussed in the Introduction to this book, and his focus on the autobiography of Paul Nizan in his discussion of elite institutions of higher education in France that I mentioned in Chapter Four. In all cases, we see the connections between travels that entail movements in social positioning and those that entail geographical migration. A Bourdieusian perspective on mobility and immobility places such personal stories and experiences within a broader analytic framework, utilizing concepts of habitus, capital, and social space.

Borders and Social Space

Bourdieu's concern with the relationship between mobility, space, and power is relevant to contemporary approaches in anthropology that question nation-state boundaries and seek new ways of understanding social connections that transcend national borders. An ethnography of social space that draws upon Bourdieu's approach can lend fresh perspectives to the study of how social and geographical boundaries come to be classified and perceived in everyday life.

Bourdieu frequently referred to social space as national social space, but he did not assume that national territory overlaps with national social space. His intent was, rather, to understand how such commonsense notions regarding the borders of social space come about. Bourdieu questioned all geographic regions and territories that were assumed to be naturally occurring, and his focus on the state and national social space was aimed at unpacking how the social space and geographic space of a nation-state came to be understood as coterminous. His work was concerned with many of the same questions that have guided others, such as Gupta and Ferguson, who have been influential in anthropology and related disciplines for their critiques of how the social sciences tend to represent space in terms of distinctive societies divided spatially and occupying "'naturally' discontinuous spaces" (1992, 6; see also 1997). These authors draw attention to the ways in which space comes to be viewed as a place with a particular identity when a demarcated physical space is associated with a particular social formation. This resonates with Bourdieu's discussion of regions and even the nation-state itself, as I discussed in Chapter Four.

In a related attempt to unpack the relationship between social and physical boundaries, Appadurai (1996, 48) suggests that what he calls "ethnoscapes" are landscapes of identity more than bounded, local places. He uses the term "locality" to refer to "actual social forms" like places, sites, and neighborhoods (ibid., 204, fn1), and he argues that locality is "primarily relational and contextual rather than scalar or spatial" (ibid., 178). He aims, as he wrote, to "get away from the idea that group identities necessarily imply that cultures need to be spatially bounded, historically unselfconscious, or ethnically homogeneous forms" (ibid., 183). Gupta and Ferguson's focus on interstitiality and Appadurai's focus on flow and scapes remind us that social space cannot be assumed to overlap with bounded physical spaces or territories.

We can also see some affinities between Bourdieu's approach and that addressed in the concepts of "non-place" (Augé [1992] 2009) and "excluded space" (Munn 1996), which suggest that the ways in which a physical or geographic space constitutes or denies a social space are complex. Mary Louise Pratt (1992) identified contact zones, which might be understood in Bourdieu's terms to be permeable borders of social spaces. This concept helps us theorize both geographic borders and the boundaries of social spaces as arenas for struggle and resistance to forms of domination. As Sarah Green has written, renewed interest in borders considers the "historical variability of the form and purpose of borders" (2013, 349). In their historical overview of the anthropological literature on boundaries, Donnan and Wilson point out that in structural-functionalist approaches, boundaries were of relevance only in order to help "define and delimit the 'edges' of their subject matter" (1999, 20). In more recent times, tropes of borders are widespread in scholarly research not for the purposes of closing off social units and investigating social identities either within units or even solely at the borders of units but, rather, in order to understand articulations of power and social practices surrounding the construction and control of borders.

Bourdieu's attention to the ways in which social and geographic boundaries are constructed by the nation-state and come to be taken for granted is one that could be taken up more by scholars in border studies. Bourdieu did not, however, focus on what happens at the borders, even if, as I have noted in this book, he did write about those who may legitimately transgress them due to the symbolic capital conferred by rites of institution. Bhabha's (2004) concept of "third space" opens up possibilities for challenges to *doxic* understandings of the spatial and social divisions of social life, as does Pratt's "contact zone." These ideas underscore the ways in which Bourdieu focused primarily on how power and domination act to create social and geographical boundaries that appear to be natural, rather than on challenges to such processes. However, his ideas of social space could be expanded to include a focus on such challenges.

In her classic critique of refugee studies, Liisa Malkki wrote that "it is doubtful that most people's social universes stop abruptly at the border of their own country" in the context of a discussion of international relocation (1995, 509). She questions the assumptions of displacement associated with refugee studies and the presumption that loss of a homeland entails loss of identity. Pointing to the need to view both displacement and emplacement as historically constructed ideas that are "ever unfinished," Malkki argues that both are the product of territorial nation-states and what she labels as "the national order of things" (ibid., 516). Bourdieu's concept of social space is similar in that he viewed territorial boundaries of the state as connected to national identity, but also understood this to be the product of a process of symbolic domination whereby nations and national borders come to be perceived as natural. Although Bourdieu focused a great deal of his early work on the emotional consequences of displacement, it was not among those who crossed national boundaries, however, but among both internal migrants and those who were located within a changing social space for which their habitus was not equipped.

Bourdieu's emphasis on the role of the state and nation in constructing and maintaining the hierarchies of social space underscores the continued relevance of the nation-state in the face of international mobilities. Craig Calhoun, who argues that "nations matter," has written, "Nations appear simultaneously as always already there cultural commonalities, as new projects occasioned by colonialism and independence struggles, and as impositions of certain constructions of the national culture over other identities and cultural projects within the ostensible nation" (2007, 21). Calhoun's cautions against adopting a postnationalist view are even more pertinent now than when he wrote them, in the face of growing nationalist and populist movements in Europe. Along similar lines, Rogers Brubaker has argued "The nation-state remains the decisive locus of membership even in a globalizing world; struggles over belonging in and to the nation-state remain the most consequential forms of membership politics" (2010, 77). States maintain ties with their citizens who live outside of their borders and also maintain control over those living within their territory who have come from elsewhere, and Brubaker notes that this control is supported by "the language of nationalism" (ibid., 78). For Brubaker, the term transborder is preferable to transnational in understanding the experiences of mobile people.

Emplacements and Moorings

Bourdieu's concept of the embodied habitus posits that our dispositions lead us to seek out people and physical locations where we feel an affinity, a sense of "home." As Jan Willem Duyvendak (2011) has pointed out, some very mobile cosmopolitan people feel at home in movement, but this may be an exception. The concept of emplacement, which has become increasingly visible in ethnographic studies of migration, addresses the desire to be "emplaced"—either not to move at all or to seek emplacement after a geographic move. Modes of emplacement or belonging are also modes of positioning in a social space. Migrants bring their dispositions and worldviews with them—including ideas about presentation of self, understandings of neighborly reciprocity, and also a set of know-how, social connections, and skills (linguistic, social, educational) that may or may not be highly valued in the host setting. Bourdieu's model of social space and the positioning of habitus within it is usefully applied to the study of emplacement.

In an essay on refugees and place, Catherine Brun (2001) identified two dominant ways of thinking about social space—neither of which, she argues, adequately captures the experiences of refugees. One views it as "a flat, immobilized surface" and considers refugees as people "torn loose" from their "natural place" in the world. This is similar to the perspective, criticized by Roger Rouse, of immigrants as "moving from one coherent and bounded social space to another." The other view identified by Brun decouples people and place and views space as "constructed from the multiplicity of social relations across all spatial scales" (2001, 15). This is the perspective associated with many attempts to focus on global flows, contact zones, and transnationalism. Brun uses the concept of social spatiality to argue that a deterritorialized view of refugees neglects their experiences and the different attitudes and policy environments in which they are placed. Her work on refugees in Sri Lanka calls attention to the strategies used by refugees who have "the contradictory experience of being physically present in one location but at the same time living with a feeling of belonging somewhere else" (ibid., 23), and she points to the spatial strategies used by refugees as they find a position in the host setting. Her argument is that even though much contemporary social theory argues that links between territories and people may be social constructs, refugees themselves use such essentialisms in thinking about place. We must not, therefore, overlook this feature of their experience in our own work.

In another approach to migration and spatiality, Anne-Marie Fortier (2000) draws upon Brah's idea of the "diaspora space"—located between the local and the transnational, and at the intersections of staying put and being displaced—to explore Italian migration to Britain. Fortier identifies critical migration studies as a movement that questions imaginings of a fluid and hypermobile world and seeks to understand "imaginative geographies" and "migrant horizons" (2006, 314). Among immigrants, Fortier writes, there is a separation between "the space of belonging and the place of residence" (ibid., 316), which implies, in Bourdieu's terminology, that they are positioned in two social spaces while residing in one geographic place. They feel that they belong in the social space of the country they left, and feel out of place in the social space of the country to which they have moved.

Maja Korac (2009) looked at the effects of both bridging and bonding networks on their emplacements in her study of refugees from the former Yugoslavia who settled in Amsterdam and Rome. She uses the metaphor of "nesting" to discuss how former refugees become emplaced in localities through ties outside their ethnic groups, and how they deploy bonding strategies with coethnics to become emplaced in transnational social spaces. Although this study does not rely heavily on Bourdieu's concepts directly, and uses "social space" differently, Korac suggests that these refugees were from similar backgrounds and therefore brought similar forms of cultural capital. Her work points to the possibilities of using Bourdieu's approach in this work to greater advantage by incorporating the ideas of social capital, affinities of habitus, and positionings in social space. It underscores Bourdieu's essential point that the displacement of mobility will be accompanied by the desire for feeling at home through modes of emplacement.

Bernard Debarbieux (2014) suggests that the critique of what he refers to as "the territorial paradigm" and "sedentary forms of knowledge"[6] has gone too far in not taking subjective attachments to place as significant and viewing all mobility as one of flux and circulation. He suggests that metaphors of anchoring and mooring are replacing those of rootedness in attempts to understand more temporary localizations. Debarbieux mentions Bourdieu's use of the spatial metaphor of rootedness (*enracinement*) in his publications on Algeria. This work was discussed in Chapter Two, and it bears repeating here that Bourdieu did not view attachment to place as being "rooted" to mean some sort of primordial attachment. Rather, he viewed this as a socially constructed feeling produced by one's position in social space.

In his discussion of spatial metaphors in Francophone academic literature,[7] Debarbieux identifies anchoring (*ancrage*), dwelling (*habiter*), rootedness (*enracinement*), and docking and mooring (*amarrage*). He considers the metaphor of mooring and its related metaphor of anchoring as different from that of rootedness, which signifies a more enduring emplacement. The relationship to place of those who are moored is temporary, and the assumption is that there will be a further movement. He notes:

> When the metaphors of rootedness, of anchoring, and mooring talk about places, they are referring to a variety of places: a nurturing place for the rooted; a temporary place whose quality depends on the relational resources, whose access is given to whoever throws anchors there; and a place of temporary dependence on local resources for those who moor there. These three metaphors evoke different ways of being in a place: an (allegedly) organic dependence, vital for rooting and a physical, mechanical contingency for anchoring and mooring. (2014, 68)

The concept of mooring as articulated by John Urry has captured the imagination of mobility scholars because it points to the pauses in mobility and flux. As Urry has argued regarding the mobility/mooring dialectic, mooring refers to "specialized periods and places involving temporary rest, storage, infra-structural immobility, disposal, and immobile zones" (2003, 126). Moorings help organize time-space and thus enable mobility, according to Urry. However, the assumption that mobility will be the norm, which is part of this construction, is questionable (see Franquesa 2011). There is also the issue, raised by a social space perspective, of what it is that people are moored to—a social space, a physical place, a space of positioning and belonging?

An earlier use of the metaphor of mooring (Racine 1997) provides an alternative. In a collaborative study of villages in rural India, the researchers examined why those in some villages were more apt to be mobile, either migrating permanently or moving temporarily to towns or cities. They used a concept of "village mooring" to discuss attachments to not only the place of a village, but also to the social and especially kin relations there (the aspects of social space involving sociality as well as spatiality). One important question asked in this project was that of why some people do not move, including entire villages that had more of a reputation than others for the mobilities (or moorings) of its natives. In the context of a mobility paradigm that sees movement as continual, needing some organization through mooring in Urry's iteration, this poses a question not always asked in mobility and migration. When the focus is so much on those who do move, it is important to also ask about those who stay behind or stay in place.

Mooring is a term that speaks to both social and geographical space in that it can refer to the place (as in where a boat is secured) or to the act of anchoring. The connotation of the word is that it is something that provides stability and to which one can adhere. Bourdieu's understanding of habitus as position in social space could be described, thus, as a mooring in social space, which can also be a location in physical space. The concept of trajectory is one that implies possibilities of mobility and immobility for habitus, connected to the idea of "social aging," and localizations that can be more or less temporary depending upon the trajectory.

The main point I have emphasized in this book is that social space is a concept that incorporates the embodied habitus as positioned in both physical and more abstract social space. Bourdieu's concept of social space is concerned with understanding mobilities and immobilities in geographic and social space. The dispositions of habitus affect aspirations and also what it means to feel at home or out of place. The habitus can be described as emplaced or displaced, moored or in motion. The concept of social space is associated with Bourdieu's world-making, his model of the social world and its hierarchy. At the same time, Bourdieu understood that the subjective experiences of emplacement or displacement felt by all social actors influence the social practices that construct this social space. The dispositions of habitus are the product of a person's social origins and trajectories over time. Affinities of habitus bring people together and create a sense of belonging; but for Bourdieu, this must be understood in terms of their position in social space.

A Critical Appraisal: Limitations and Possibilities

In addition to the many possible applications of Bourdieu's approach to the study of migration and mobility more broadly that I have emphasized throughout this book, it is important also to draw attention to several enduring limitations with his concept of social space that can be overcome with further exploration and adaptation of social space in new contexts. These limitations have been mentioned in earlier chapters of this book, but I return to them here before also reiterating some of the major contributions Bourdieu's concept of social space can make to ethnographic studies of migration and mobility.

One criticism is that Bourdieu's analyses primarily focused on males who felt out of place due to geographic mobility, social mobility, or immobility when the world around them changed. It is important to investigate the positions and positionings of females in social space in order to correct this bias. Although Bourdieu did address gender in his book *Masculine Domination* (1998b/2001), largely in a response to feminist criticisms that he did not sufficiently consider women's positionings in social space, most of his writings on social space deal with male subjects. In the Introduction to this book, I provided some examples of feminist approaches to social space that used Bourdieu's ideas, but more needs to be done in studies of mobility and immobility to better understand gendered aspects of spatial practices and experiences of mobility.

Another important limitation in Bourdieu's approach is that he tended to describe social space as "enclosed." What does this mean? Although he viewed territorial and social boundaries as socially constructed, he devoted little attention to border zones or interstitial spaces that might exist at the threshold of social space. He also, however, noted the "elasticity of the social world" (2013, 219), which meant that it was partially created by representations of it by those who lived in it. This seems to indicate that the thresholds of social space are elastic and can shift when representations of it shift. In Chapter Two, I demonstrated that Bourdieu conceptualized social space as possibly opening and enlarging by using examples from his earlier work among peasant societies, and especially his work in rural France. This leads to the possibility that it can also contract. This is a topic, however, that requires further exploration using Bourdieu's concepts while also adapting them in order to avoid the residue of structuralism that was present in some of his earlier writings (such as that on the Kabyle house).

There are also enduring questions about Bourdieu's understanding of state power and its reach. At times, Bourdieu described state power in national social space as universally present, while at other times, he suggested that this universal reach of the state is part of the *doxa* that becomes common sense. For Bourdieu, as I discussed in Chapter Four, education is a major vehicle for the imposition of symbolic power and the symbolic violence that legitimizes those who are dominant and creates social divisions in the world. This leads me to the question of where to locate the "margins of the state" (Das and Poole 2004) in Bourdieu's thinking. Although he acknowledged that he was more interested in the study of power and domination than in the question of resistance or challenges to it, and he was not unaware of resistance, he presented a fairly totalizing view of symbolic power in social space. Symbolic power and symbolic violence lead people to either stay in their place or move, if that is their destiny due to the dispositions of habitus. Staying in place can be understood in terms of one's position in the social hierarchy as well as one's location in geographic place. Even if we do accept, as I propose, that the nation-state continues to be central to mobility and immobility, more attention should be placed on the limits to the symbolic power of the state as maintained in national social space or in the European Union.

Bourdieu was adamant that his concepts were all tools of research and not "real" things. He used them to make sense of the world and to critique systems of power and domination that led to inequalities. My own approach to Bourdieu's thought (drawing upon his claims that these were analytic constructs) is to not take his approach too literally while also taking seriously that his concepts work together—with the implication that any reference to social space must include consideration of habitus, capital, field, and symbolic power. These associated notions cannot be separated from the concept of social space if one is to avoid the methodological individualism that Bourdieu worked against in his approach to the social world.

The enduring advantage of Bourdieu's approach to social space, viewed over the course of his career and in its many iterations, is that it makes us more aware of the connections between geographic and social space. It can help us to view mobility as movement across boundaries that are social and geographic, and to see how these are related, while also understanding that boundaries themselves are social constructions. Moreover, the concept of the embodied habitus helps us understand the role of emotion in mobility and immobility. I end this book with a call for an ethnography of social space, for more anthropological work that takes up Bourdieu's concept of social space in order to view mobility in terms of trajectories within and across it, as well as emplacements. Adapting Bourdieu's ideas can help provide an alternative to preoccupations with flows and mobilities—not as a return to ideas of bounded spaces as in "one place, one culture," but, rather, as a way to understand ideas and feelings of affinity, and the institutional structures and practices that work to contain and mold commonsense understandings of "the sense of one's place." Bourdieu's approach situates power at the center of studies of mobility, encouraging us to investigate the structured inequalities that prevail in spatial choices and practices.

NOTES

1. See Reed-Danahay (2017a) for a more preliminary discussion of Bourdieu, auto-ethnography, and migration.
2. For an overview of this approach, see Caroline Brettell's chapter on "Migration Stories" in Brettell (2003).
3. Examples of this from my own work include Reed-Danahay 1997; 2002; 2005a; and 2015b.
4. In referring to this statement by Bourdieu, I was reminded that when I was undertaking fieldwork on education in rural Auvergne in the early 1980s, when I had first gotten to know Bourdieu, he suggested to me that I find village monographs written by local teachers to help me better understand the local region and construct the history of schooling there.
5. See Reed-Danahay (2005b) for a more extended discussion of Bourdieu and personal narrative, which does not, however, focus on social space and mobility as I do here.
6. He cites as examples such writers as Gupta and Ferguson (1992); Appadurai (1996); Massey (2005); and Amselle (2000).
7. For related discussions of the prevalence of spatial metaphors in everyday speech, see Sorokin (1927); Silber (1995); Urry (2000); and Vandebroeck (2018).

References

Bourdieu and Coauthors

1958. *Sociologie de l'Algérie*. Paris: Presses Universitaires de France.

1962. "Célibat et Condition Paysanne." *Etudes Rurales* 5–6: 32–135.

1963a. "The Attitude of the Algerian Peasant toward Time." In *Mediterranean Country-men. Essays in the Social Anthropology of the Mediterranean*, edited by Julian A. Pitt-Rivers. Translated by Gerald E. Williams, 55–72. Paris: Mouton and Co.

1963b (and Alain Darbel, Jean-Pierre Rivet, and Claude Seibel). *Travail et Travailleurs en Algérie*. Paris: Mouton and Co.

1964a (and Abdelmalek Sayad). *Le Déracinement: La Crise de l'Agriculture Traditionnelle en Algérie*. Paris: Éditions de Minuit.

1964b (and Abdelmalek Sayad). "Paysans Déracinés: Bouleversements Morphologiques et Changements Culturels en Algérie." *Etudes Rurales* (Paris) 12: 56–94.

1964c (and Jean-Claude Passeron). *Les Héritiers. Les Etudiants et la Culture*. Paris: Editions de Minuit.

1965a. *Un Art Moyen*. Paris: Les Editions de Minuit.

1965b (and Marie-Claire Bourdieu). "Le Paysan et la Photographie." *Revue Française de Sociologie* 6, no. 2: 164–74.

1966a. "Champ Intellectuel et Projet Créateur`." *Les Temps Modernes* 22: 865–906.

1966b. "The Sentiment of Honour in Kabyle Society." In *Honor and Shame: The Values of Mediterranean Society*, edited by John G. Peristiany. Translated by Philip Sharrard, 192–241. Chicago: University of Chicago Press.

1967. "Postface." In *Architecture Gothique et Pensée Scholastique*, written by E. Panofsky, 133–67. Paris: Les Editions de Minuit.

1970a. "La Maison Kabyle ou le Monde Renversé." In *Echanges et Communications: Mé-langes Offerts à Claude Lévi-Strauss à l'Occasion de son 60ᵉᵐᵉ Anniversaire*, edited by J. Puillon and P. Maranda, 739–59. Paris: Mouton and Co.

1970b (and Jean-Claude Passeron). *La Reproduction: Eléments pour une Théorie du Système d'Enseignement*. Genève: Librairie Droz.

1970c. "The Berber House or the World Reversed." *Social Science Information* 9: 151–70.

1971. "Genèse et Structure du Champ Religieux." *Revue Française de Sociologie* 12, no. 3: 295–334.

1972a. *Esquisse d'une Théorie de la Pratique*. Genève: Libraire Droz.

1972b. "Les Stratégies Matrimoniales dans le Système de Reproduction." *Annales: Economies, Sociétés, Civilisations* 27, no. 4/5: 1105–27.

1975. "L'Invention de la Vie d'Artiste." *Actes de la Recherche en Sciences Sociales* 1, no. 2: 67–93.

1976a (and Luc Boltanski). "La Production de l'Idéologie Dominante." *Actes de la Recherche en Sciences Sociales* 2, no. 2–3: 3–73.

1976b (and Monique de St. Martin). "Anatomie du Goût." *Actes de la Recherche en Sciences Sociales* 5: 5–81.

1977a. *Algérie 1960: Structures Économiques et Structures Sociales.* Paris : Editions de Minuit.

1977b. "Une Classe Objet." *Actes de la Recherches en Sciences Sociales* 17/18: 2–5.

1977c. *Outline of a Theory of Practice.* Translated by Richard Nice. Cambridge, UK: Cambridge University Press.

1977d. (and Jean-Claude Passeron). *Reproduction in Education, Culture and Society.* London: Sage Publications.

1979a. *Algeria 1960.* Translated by Richard Nice. Cambridge: Cambridge University Press.

1979b. *La Distinction: Critique Social du Jugement.* Paris: Editions de Minuit.

1979c. "Les Trois États du Capital Culturel." *Actes de la Recherche en Sciences Sociales* 30: 3–6.

1980a. "L'Identité et la Représentation: Eléments pour une Réflexion Critique sur l'Idée de Région." *Actes de la Recherches en Sciences Sociales* 35: 62–72.

1980b. *Le Sens Pratique.* Paris: Les Editions de Minuit.

1982a. *Ce que Parler Veut Dire: L'Economie des Echanges Linguistiques.* Paris: Librairie Arthème Fayard.

1982b. "Les Rites comme Actes d'Institution." *Actes de la Recherche en Sciences Sociales* 43: 58–63.

1983. "The Field of Cultural Production, or: The Economic World Reversed." Translated by Richard Nice. *Poetics* 12, no. 4–5: 311–56.

1984a. *Distinction: A Social Critique of the Judgement of Taste.* Translated by Richard Nice. Cambridge, MA: Harvard University Press.

1984b. *Homo Academicus.* Paris: Editions de Minuit.

1985a. "The Genesis of the Concepts of *Habitus* and *Field.*" Translated by Channa Newman. *Sociocriticism* 2: 11–24.

1985b. "Social Space and the Genesis of Groups." *Theory and Society* 14: 723–44.

1986a. "The Forms of Capital." In *Handbook of Theory and Research in the Sociology of Education,* edited by John G. Richardson, 241–58. New York: Greenwood Press.

1986b. "L'Illusion Biographique." *Actes de la Recherches en Sciences Sociales* 62–63: 69–72.

1987. "The Invention of the Artist's Life." Translated by E. Koch. *Yale French Studies* 73: 75–103.

1988a. "Flaubert's Point of View." *Critical Inquiry* 14, no. 3: 539–62.

1988b. *Homo Academicus.* Translated by Peter Collier. Stanford: Stanford University Press.

1989a. *La Noblesse d'Etat: Grandes Ecoles et Esprit de Corps.* Paris: Les Editions de Minuit.

1989b. "Reproduction Interdite: La Dimension Symbolique de la Domination Economique." *Etudes Rurales* 113–14: 15–36.

1989c. "Social Space and Symbolic Power." *Sociological Theory* 7, no. 1: 14–25.

1990. *The Logic of Practice*. Translated by Richard Nice. Stanford: Stanford University Press.

1991a. "First Lecture. Social Space and Symbolic Space: An Introduction to a Japanese Reading of Distinction." *Poetics Today* 12, no. 4: 627–38.

1991b. *Language and Symbolic Power*. Translated by John B. Thompson. Cambridge, MA: Harvard University Press.

1992a. (and Loïc J.D. Wacquant). *An Invitation to Reflexive Sociology*. Chicago: University of Chicago Press.

1992b. *Les Règles de l'Art: Genèse et Structure du Champ Littéraire*. Paris: Editions du Seuil.

1992c. "Rites as Acts of Institution." In *Honor and Grace in Anthropology*, edited by J. G. Peristiany and J. Pitt-Rivers. Translated by Peter Just, 79–89. Cambridge, UK: Cambridge University Press.

1993a. "Esprits d'Etat: Genèse et Structure du Champ Bureaucratique." *Actes de la Recherche en Science Sociales* 96–97: 49–62.

1993b. *The Field of Cultural Production: Essays on Art and Literature*, edited and introduced by Randal Johnson. New York: Columbia University Press.

1993c (et. al). *La Misère du Monde*. Paris: Editions du Seuil.

1994a. *Raisons Pratiques*. Paris: Editions du Seuil.

1994b. "Rethinking the State: Genesis and Structure of the Bureaucratic Field." Translated by Loïc J. D. Wacquant and Samar Farage. *Sociological Theory* 12, no. 1: 1–18.

1996a. *Physical Space, Social Space and Habitus*. Rapport 10: 1996. Oslo: Institutt for sosiologi og samfunnsgeografi, University of Oslo.

1996b. *The Rules of Art: Genesis and Structure of the Literary Field*. Translated by Susan Emanuel. Stanford: Stanford University Press.

1996c. *The State Nobility*. Translated by Lauretta C. Clough. Stanford: Stanford University Press.

1997. *Méditations Pascaliennes*. Paris: Editions du Seuil.

1998a. *Acts of Resistance: Against the Tyranny of the Market*. Translated by Richard Nice. Oxford: Polity Press.

1998b. *La Domination Masculine*. Paris: Editions du Seuil.

1998c. "The Essence of Neoliberalism." Translated by Jeremy J. Shapiro. *Le Monde Diplomatique* (Paris). December 1–7. http://mondediplo.com/1998/12/08bourdieu.

1998d. *Practical Reason: On the Theory of Action*. Stanford: Stanford University Press.

1999a. "Pour un Mouvement Social Européen." *Le Monde Diplomatique* (Paris). June 16–17. http://www.monde-diplomatique.fr/1999/06/BOURDIEU/12158.html.

1999b (et al.). *The Weight of the World*. Translated by Priscilla P. Ferguson et al. Stanford: Stanford University Press.

2000a. "The Biographical Illusion." In *Identity: A Reader*, edited by Paul du Gay et al. Translated by Yves Winkin and Wendy Leeds-Hurwitz, 297–303. London: Sage Publications.

2000b. "Making the Economic Habitus: Algerian Workers Revisited." Translated by Richard Nice and Loïc Wacquant. *Ethnography* 1, no. 1: 17–41.

2000c. *Pascalian Meditations*. Translated by Richard Nice. Stanford: Stanford University Press.

2000d. *Les Structures Sociales de l'Economie*. Paris: Editions du Seuil.

2001. *Masculine Domination*. Translated by Richard Nice. Stanford: Stanford University Press.

2002a. *Le Bal des Célibataires: Crise de la Société Paysanne en Béarn*. Paris: Editions du Seuil.

2002b. *Interventions 1961–2001: Science Sociale et Action Politique*, edited by Franck Poupeau and Thierry Discipelo. Marseille: Agone.

2002c. "Habitus." In *Habitus: A Sense of Place*, edited by Jean Hillier and Emma Rooksby, 27–34. Aldershot, UK: Ashgate.

2002d. "The Role of Intellectuals Today." *Theoria* 99: 1–6.

2003a. *Images d'Algérie: Une Affinité Elective*, edited by Franz Shultheis. Arles: Actes Sud.

2003b. "Participant Objectivation." *Journal of the Royal Anthropological Institute* 9: 281–94.

2004a. *Esquisse pour une Auto-analyse*. Paris: Editions Raisons d'Agir.

2004b. "The Peasant and His Body." Translated and adapted by Richard Nice and Loïc Wacquant. *Ethnography* 5, no. 4: 579–99.

2005. *The Social Structures of the Economy*. Translated by Chris Turner. Cambridge, UK: Polity Press.

2007. *Sketch for a Self-Analysis*. Translated by Richard Nice. Chicago: University of Chicago Press.

2008a. *The Bachelor's Ball*. Translated by Richard Nice. Chicago: University of Chicago Press.

2008b. *Esquisses Algériennes*. Edited and presented by Tassadit Yacine. Paris: Editions du Seuil.

2008c. *Political Interventions: Social Science and Political Action*, edited by Franck Poupeau and Thierry Discipelo. Translated by David Fernbach and Gregory Elliott. London: Verso.

2012. *Sur l'Etat*. Paris: Editions Raisons d'Agir/Editions du Seuil.

2013. *Algerian Sketches*, edited and presented by Tassadit Yacine. Translated by David Fernbach. Cambridge, UK: Polity Press.

2014. *On the State: Lectures at the Collège de France, 1989–1992*. Translated by David Fernbach. Cambridge, UK: Polity Press.

2018. "Social Space and the Genesis of Appropriated Physical Space." Translated and edited by Loïc Wacquant. *International Journal of Urban and Regional Research* 42, no. 1: 106–14.

Other Authors

Adkins, Lisa, and Beverly Skeggs, eds. 2005. *Feminism after Bourdieu*. Oxford: Blackwell Publishing.

Adler-Nissen, Rebecca, ed. 2013. *Bourdieu in International Relations*. New York: Routledge.

Amelina, Anna, et al., eds. 2012. *Beyond Methodological Nationalism: Research Methodologies for Cross-Border Studies*. New York: Routledge.

Amit, Vered, ed. 2007. *Going First Class? New Approaches to Privileged Travel and Movement*. New York: Berghahn Books.

———, ed. 2015. *Thinking through Sociality: An Anthropological Interrogation of Key Concepts.* Oxford: Berghahn Books.

Amselle, Jean-Loup. 2000. *Branchements: Anthropologie de l'Universalité des Cultures.* Paris: Flammarion.

Anderson, Benedict. (1983) 1991. *Imagined Communities: Reflections on the Origin and Spread of Nationalism,* revised ed. London: Verso.

Appadurai, Arjun. 1996. *Modernity at Large: Cultural Dimensions of Globalization.* Minneapolis: University of Minnesota Press.

Ardener, Shirley, ed. 1993. *Women and Space: Ground Rules and Social Maps.* Oxford: Berg Publishers.

Armand, Louis, and Valéry Giscard d'Estaing. 1969. *Quel Avenir pour l'Europe: Dialogue entre Louis Armand et Valéry Giscard d'Estaing.* Paris: Publicis Conseil.

Atkinson, Will. 2017. *Class in the New Millennium: The Structure, Homologies and Experience of the British Social Space.* London: Routledge.

Augé, Marc. 1990. "Ten Questions Put to Claude Lévi-Strauss." *Current Anthropology* 31, no. 1: 85–90.

———. (1992) 2009. *Non-Places: An Introduction to Supermodernity.* Translated by John Howe. London: Verso.

Bachelard, Gaston. (1958) 1964. *The Poetics of Space.* Translated by Maria Jolas. Boston: Beacon Press.

Balibar, Étienne. (2001) 2004. *We, the People of Europe? Reflections on Transnational Citizenship.* Translated by James Swenson. Princeton: Princeton University Press.

Barth, Fredrik, ed. 1969. *Ethnic Groups and Boundaries: The Social Organization of Cultural Difference.* Boston: Little, Brown, and Co.

Basch, Linda, Nina Glick Schiller, and Cristina Szanton Blanc. 1994. *Nations Unbound: Transnational Projects, Postcolonial Predicaments, and Deterritorialized Nation-Sates.* The Netherlands: Gordon and Breach Science Publishers.

Baudin, Gérard, and Philippe Bonnin, eds. 2009. *Faire Territoire.* Paris: Editions Recherches.

Beamon, Jean. 2017. *Citizen Outsiders: Children of North African Immigrants in France.* Berkeley: University of California Press.

Benson, Michaela, and Karen O'Reilly. 2009. "Migration and the Search for a Better Way of Life: A Critical Exploration of Lifestyle Migration." *The Sociological Review* 57, no. 4: 608–25.

Bhabha, Homi. 2004. *The Location of Culture.* New York: Routledge.

Bigo, Didier, Philippe Bonditti, and Christian Olsson. (2010) 2016. "Mapping the European Field of Security Professionals." In *Europe's 21st Century Challenge: Delivering Liberty,* edited by Didier Bigo et al., 49–64. New York: Routledge.

Billig, Michael. 1995. *Banal Nationalism.* London: Sage Publications.

Bon, Nataša G., and Jaka Repič, eds. 2016. *Moving Places: Relations, Return, and Belonging.* New York: Berghahn Books.

Brenner, Neil, and Stuart Elden. 2009. "Henri Lefebvre on State, Space, Territory." *International Political Sociology* 3, no. 4: 353–377.

Brettell, Caroline. 2003. *Anthropology and Migration: Essays on Transnationalism, Ethnicity, and Identity.* Walnut Creek, CA: Alta Mira Press.

Brettell, Caroline, and Deborah Reed-Danahay. 2012. *Civic Engagements: The Citizenship Practices of Indian and Vietnamese Immigrants*. Stanford, CA: Stanford University Press.

Brousse, Cécile. 2017. "L'Union Européenne, un Espace Social Unifié?" *Actes de la Recherche en Sciences Sociale* 219: 12–41.

Brubaker, Rogers. 2010. "Migration, Membership, and the Modern Nation-State: Internal and External Dimensions of the Politics of Belonging." *Journal of Interdisciplinary History* 151, no. 1: 61–78.

Brun, Catherine. 2001. "Reterritorializing the Relationship between People and Place in Refugee Studies." *Geografiska Annaler* 83B, no. 1: 15–25.

Bruno, G. 1877. *La Tour de la France par Deux Enfants*. Paris: Belin.

Butimi, Alessandra. 2018. "'An Uplifting Tale of Europe': Jacques Delors and the Contradictory Quest for a European Social Model in the Age of Reagan." *Journal of Transatlantic Studies* 16, no. 3: 203–21.

Butler, Judith. 1997. *Excitable Speech: A Politics of the Performance*. London: Routledge.

Buttimer, Anne. 1969. "Social Space in Interdisciplinary Perspective." *Geographical Review* 59, no. 3: 417–26.

Cairns, David, et al. 2017. *The Consequences of Mobility: Reflexivity, Social Inequality, and the Reproduction of Precariousness in Highly Skilled Migration*. New York: Palgrave Macmillan.

Calhoun, Craig. 2007. *Nations Matter: Culture, History, and the Cosmopolitan Dream*. London: Routledge.

Carsten, Janet, and Stephen Hugh-Jones. 1995. "Introduction." In *About the House: Lévi-Strauss and Beyond*, edited by Janet Carsten and Stephen Hugh-Jones, 1–46. Cambridge, UK: Cambridge University Press.

Certeau, Michel de. 1984. *The Practice of Everyday Life*. Translated by Steven Rendall. Berkeley: University of California Press.

——. (1974) 1997. *Culture in the Plural*. Translated Tom Conley. Minneapolis: University of Minnesota Press.

Chombart de Lauwe, Paul-Henri. 1965. *Paris: Essais de Sociologie 1952–1964*. Paris: Editions Ouvrières.

Claval, Paul. 1984. "The Concept of Social Space and the Nature of Social Geography." *New Zealand Geographer* 40, no. 2: 104–9.

Cohen, Marilyn, ed. 2013. *Novel Approaches to Anthropology: Contributions to Literary Anthropology*. Lanham, MD: Lexington Books.

Cole, Jennifer. 2014. "The Téléphone Malgache: Transnational Gossip and Social Transformation among Malagasy Marriage Migrants in France." *American Ethnologist* 41, no. 2: 276–89.

Coleman, Simon, and Peter Collins, eds. 2006. *Locating the Field: Space, Place and Context in Anthropology*. Oxford: Berg Publishers.

Condominas, Georges. 1980. *L'Espace Social—A Propos de l'Asie du Sud-est*. Paris: Flammarion.

Conradson, David, and Alan Latham. 2005. "Transnational Urbanism: Attending to Everyday Practices and Mobilities." *Journal of Ethnic and Migration Studies* 31, no. 2: 227–33.

Conradson, David, and Deirdre McKay. 2007. "Translocal Subjectivities: Mobility, Connection, Emotion." *Mobilities* 2, no. 2: 167–74.

Corsin Jiménez, Alberto. 2003. "On Space as a Capacity." *Journal of the Royal Anthropological Institute* 9: 137–53.

Coulangeon, Philippe, and Julien Duval, eds. 2013. *Trente ans Après La Distinction de Pierre Bourdieu*. Paris: Editions La Découverte.

———, eds. 2015. *The Routledge Companion to Bourdieu's Distinction*. London: Routledge.

Cresswell, Tim. 2006. *On the Move: Mobility in the Modern Western World*. New York and London: Taylor and Francis.

Crossley, Nick. 2005. *Key Concepts in Critical Social Theory*. London: Sage Publications.

Das, Veena, and Deborah Poole, eds. 2004. *Anthropology at the Margins of the State*. Santa Fe: School of American Research Press.

Debarbieux, Bernard. 2014. "Enracinement – Ancrage – Amarrage: Raviver les Metaphores." *L'Espace Geographique* 1, no. 43: 68–80.

Demossier, Marion, ed. 2007. *The European Puzzle: The Political Structuring of Cultural Identities at a Time of Transition*. New York: Berghahn Books.

Donnan, Hastings, and Thomas M. Wilson. 1999. *Borders: Frontiers of Identity, Nation, and State*. Oxford: Berg Publishers.

Dosse, François. (1992) 1997. *History of Structuralism. Volume 2: The Sign Sets, 1967–Present*. Translated by Deborah Glassman. Minneapolis: University of Minnesota Press.

Duchêne-Lacroix, Cédric, and Angeliki Koukoutsaki-Monnier. 2016. "Mapping the Social Space of Transnational Migrants on the Basis of Their (Supra) National Belongings: The Case of French Citizens in Berlin." *Identities: Global Studies in Culture and Power* 23, no. 2: 136–54.

Dunning, Eric, and Stephen Mennell. 1996. "Preface." In *The Germans*, written by Norbert Elias. Oxford: Blackwell Publishers.

Durkheim, Emile. (1897) 1951. *Suicide: A Study in Sociology*. Translated by John A. Spaulding and George Simpson. Glencoe, IL: The Free Press.

———. (1912) 1995. *The Elementary Forms of Religious Life*. Translated by Karen E. Fields. New York: The Free Press.

Durkheim, Emile, and Marcel Mauss. 1963. *Primitive Classification*. Translated by Rodney Needham. Chicago: University of Chicago Press.

Duyvendak, Jan Willem. 2011. *The Politics of Home: Belonging and Nostalgia in Western Europe and the United States*. New York: Palgrave Macmillan.

Elias, Norbert. 1987. *The Society of Individuals*. Translated by Edmund Jephcott. Oxford: Basil Blackwell.

Encrevé, Pierre, and Rose-Marie Lagrave, eds. 2003. *Travailler avec Bourdieu*. Paris: Flammarion.

Englund, Harri. 2002. "Ethnography after Globalism: Migration and Emplacement in Malawi." *American Ethnologist* 29, no. 2: 261–86.

Erel, Umut. 2010. "Migrating Cultural Capital: Bourdieu in Migration Studies." *Sociology* 44, no. 4: 642–60.

Eribon, Didier, and René Pierre. 1981. "Retrouver la Tradition Libertaire de la Gauche." Interview with Pierre Bourdieu. *Libération*, 23 December.

Eriksen, Thomas Hylland. 2006. "Cultural Contagion in a New Key." *Ethnos* 71, no. 2: 265–72.

Escobar, Arturo. 2001. "Culture Sits in Places: Reflections on Globalism and Subaltern Strategies of Localization." *Political Geography* 20: 137–74.

Fabiani, Jean-Louis. 2016. *Pierre Bourdieu: Un Structuralisme Héroïque*. Paris: Editions du Seuil.

Faist, Thomas. 2004. "The Border-Crossing Expansion of Social Space: Concepts, Questions and Topics." In *Transnational Social Spaces: Agents, Networks, and Institutions*, edited by Thomas Faist and Eyüp Özveron, 1–36. Aldershot, UK: Ashgate.

———. 2012. "Toward a Transnational Methodology: Methods to Address Methodological Nationalism, Essentialism, and Positionality." *Revue Européenne des Migrations Internationales* 28, no. 1: 51–70.

———. 2013. "The Mobility Turn: A New Paradigm for the Social Sciences?" *Ethnic and Racial Studies* 36, no. 11: 1637–46.

Faist, Thomas, and Eyüp Özveron, eds. 2004. *Transnational Social Spaces: Agents, Networks, and Institutions*. Aldershot, UK: Ashgate.

Fassin, Didier. (2013) 2015. "Introduction: Governing Precarity." In *At the Heart of the State: The Moral World of Institutions*, edited by Didier Fassin et al., 1–11. London: Pluto Books.

Fassin, Didier, et al. (2013) 2015. *At the Heart of the State: The Moral World of Institutions*. London: Pluto Books.

Fassin, Didier, and Sara Mazouz. 2009. "What Is It to Become French? Naturalization as a Republican Rite of Institution." *Revue Française de Sociologie* 50, no. 5: 37–64.

Favell, Adrian. 2008. *Eurostars and Eurocities: Free Movement and Mobility in an Integrating Europe*. Malden, MA: Blackwell Publishing.

Favell, Adrian, and Ettore Recchi. 2011. "Social Mobility and Spatial Mobility." In *Sociology of the European Union*, edited by Adrian Favell and Virginie Guiraudon, 50–75. New York: Palgrave Macmillan.

Feldman, Gregory. 2011. *The Migration Apparatus: Security, Labor, and Policymaking in the European Union*. Stanford: Stanford University Press.

Fisher, Max. 2018. "Europe Could Melt Down over a Simple Question of Borders." *New York Times*. 6 July 2018.

Fogle, Nikolaus. 2011. *The Spatial Logic of Social Struggle: A Bourdieuian Topology*. Lanham, MD: Lexington Books.

Fortier, Anne-Marie. 2000. *Migrant Belongings: Memory, Space, Identity*. Oxford: Berg Publishers.

———. 2006. "The Politics of Scaling, Timing and Embodying: Rethinking the 'New Europe.'" *Mobilities* 1, no. 3: 313–31.

Franquesa, Jaume. 2011. "'We've Lost Our Bearings': Place, Tourism, and the Limits of the 'Mobility Turn.'" *Antipode* 43, no. 4: 1012–33.

Friedman, Victor. 2011. "Revisiting Social Space: Relational Thinking about Organizational Change." *Research in Organizational Change and Development* 19: 233–57.

Frisby, David, and Mike Featherstone. (1997) 2000. "Introduction to the Texts." In *Simmel on Culture: Selected Writings*, edited by David Frisby and Mike Featherstone, 1–28. London: Sage Publications.

Geddes, Andrew. 2008. *Immigration and European Integration: Beyond Fortress Europe?* 2nd ed. Manchester: Manchester University Press.

Glick Schiller, Nina. 2005. "Transnational Social Fields and Imperialism: Bringing a Theory of Power to Transnational Studies." *Anthropological Theory* 5, no. 4: 439–61.

Glick Schiller, Nina, Linda Basch, and Cristina Szanton Blanc. 1995. "From Immigrant to Transmigrant: Theorizing Transnational Migration." *Anthropological Quarterly* 68, no. 1: 48–63.

Glick Schiller, Nina, and Ayse Çaglar. 2009. "Towards a Comparative Theory of Locality in Migration Studies: Migrant Incorporation and City Scale." *Journal of Ethnic and Migration Studies* 35, no. 2: 177–202.

Go, Julian, and Monika Krause. 2010. "Fielding Transnationalism: An Introduction." *The Sociological Review* 64, no. 2: 6–30.

Goffman, Erving. 1959. *The Presentation of Self in Everyday Life*. New York: Doubleday.

———. 1963. *Behavior in Public Places: Notes on the Social Organization of Gathering*. New York: The Free Press.

———. 1971. *Relations in Public: Microstudies of the Social Order*. New York: Harper Colophon Books.

Goodman, Jane E. 2009. "The Proverbial Bourdieu: Habitus and the Politics of Representation in the Ethnography of Kabylia." In *Bourdieu in Algeria: Colonial Politics, Ethnographic Practices, Theoretical Developments*, edited by Jane E. Goodman and Paul A. Silverstein, 94–132. Lincoln: University of Nebraska Press.

Goodman, Jane E., and Paul A. Silverstein, eds. 2009. *Bourdieu in Algeria: Colonial Politics, Ethnographic Practices, Theoretical Developments*. Lincoln: University of Nebraska Press.

Goodman, Nelson. 1978. *Ways of Worldmaking*. Indianapolis: Hackett Publishing.

Gorski, Philip S., ed. 2013. *Bourdieu and Historical Analysis*. Durham and London: Duke University Press.

Gray, Breda. 2008. "Putting Emotion and Reflexivity to Work in Researching Migration." *Sociology* 42, no. 5: 935–52.

Green, Sarah. 2013. "Borders and the Relocation of Europe." *Annual Review of Anthropology* 42: 345–61.

Greiner, Clemens, and Patrick Sakdapolrak. 2013. "Translocality: Concepts, Applications and Emerging Research Perspectives." *Geography Compass* 7, no. 5: 373–84.

Grenfell, Michael, et al. 2011. *Bourdieu, Language, and Linguistics*. London: Continuum.

Gupta, Akhil. 1992. "The Song of the Nonaligned World: Transnational Identities and the Reinscription of Space in Late Capitalism." *Current Anthropology* 7, no. 1: 63–79.

Gupta, Akhil, and James Ferguson. 1992. "Beyond 'Culture': Space, Identity, and the Politics of Difference." *Cultural Anthropology* 7, no. 1: 6–23.

———, eds. 1997. *Culture, Power, Place*. Durham, NC: Duke University Press.

Gürsel, Zeynep. 2016. *Image Brokers: Visualizing World News in the Age of Digital Circulation*. Berkeley, CA: University of California Press.

Halbwachs, Maurice. (1950) 1980. *On Collective Memory*. Translated by Francis J. Ditter Jr. and Vida Yazdi Ditter. New York: Harper and Row.

Hall, Edward T. 1966. *The Hidden Dimension*. Garden City, NY: Doubleday.

Hammoudi, Abdellah. 2009. "Phenomenology and Ethnography: On Kabyle Habitus in the Work of Pierre Bourdieu." In *Bourdieu in Algeria: Colonial Politics, Ethnographic Prac-*

tices, Theoretical Developments, edited by Jane E. Goodman and Paul A. Silverstein, 199–254. Lincoln: University of Nebraska Press.

Handler, Richard, and Daniel Segal. (1990) 1999. *Jane Austin and the Fiction of Culture: An Essay on the Narration of Social Realities*. Updated version. Lanham, MD: Rowman and Littlefield Publishers, Inc.

Hannerz, Ulf. 1996. *Transnational Connections*. London: Routledge.

Hantrais, Linda. 2007. *Social Policy in the European Union*. 3rd ed. London: Palgrave Macmillan.

Hardy, Cheryl. 2014. "Social Space." In *Pierre Bourdieu: Key Concepts*. 2nd ed., edited by Michael Grenfell, 229–49. London: Routledge.

Harvey, David. 1990. "Between Space and Time: Reflections on the Geographical Imagination." *Annals of the Association of American Geographers* 80, no. 3: 418–34.

———. 2005. "The Sociological and Geographical Imaginations." *International Journal of Politics, Culture, and Society* 18, no. 3/4: 211–55.

Haywood, Elizabeth. 1993. "The European Policy of François Mitterrand." *Journal of Common Market Studies* 31, no. 2: 269–82.

Herzfeld, Michael. 1992. *The Social Production of Indifference: Exploring the Symbolic Roots of Western Bureaucracy*. Chicago: University of Chicago Press.

———. 1997. *Portrait of a Greek Imagination: An Ethnographic Biography of Andreas Nenedakis*. Chicago: University of Chicago Press.

———. (2005) 2016. *Cultural Intimacy: Social Poetics and the Real Life of States, Societies, and Institutions*. 3rd ed. New York: Routledge.

Hilgers, Mathieu, and Eric Mangez. 2015a. "Afterword: Theory of Fields in the Postcolonial Age." In *Bourdieu's Theory of Social Fields: Concepts and Applications*, edited by Mathieu Hilgers and Eric Mangez, 257–73. New York: Routledge.

———. 2015b. "Introduction to Pierre Bourdieu's Theory of Social Fields." In *Bourdieu's Theory of Social Fields: Concepts and Applications*, edited by Mathieu Hilgers and Eric Mangez, 1–36. New York: Routledge.

Hillier, Jean, and Emma Rooksby, eds. 2002. *In Habitus: A Sense of Place*. Aldershot, UK: Ashgate.

Hobsbawm, Eric. 1983. "Mass-Producing Traditions: Europe 1870–1914." In *The Invention of Tradition*, edited by Eric Hobsbawm and Terence Ranger, 263–307. Cambridge, UK: Cambridge University Press.

Hoggart, Richard. (1957) 1992. *The Uses of Literacy*. New Brunswick, NJ: Transaction Publishers.

Hubbard, Phil, and Rob Kitchin, eds. *Key Thinkers on Space and Place*. 2nd ed. London: Sage Publications.

Hunter, Lisa. 2004. "Bourdieu and the Social Space of the PE Class: Reproduction of Doxa through Practice." *Sport, Education, and Society* 9, no. 2: 175–94.

Ilkan, Susan. 1999. "Social Spaces and the Micropolitics of Differentiation: An Example from Northwestern Turkey." *Ethnology* 38, no. 3: 243–56.

Ingold, Tom. 2016. "Foreword to the Second Edition." In *The Invention of Culture*. 2nd ed. Edited by Roy Wagner, x–xv. Chicago: University of Chicago Press.

INSEE. 2017. *France, Portrait Social, Edition 2017*. Paris: Insee Références.

Jenkins, Tim. 2006. "Bourdieu's Béarnais Ethnography." *Theory, Culture and Society* 23, no. 6: 45–72.

———. 2010. *The Life of Property: House, Family, and Inheritance in Béarn, Southwest France*. New York: Berghahn Books.

Jiménez Zunino, Cecilia. 2014. "Symbolic Strategies in Migrant Contexts: Middle-Class Argentineans in Spain." *Migraciones Internacionales* 7, no. 4: 39–67.

Johnson, Randal. 1993. "Editor's Introduction." In *The Field of Cultural Production*, edited by Pierre Bourdieu, 1–25. New York: Columbia University Press.

Kauppi, Niilo. 2003. "Bourdieu's Political Sociology and the Politics of European Integration." *Theory and Society* 32, no. 5/6: 775–89.

———. 2018. "Transnational Social Fields." In *The Oxford Handbook of Pierre Bourdieu*, edited by Thomas Medvitz and Jeffrey J. Sallaz, 183–99. New York: Oxford University Press.

Kearney, Michael. 1991. "Borders and Boundaries of State and Self at the End of Empire." *Journal of Historical Sociology* 4, no. 1: 52–74.

Korac, Maja. 2009. *Remaking Home: Reconstructing Life, Place and Identity in Rome and Amsterdam*. Oxford: Berghahn Books.

Kuper, Hilda. 1972. "The Language of Sites in the Politics of Space." *American Anthropologist* 74: 411–25.

Lagrave, Rose-Marie. 1980. *Le Village Romanesque*. Le Paradou: Actes du Sud.

Lahire, Bernard. 2010. "The Double Life of Writers." Translated by Gwendolyn Wells. *New Literary History* 41: 443–65.

———. (2001) 2011. *The Plural Actor*. Translated by David Fernbach. Cambridge, UK: Polity Press.

———. 2013. "La Culture à l'Echelle Individuelle: La Transférabilité en Question." In *Trente ans Après La Distinction de Pierre Bourdieu*, edited by Philippe Coulangeon and Julien Duval, 165–76. Paris: Editions La Découverte.

Lamont, Michèle. 1992. *Money, Morals, and Manners: The Culture of the French and American Upper-Middle Class*. Chicago: University of Chicago Press.

Laval, Christian. 2018. *Foucault, Bourdieu, et la Question Néolibérale*. Paris: La Découverte.

Lechner, Frank J. 1991. "Simmel on Social Space." *Theory, Culture and Society* 8: 195–201.

Leclercq, Catherine, Wenceslas Lizé, and Hélène Stevens, eds. 2015. *Bourdieu et les Sciences Sociales: Réception et Usages*. Paris: La Dispute.

Lefebvre, Henri. (1974) 1991. *The Production of Space*. Translated by Donald Nicholson-Smith. Malden, MA: Blackwell Publishing.

Lemert, Charles. 2006. *Durkheim's Ghosts: Cultural Logics and Social Things*. Cambridge, UK: Cambridge University Press.

Le Play, Frédéric. 1865. *Petite Bibliotèque Economique*. Paris: Guillaumin.

———. 1884. *L'Organisation de la Famille Selon le Vrai Modèle Signalé par l'Histoire de Toutes les Races et de Tous les Temps*. 3rd ed. Paris: Téqui.

Lévi-Strauss, Claude. (1958) 1963. *Structural Anthropology*. Translated by Claire Jacobson and Brooke Shoepf. New York: Basic Books.

Levitt, Peggy, and Nina Glick Schiller. 2004. "Conceptualizing Simultaneity: A Transnational Field Perspective on Society." *International Migration Review* 38, no. 3: 1002–39.

Lewin, Kurt. 1964. *Field Theory in Social Science: Selected Papers*, edited by Dorwin Cartwright. New York: Harper and Row.

———. (1939) 1967. "Experiments in Social Space." *Reflections* 1, no. 1: 8–13.

Lipstadt, Hélène. 2008. "'Life as a Ride in the Metro': Pierre Bourdieu on Biography and Space." In *Biographies and Space: Placing the Subject in Art and Architecture*, edited by Dana Arnold and Joanna Sofaer, 35–54. New York: Routledge.

Löfgren, Orvar. 1987. "Deconstructing Swedishness: Culture and Class in Modern Sweden." In *Anthropology at Home*, edited by Anthony Jackson, 74–93. London: Tavistock.

Low, Setha M. 2003. "Anthropological Theories of Body, Space, and Culture." *Space and Culture* 6, no. 1: 9–18.

———. 2016. *Spatializing Culture*. New York: Routledge.

Low, Setha M., and Denise Lawrence. 2003. *The Anthropology of Space and Place: Locating Culture*. London: Blackwell.

Loyal, Steven. 2017. *Bourdieu's Theory of the State: A Critical Introduction*. New York: Palgrave Macmillan.

MacDonald, Sharon, ed. 1993. *Inside European Identities: Ethnography in Western Europe*. Oxford: Berg Publishers.

Malkki, Liisa. 1995. "Refugees and Exile: From 'Refugee Studies' to the Natural Order of Things." *Annual Review of Anthropology* 24: 495–523.

Marchetti, Maria Christina. 2011. "Space, Mobility and New Boundaries: The Redefinition of Social Action." In *The Politics of Proximity: Mobility and Immobility in Practice*, edited by Giuseppina Pellegrino, 17–30. Farnham, Surrey, UK: Ashgate Publishing.

Massey, Doreen. 2005. *For Space*. London: Sage Publications.

Mauss, Marcel. 1935. "Les Techniques du Corps." *Journal de Psychologie Normale et Pathologique* 3–4: 271–93.

———. (1950) 1979. "Body Techniques." In *Sociology and Psychology: Essays*. Translated by Ben Brewster, 97–123. London and Henley: Routledge and Kegan Paul.

Medvetz, Thomas, and Jeffrey J. Sallaz eds. 2018. *The Oxford Handbook of Pierre Bourdieu*. Oxford: Oxford University Press.

Mitchell, Peta. 2012. *Contagious Metaphor*. London: Bloomsbury Academic.

Moch, Leslie Page. 2003. *Moving Europeans: Migration in Western Europe since 1650*. 2nd ed. Bloomington: Indiana University Press.

Moore, Henrietta L. 1986. *Space, Text and Gender: An Anthropological Study of the Markwet of Kenya*. Cambridge, UK: Cambridge University Press.

Morgan, Kimberly J., and Anna Shola Orloff. 2017. "Introduction: The Many Hands of the State." In *The Many Hands of the State: Theorizing Political Authority and Social Control*, edited by Kimberly J. Morgan and Anna Shola Orloff, 1–32. Cambridge, UK: Cambridge University Press.

Munn, Nancy D. 1996. "Excluded Spaces: The Figure in the Australian Aboriginal Landscape." *Critical Inquiry* 22: 446–65.

Murphy-Lejeune, Elizabeth. 2002. *Student Mobility and Narrative in Europe: The New Strangers*. New York: Routledge.

Nader, Laura. 1997. "Controlling Processes: Tracing the Dynamic Components of Power." *Current Anthropology* 38, no. 5: 711–37.

Nageeb, Salma Ahmed. 2004. *New Spaces and Old Frontiers: Women, Social Space, and Islamization in Sudan*. Lanham, MD: Lexington Books.

Oliver, Caroline, and Karen O'Reilly. 2010. "A Bourdieusian Analysis of Class and Migration: Habitus and the Individualizing Process." *Sociology* 44, no. 1: 49–66.

Ozouf, Jacques, and Mona Ozouf. 1984. "La Tour de la France par Deux Enfants: Le Petit Livre Rouge de la République." In *Les Lieux de Mémoire. Volume I: La République*, edited by Pierre Nora, 277–301. Paris: Editions Gallimard.

Painter, Joe. 2000. "Pierre Bourdieu." In *Thinking Space*, edited by Mike Crang and Nigel Thrift, 239–59. London: Routledge.

Park, Robert E. 1924. "The Concept of Social Distance: As Applied to the Study of Race Relations." *Journal of Applied Sociology* 8, no. 5: 339–44.

———. 1952. *Human Communities: The City and Human Ecology*. Glencoe, IL: The Free Press.

Pellow, Deborah, ed. 1996. *Setting Boundaries: The Anthropology of Spatial and Social Organization*. Westport, CT: Bergin and Garvey.

Pernicka, Susanne, and Christian Lahusen. 2018. "Power and Counter Power in Europe: The Transnational Structuring of Social Spaces and Social Fields." *Osterrich Z. Sociologie* 43 (Supplement 1): 1–11.

Pierce, Joseph, and Deborah G. Martin. 2015. "Placing Lefebvre." *Antipode* 47, no. 5: 1279–99.

Pratt, Mary Louise. 1992. *Imperial Eyes: Travel Writing and Transculturation*. London: Routledge.

Pries, Ludger. 2001. "The Approach of Transnational Social Spaces: Responding to New Configurations of the Social and the Spatial." In *New Transnational Social Spaces*, edited by Ludger Pries. New York: Routledge.

Pullano, Teresa. 2014. *La Citoyenneté Européenne: Une Espace Quasi Etatique*. Paris: Presses de Sciences Po.

Racine, Jean-Luc, ed. 1997. *Peasant Moorings: Village Ties and Mobility Rationales in South India*. Pondicherry, India: The French Institute; and Thousand Oaks: Sage Publications.

Rapport, Nigel. 1994. *The Prose and the Passion: Anthropology, Literature, and the Writing of E. M. Forster*. Manchester: Manchester University Press.

Raulin, Anne, and Susan Carol Rogers, eds. 2012. *Parallaxes Transatlantiques: Vers une Anthropologie Réciproque*. Paris: CNRS Editions.

Recchi, Ettore. 2015. *Mobile Europe: The Theory and Practice of Free Movement in the EU*. New York: Palgrave Macmillan.

Reed-Danahay, Deborah. 1993. "Talking About Resistance: Ethnography and Theory in Rural France." *Anthropological Quarterly* 66, no. 4: 221–29.

———. 1995. "The Kabyle and the French: Occidentalism in Bourdieu's Theory of Practice." In *Occidentalism: Images of the West*, edited by James Carrier, 61–84. Oxford: Oxford University Press.

———. 1996. *Education and Identity in Rural France: The Politics of Schooling*. Cambridge, UK: Cambridge University Press.

———. 1997. "Leaving Home: Schooling Stories and the Ethnography of Autoethnography in Rural France." In *Auto/Ethnography: Rewriting the Self and the Social*, edited by D. Reed-Danahay, 123–43. Oxford: Berg Publishers.

———. 2002. "Sites of Memory: Autoethnographies from Rural France." *Biography: An Interdisciplinary Quarterly* 25, no. 1 (Special Issue on Biography and Geography): 95–109.

———. 2004. "Tristes Paysans: Bourdieu's Early Ethnography in Béarn and Kabylia." *Anthropological Quarterly* 77, no. 1: 87–106.

———. 2005a. "Desire, Migration, and Attachment to Place: Life Stories of Rural French Women." In *Women on the Verge of Home: Narratives of Home and Transgressive Travel*, edited by Bilinda Straight, 129–48. Albany: SUNY Press.

———. 2005b. *Locating Bourdieu*. Bloomington: Indiana University Press.

———. 2007. "Citizenship Education in the 'New Europe': Who Belongs?" In *Reimagining Civic Education: How Diverse Societies Form Democratic Citizens*, edited by Bradley Levinson and Doyle Stevick, 197–215. Lanham, MD: Rowman and Littlefield, Pubs.

———. 2008. "From the 'Imagined Community' to 'Communities of Practice': Immigrant Belonging Among Vietnamese Americans." In *Citizenship, Political Engagement, and Belonging: Immigrants in Europe and the United States*, edited by Deborah Reed-Danahay and Caroline B. Brettell, 78–97. New Brunswick, NJ: Rutgers University Press.

———. 2009. "Bourdieu's Ethnography in Béarn and Kabylia: The Peasant Habitus." In *Bourdieu in Algeria: Colonial Policies, Theoretical Developments*, edited by Jane Goodman and Paul A. Silverstein, 133–63. Lincoln: University of Nebraska Press.

———. 2010. "Citizenship, Immigration, and Embodiment: Vietnamese Americans in North-Central Texas." In *Contested Spaces: Citizenship and Belonging in Contemporary Times*, edited by Meenakshi Thapan, 101–19. New Delhi: Orient Blackswan.

———. 2012. "La Notion de 'Communauté' à l'Épreuve des Terrains: Des Espaces Sociaux de la France Rurale à la Diaspora Vietnamienne." In *Parallaxes Transatlantiques: Vers une Anthropologie Réciproque*, edited by Anne Raulin and Susan Carol Rogers, 159–80. Paris: CNRS Editions.

———. 2013. "Habitus." In *Theory in Social and Cultural Anthropology: An Encyclopedia*, edited by R. Jon McGee and Richard L. Warms, 374–76. Thousand Oaks: Sage Publications.

———. (2012) 2015a. "Confronting Community: From Rural France to the Vietnamese Diaspora." In *Transatlantic Parallaxes: Toward Reciprocal Anthropology*, Revised English version, edited by Anne Raulin and Susan Carol Rogers, 125–42. Oxford: Berghahn Books.

———. 2015b. "'Like a Foreigner in my own Homeland': Writing the Dilemmas of Return in the Vietnamese American Diaspora." *Identities: Global Studies in Culture and Power* 22, no. 5: 603–18.

———. 2015c. "Social Space: Distance, Proximity, and Thresholds of Affinity." In *Thinking Through Sociality: An Anthropological Interrogation of Key Concepts*, edited by Vered Amit, 69–96. Oxford: Berghahn Books.

———. 2017a. "Bourdieu and Critical Autoethnography: Implications for Research, Writing, and Teaching." *International Journal of Multicultural Education* 19, no. 1: 144–54.

———. 2017b. "Bourdieu, Social Space, and the Nation-State: Implications for Migration Studies." *Sociologica* 2: 1–22. http://www.sociologica.mulino.it/journal/issue/index/Issue/Journal:ISSUE:33.

———. 2019. "Autoethnography. Flagship Entry." In *Sage Research Methods Foundations*, edited by Paul Atkinson et al. London: Sage. doi: 10.4135/9781526421036815143.

Richter, Marina. 2012. "Researching Transnational Social Spaces: A Qualitative Study of the Spanish Second Generation in Switzerland." *Forum: Qualitative Social Research* 13, no. 3. http://www.qualitative-research.net/index.php/fqs/article/view/1678.

Robbins, Derek. 2011. "From Solidarity to Social Inclusion: The Political Transformations of Durkheimianism." *Durkheimian Studies / Études Durkheimiennes* 17: 80–102.

Roberts, Les. 2012. *Mapping Cultures: Place, Practice, Performance*. Basingstoke: Palgrave Macmillan.

Rogers, Alisdair. 2004. "A European Space for Transnationalism?" In *Transnational Spaces*, edited by Peter Jackson, Philip Crang, and Claire Dwyer, 164–82. New York: Routledge.

Rouse, Roger. 1991. "Mexican Migration and the Social Space of Postmodernism." *Diaspora* 1, no. 1: 8–23.

Rumford, Chris. 2003. "European Civil Society or Transnational Social Space? Conceptions of Society in Discourses of EU Citizenship, Governance and the Democratic Deficit: An Emerging Agenda." *European Journal of Social Theory* 6, no. 1: 25–43.

St. Martin, Monique de. 2015. "'Anatomie du Goût' to *La Distinction*: Attempting to Construct the Social Space. Some Markers for the History of the Research." In *The Routledge Companion to Bourdieu's Distinction*, edited by Philippe Coulangeon and Julien Duval. Translated by Kristin Cooper, 15–28. London: Routledge.

Salazar, Noel. 2018. *Momentous Mobilities: Anthropological Musings on the Meanings of Travel*. New York: Berghahn Books.

Salazar, Noel, and Kiran Jarayim, eds. 2016. *Keywords of Mobility: Critical Engagements*. New York: Berghahn Books.

Sapiro, Gisèle, ed. 2010. *Sociology as a Martial Art: Political Writings by Pierre Bourdieu*. Translated by Priscilla Parkhurst Ferguson, Richard Nice, and Loïc Wacquant. New York: The New Press.

———. 2018. "Field Theory from a Transnational Perspective." In *The Oxford Handbook of Pierre Bourdieu*, edited by Thomas Medvetz and Jeffrey J. Sallaz, 162–82. Oxford: Oxford University Press.

Savage, Mike. 2011. "The Lost Urban Sociology of Pierre Bourdieu." In *The New Blackwell Companion to the City*, edited by Gary Bridge and Sophie Watson, 511–20. Malden, MA: Blackwell Publishing Ltd.

Sayad, Abdelmalek. (1991) 2004. *The Suffering of the Immigrant*. Preface by Pierre Bourdieu. Translated by David Macey. Cambridge, UK: Polity Press.

Scott, James C. 1998. *Seeing Like a State: How Certain Schemes to Improve the Human Condition Have Failed*. New Haven, CT: Yale University Press.

Sheller, Mimi. 2017. "From Spatial Turn to Mobilities Turn." *Current Sociology* 65, no. 4: 623–39.

Sheller, Mimi, and John Urry. 2006. "The New Mobilities Paradigm." *Environment and Planning A: Economy and Space* 38, no. 2: 207–26.

Shepherd, Todd. 2006. *The Invention of Decolonization: The Algerian War and the Remaking of France*. Ithaca: Cornell University Press.

Silber, Ilana Friedrich. 1995. "Space, Fields, Boundaries: The Rise of Spatial Metaphors in Contemporary Sociological Theory." *Social Research* 62, no. 2: 323–55.

Silverstein, Paul A. 2009. "Of Rooting and Uprooting: Kabyle Habitus, Domesticity, and Structural Nostalgia." In *Bourdieu in Algeria: Colonial Politics, Ethnographic Practices, Theoretical Developments*, edited by Jane E. Goodman and Paul A. Silverstein, 164–98. Lincoln: University of Nebraska Press.

Simon, Patrick. 2012. *French National Identity and Integration: Who Belongs to the National Community?* Washington, DC: Migration Policy Institute.

Simonsen, Kirsten. 1996. "What Kind of Space in What Kind of Social Theory?" *Progress in Human Geography* 20, no. 4: 494–512.

Smith, Michael Peter. 1992. "Postmodernism, Urban Ethnography, and the New Social Space of Ethnicity." *Theory and Society* 21, no. 4: 493–531.

Soja, Edward W. 1989. *Postmodern Geographies: The Reassertion of Space in Critical Social Theory*. London: Verso.

Sorokin, Pitirim. 1927. *Social Mobility*. New York: Harper and Brothers.

Speller, John R. W. 2011 *Bourdieu and Literature*. Cambridge, UK: Open Book Publishers.

Stacul, Jaro, Christina Moutsou, and Helen Kopnina, eds. 2006. *Crossing European Boundaries: Beyond Conventional Geographical Categories*. New York: Berghahn Books.

Susen, Simon. 2014. "The Place of Space in Social and Cultural Theory." In *Routledge Handbook of Social and Cultural Theory*, edited by Anthony Elliott, 333–57. New York: Routledge.

Susen, Simon, and Bryan S. Turner. 2011a. "Introduction: Preliminary Reflections on the Legacy of Pierre Bourdieu." In *The Legacy of Pierre Bourdieu: Critical Essays*, edited by Simon Susen and Bryan S. Turner, xiii–xxix. London: Anthem Press.

——, eds. 2011b. *The Legacy of Pierre Bourdieu: Critical Essays*. London: Anthem Press

Svašek, Maruška, ed. 2012. *Emotions and Human Mobility: Ethnographies of Movement*. New York: Routledge.

Swartz, David L. 2013. *Symbolic Power, Politics, and Intellectuals: The Political Sociology of Pierre Bourdieu*. Chicago: University of Chicago Press.

Swartz, David L., and Vera L. Zolberg, eds. 2004. *After Bourdieu: Influence, Critique, Elaboration*. New York: Kluwer Academic Publishing.

Tally, Robert T. 2013. *Spatiality*. Abington: Routledge.

Thatcher, Jenny, et al. 2015. *Bourdieu: The Next Generation*. London: Routledge.

Thatcher, Jenny, and Kristoffer Halvorsrud. 2015. "Migrating Habitus: A Comparative Case Study of Polish and South African Migrants in the U.K." In *Bourdieu: The Next Generation*, edited by Jenny Thatcher et al., 88–106. London: Routledge.

Thompson, E. P. (1963) 1966. *The Making of the English Working Class*. New York: Vintage Books.

Thompson, John B. 1991. "Editor's Introduction." In *Language and Symbolic Power*, edited by Pierre Bourdieu, 1–31. Cambridge, MA: Harvard University Press.

Tönnies, Ferdinand. (1887) 1957. *Community and Society*. Translated by C. P. Loomis. East Lansing: Michigan State University Press.

Turner, Victor. 1969. *The Ritual Process: Structure and Anti-Structure*. Ithaca: Cornell University Press.

Tsing, Anna. 2000. "The Global Situation." *Cultural Anthropology* 15, no. 3: 327–60.

Urry, John. 2000. *Sociology Beyond Societies: Mobilities for the Twenty-first Century.* London: Routledge.

———. 2003. *Global Complexity.* Cambridge, UK: Polity Press.

———. 2007. *Mobilities.* Cambridge, UK: Polity Press.

Vandebroeck, Dieter. 2018. "Toward a European Social Topography: The Contemporary Relevance of Pierre Bourdieu's Concept of 'Social Space.'" *European Societies* 20, no. 3: 359–74.

Van Gennep, Arnold. 1909. *The Rites of Passage.* Translated by Monika B. Vizedom and Gabrielle L. Caffee. London: Routledge and Kegan Paul.

Venturini, Patrick. 1989. *1992: The European Social Dimension.* Luxembourg: Office for Official Publications of the European Commission.

Wacquant, Loïc. 1996. "Foreword." In *The State Nobility*, by Pierre Bourdieu, translated by Lauretta C. Clough, ix–xxii. Stanford: Stanford University Press.

Wagner, Roy. (1975) 2016. *The Invention of Culture.* 2nd ed. Chicago: University of Chicago Press.

Warf, Barney, and Santa Arias, eds. 2009. *The Spatial Turn: Interdisciplinary Perspectives.* Abington: Routledge.

Webster, Helena. 2011. *Bourdieu for Architects.* New York: Routledge.

Weil, Patrick. (2002) 2008. *How to be French: Nationality in the Making Since 1789.* Translated by Catherine Porter. Durham, NC: Duke University Press.

Wiles, Janine. 2008. "Sense of Home in a Transnational Social Space: New Zealanders in London." *Global Networks* 8, no. 1: 116–37.

Williams, Raymond. 1973. *The Country and the City.* New York: Oxford University Press.

Wilson, Thomas M., and Hastings Donnan, eds. 2012. *A Companion to Border Studies.* Malden, MA: Blackwell Publishing.

Wimmer, Andreas, and Nina Glick Schiller. 2002. "Methodological Nationalism and Beyond: Nation-State Building, Migration, and the Social Sciences." *Global Networks* 2, no. 4: 301–34.

Wise, John M. 1997. *Exploring Technology and Social Space.* London: Sage Publications.

Wolff, Kurt H. 1950. *The Sociology of Georg Simmel.* New York: The Free Press.

Yacine, Tassadit. (2008) 2013. "At the Origins of a Singular Ethnosociology." In *Algerian Sketches*, by Pierre Bourdieu. Edited and presented by Tassadit Yacine. Translated by David Fernbach, 13–34. Cambridge, UK: Polity Press.

Zieleniec, Andrzej. 2007. *Space and Social Theory.* London: Sage Publications.

Index